The Power to Probe

A Study of
Congressional Investigations

James Hamilton

The
POWER
to
PROBE

A Study of
Congressional Investigations

Introduction by Senator Sam J. Ervin, Jr.

Random House · New York

Copyright © 1976 by James Hamilton

All rights reserved under International and Pan-American
Copyright Conventions. Published in the United States by
Random House, Inc., New York, and simultaneously in Canada
by Random House of Canada Limited, Toronto.

Library of Congress Cataloging in Publication Data
Hamilton, James, 1938–
The power to probe.
Includes index.
1. Governmental investigations—United States.
2. United States. Congress—Powers and duties.
I. Title.
KF4942.H34   328.73′07′45   75-35911
ISBN 0-394-49796-1

Manufactured in the United States of America
9 8 7 6 5 4 3 2
First Edition

To my parents

Acknowledgments

This book could not have been produced without the assistance of many people. In particular I want to express my gratitude to a few whose help has been invaluable: first and foremost, to Peg Cuthbertson, who edited, typed, researched, encouraged and generally prodded the book to completion—it is impossible for me to convey my appreciation fully for her indispensable aid; to the Ford Foundation, whose generous support helped finance the writing of this book; to my brother-in-law, Dr. John Kuhnle, who devoted many hours of his considerable literary talents to editing the early manuscript; to erudite Washington attorney Michael Boudin and to David Dorsen, my wise and trusted fellow assistant chief counsel on the Senate Select Committee on Presidential Campaign Activities, who read this book in draft and made many helpful suggestions; to Barbara Evans (for years secretary and confidante to the late Dean Acheson), who typed a large portion of the manuscript and brought to the task the same care and expertise she devoted to Mr. Acheson's numerous works; to Brian Kenner, my perceptive, industrious research assistant (currently perched near the top of his class at George Washington Law School), who verified the accuracy of most of the legal and historical statements in this book and also recommended a number of useful additions to the final product; to Jason Epstein, my Random House editor, who pruned with an experienced and artful eye but allowed me to write the type of book I wanted; and to the staff and consultants of the Senate Select Committee on Presidential Campaign Activities who participated in the development of many of the ideas set forth in this book.*

---

* Lawyers may be interested in the 2,100-page Legal Appendix to the committee's final report where legal documents (briefs, memoranda, etc.) discussing many of the issues dealt with in this book are presented; the committee's documents in most instances (but not always) contain accurate statements of relevant law. It should be stressed, however, that the views expressed in this book do not

Finally, I must thank Senator Sam Ervin, not only for writing the Introduction to this book but also for providing moral leadership to the nation when it was sorely needed.

J.H.

October 1975

necessarily reflect the opinions of any member of that Ervin committee or of its staff or consultants. Nor do my views necessarily comport with the opinions of any members of the law firm I have joined since this book was written, nor with the views of its present or former clients.

Contents

Introduction

When Jim Hamilton, the author of this book, joined the legal staff of the Senate Select Committee on Presidential Campaign Activities, he brought to the committee an alert mind, intellectual integrity, a remarkable knowledge and understanding of law and people, a dedication to our constitutional system of government, and an untiring willingness to perform with diligence every task assigned to him. By virtue of these qualifications, Mr. Hamilton rendered services of great value to the Select Committee by giving it wise advice in respect to legal matters and practical considerations, by heading several of its investigations, and by arguing with rare ability before the federal courts of the District of Columbia important litigation in which the committee became involved.

During his services on the committee, he made a profound study of the constitutional principles, congressional rules, and congressional precedents relating to investigations by congressional committees, and of the decisions of the Supreme Court of the United States and the other federal courts construing these principles, rules, and practices. Since the Senate Select Committee terminated its activities Mr. Hamilton has continued this study. As a consequence, he has become an outstanding authority on the subject of congressional investigations.

I have read his book with delight and commend its study to the members and staffs of every congressional investigating committee, to all witnesses who may hereafter appear before any such committee, and to the attorneys who may represent such witnesses.

This book represents the most recent, the most complete, and the most authoritative study of congressional investigations which are becoming of increasing importance to the Congress and our country. In writing it, Mr. Hamilton has rendered a most important public service. This is so for reasons I set forth below.

The congressional investigation can be an instrument of freedom. Or it can be freedom's scourge.

A legislative inquiry can serve as the tool to pry open the barriers that hide governmental corruption. It can be the catalyst that spurs Congress and the public to support vital reforms in our nation's laws. Or it can debase our principles, invade the privacy of our citizens, and afford a platform for demagogues and the rankest partisans.

Hopefully, the Watergate investigations—although not without fault—were attuned to the higher precepts that should guide congressional probes. But it has not always been so. The wounds of the McCarthy era are not forgotten. Nor should they be, for remembrances of past assaults on our liberties are needed to hold us vigilant for the future.

To help ensure that legislative probes to come are conducted fairly and effectively, we must understand the legal framework in which the investigatory process functions. Public knowledge of what is allowed and what is not will at least increase the chances that the enormous power inherent in the investigatory process is channeled to beneficent ends, not spent in pernicious pursuits. Unfortunately, those who should know the ground rules—congressmen and their staff, witnesses and their counsel, the press —often do not.

Congress can probe into every matter where there is legitimate federal interest. In the modern age, where government is involved in multifaceted aspects of our daily lives, there are increasingly few areas where Congress may not delve. It may, for example, look deeply into criminal conduct affecting federal interests even though others— prosecutors, grand juries, the federal courts—also operate in this sphere.

Of considerable importance is Congress's power to investigate the executive branch. We do not live in a monarchy but in a democracy where governmental functions are shared by three equal branches. The White House is the people's house, not an imperial palace. The executive branch is not above the law. It cannot autocratically and arbitrarily block Congress from inquiring into its operations.

The Constitution and statutes give Congress a solemn duty to oversee the activities of the executive branch. How else can Congress fully comprehend whether existing laws are adequate and properly administered? How else can Congress determine with confidence what specific additional laws are needed to guide the nation?

The President should not be allowed to emasculate the oversight function by sweeping assertions of executive privilege. Nor should the courts establish judicial precedents that seriously debilitate this responsibility. All branches of government must fully appreciate that the oversight function is a vital tool for keeping the nation free. It is a shield against creeping executive imperialism of the sort that unfortunately our nation has witnessed in the recent past.

Congress also has the duty and the right to publicize its findings on corruption and maladministration. Indeed, fulfilling its responsibility to inform the public about the state of government is one of Congress's most significant functions. It is a crucial responsibility if the people are to participate in the democratic process. The people govern best when fully informed. Of course, where criminal conduct is involved and criminal trials which could be prejudiced are imminent, the informing function must be exercised with prudence.

Congress has awesome equipment to conduct its probes. Its staffs are large and burgeoning every year. So, too, grow the amounts of funds devoted to the investigatory process.

Congress has inherent subpoena power to force production of information needed for its legislative tasks. It can place witnesses before it under oath, and they must testify truthfully or suffer prosecution for perjury. Congress, with the aid of the federal courts, can grant limited immunity to witnesses to force their testimony even though they assert their Fifth Amendment privilege against self-incrimination. Witnesses given immunity are protected from the use of their testimony, or the fruits of their testimony, against them in any subsequent criminal prosecution.

Congress, moreover, has sizable powers to remedy contempts of its authority. It can dispatch its sergeants at arms to arrest and imprison those who obstruct its processes. Or, when witnesses under subpoena or order refuse to answer questions or produce records, Congress can initiate proceedings that may lead to criminal prosecutions for contempt of Congress.

Our legislators may perform these various functions without fear of reprisals. The Constitution protects congressmen from criminal prosecution or civil suits based on the performance of legislative acts.

But as great as Congress's powers are, they are subject to weighty limitations. Congress must act with valid legislative purpose. It cannot probe purely private affairs nor expose private activity solely for the sake of exposure. It cannot usurp the functions of the executive and judicial branches and prosecute, try, and convict for criminal offenses. The legislative trials of the loyalty investigations era are a black mark on the history of congressional inquiries.

Moreoever, the fundamental freedoms enshrined in the Constitution's Bill of Rights cannot be abridged by Congress. Congress, under the Fifth Amendment, cannot force a witness to incriminate himself unless given immunity. Under the Fourth Amendment, Congress cannot subject individuals to unreasonable search and seizure. It cannot unjustifiably force revelation of thoughts and beliefs, nor without substantial warrant seek to evoke the secrets of past associations. The First Amendment protects against such intrusions.

A congressional committee cannot venture beyond the responsibilities given it by its parent House through authorizing or enabling resolutions. A committee may seek only information pertinent to the subject under investigation and must inform witnesses before it why the information sought is relevant. A panel must follow its rules of procedure established to protect the rights of those under scrutiny. It should, for instance, ensure that materials deemed confidential under its rules are kept that way—not leaked—until revelation is properly authorized. Shamefully, some of those connected with the investigations of the Senate Select Committee on Presidential Campaign Activities demonstrated scant appreciation of this precept. Leaking confidential information may have severe legal consequences. I join Mr. Hamilton in deploring the inexcusable leaks of confidential information by persons whose identities Sam Dash, the chief counsel for the Senate Select Committee, and I were unable to determine.

These—in the sparsest of outlines—are the basic principles that govern congressional investigations. They are explained in depth in this book. They should be fully understood by all who participate in the investigatory process.

But an understanding of the laws that govern congressional investigation will not alone ensure that such investigations will be conducted in a lawful, fair, and efficacious manner. Those who understand the law often can most effectively pervert and abuse it. More is needed from our representatives—judgment, character, dedication. We will not see congressional investigations that live up to democratic ideals until we send men to Congress who share those ideals, men who have the fortitude and the ability to see that those ideals are put into practice, men who believe—to repeat Grover Cleveland's thought—that public office is a public trust. If our representatives abuse or misuse Congress's investigatory powers, it is the responsibility of the people to replace them with men and women more faithful to the public trust, more devoted to the public weal.

—Senator Sam J. Ervin, Jr.

The Power to Probe

A Study of
Congressional Investigations

·I·
Problems and Perplexities

When Chester Davis, a lawyer for Howard Hughes, appeared before Senator Sam Ervin's Watergate committee, he was confused. He told the committee's staff: "I am not particularly well versed in your rules of procedure. I don't understand how you operate in this arena."

Mr. Davis is not alone.

The congressional investigation is hardly an unfamiliar institution. It is reasonable to assume that the front pages of your morning newspaper carry a report of some congressional probe. The investigation may concern an inquiry into the background and finances of a presidential nominee for a Cabinet post, an ambassadorship or Vice President to discover conflicts of interest or past misdeeds. It may involve CIA assassination plots or the causes of whatever economic malaise besets us at the time. Or it may relate to a wholly different subject. But most likely some congressional investigation appears prominently in your morning paper, for congressional inquiries are the daily fare of American life.

Because of the impact that congressional investigations have on our nation's affairs, one would think that the ground rules for the investigatory process would be well defined—that the powers of Congress to probe into matters affecting the nation would be definitively prescribed and the rights afforded individuals touched by legislative investigations authoritatively delineated. And it might be thought that those most immediately concerned—congressmen, their staffs, witnesses, the bar, the Washington press corps—would understand the ground rules.

Not so. While there are standards that govern the conduct of congressional investigations, they are, in many instances, ill-defined or incomplete. And what rules there are often are not fully perceived or understood by those who should have the most comprehensive grasp of the process. From my vantage point as assistant chief counsel to Senator Ervin's Watergate committee I discovered that it was not only witnesses before the committee or those under its subpoenas who were confused. There was considerable lack of understanding of basic principles in the supposedly sophisticated Washington press corps. Attorneys representing those called on by the committee to testify or produce records were often unsure of their clients' rights and potential liabilities. Even congressmen and their staffs were frequently confused as they applied Congress's investigatory powers.

This book is an attempt, for laymen as well as lawyers, to bring some form to the investigatory process. It is an effort not only to explain the rules that control congressional investigations, which have undergone considerable changes in the last twenty years, but also to suggest needed alterations to governing principles.

Congressional investigations are, of course, no new phenomenon. Legislative inquiries, the Supreme Court said in 1951, are "an established part of representative government"* and, in fact, Congress has exercised its investigatory powers since the beginning of the republic. The first congressional investigation, launched by a select committee of the House of Representatives in 1792, involved the disastrous Ohio frontier defeat by Indian tribes of American troops under the command of General Arthur St. Clair. The Senate's first major investigation, which concerned the Seminole campaign of General Andrew Jackson, came in 1818. But the investigatory function of legislatures was already long established, having been exercised by the English Parliament, the Continental Congress, and the colonial legislatures.

Until 1900 most investigations by Congress concerned the civil and military affairs of the executive branch. Two nineteenth-century investigations were of particular importance. In 1861, after the Union's defeats at Bull Run and Balls Bluff, the Senate and the House established a Joint Committee on the Conduct of the [Civil] War. This committee, the first joint committee in Congress's history, was controlled by radical Republicans vehement in their opposition to President Lincoln. The committee probed deeply into the conduct of war, examining past and future battle plans, the conduct of generals, war supplies, naval installations, and a host of other military-related subjects. The committee even demanded the dismissals of several generals whose political persuasions differed from those of its members. So aggressively did it pursue its inquiries that it was accused of attempting to assume at least partial control of military operations. Because of its partisan, overreaching tactics, the committee's activities were—until the McCarthy era—regarded as the nadir of congressional investigatory performance.

The other major investigation of the nineteenth century concerned the notorious Credit Mobilier affair. Conducted in 1872–73, this investigation was particularly arresting

---

* *Tenney* v. *Brandhove*, 341 U.S. 367, 377 (1951).

because the Congress—acting through one Senate and two House committees—diligently examined the part played in the scandal by its own members. The last portion of the Union Pacific Railroad, which received substantial government subsidies, had been constructed by the Credit Mobilier of America. Credit Mobilier, controlled by backers of the railroad, had realized fraudulent profits from the construction. Congressman Oakes Ames of Massachusetts, a major shareholder in both Union Pacific and Credit Mobilier, had used Credit Mobilier stock in an effort to bribe prominent congressmen and other government officials, such as Vice President Schuyler Colfax and President-to-be James A. Garfield, then a congressman. Ames's goal had been to forestall congressional investigation of the railroad's affairs that might have uncovered Credit Mobilier's illicit dealings. But the investigations exposed the seamy aspects of the scandal, and several congressmen were disgraced. Ames and another congressman, James Brooks of New York, who had purchased stock at rock-bottom prices through a nominee, were censured by the House, and Colfax and Garfield never successfully explained their involvement in the affair.

The legislative investigation, for better or for worse, found its heyday in the present century.

The 1912–13 "Money Trust" investigation into the nation's growing concentration of economic power was the first major twentieth-century congressional inquiry. A subcommittee of the House Banking and Currency Committee—guided by its counsel, the prominent New York lawyer Samuel Untermeyer—summoned most of the major financiers of the day, including J.P. Morgan, to testify. The investigation discovered a dangerous conglomeration of economic might; it revealed, for example, the existence of interlocking directorships between New York banks dominated by Morgan and Rockefeller interests and a hundred and twelve of the nation's leading banking, public utilities, transporation, insurance, manufacturing, and trading corporations. The investigation's revelations were

instrumental in the passage of the Federal Reserve Act of
1913, the Clayton Antitrust Act of 1914, and the Federal
Trade Commission Act of 1914. The subcommittee also
made other legislative recommendations, similar to statutes later passed in the New Deal era, to regulate the
securities and banking industries.

In the early 1920's two Senate committees sct out to
examine the scandals in the administration of Warren
Harding (who, perhaps mercifully, died before the inquiries were finished). Will Rogers branded the scene as the
"great morality panic of 1924." Before the investigations
had run their course, damning evidence had been uncovered against several of Harding's cronies whom he had
elevated to high office. It was revealed that Secretary of the
Interior Albert B. Fall had granted leases for two
government-owned oil reserves—the Wyoming Teapot
Dome field and the California Elk Hills area—to individuals who had "loaned" him substantial sums of money. It
was discovered that the chief of the Veterans Bureau and
the alien property custodian were receiving kickbacks from
government contractors. Perhaps worst of all, the investigations showed that Attorney General Harry Daugherty,
Harding's political mentor, had known about this corruption but had failed to arrest it or prosecute the wrongdoers. Daugherty, in fact, had his own sideline going; he
was pocketing graft money from persons on the wrong
side of the prohibition laws. The Senate investigations led
to the appointment of a special prosecutor who eventually
brought some of the miscreants, including Fall, to justice.

The congressional investigations of the New Deal
period were basically of a different stamp. Here the principal task was to identify the social and economic conditions
that had caused, and had been the product of, the Great
Depression and to formulate and gain support for legislation to prevent their recurrence. The investigations
explored, among other things, the operations of stock
exchanges and public utility holding companies, unfair
labor practices, lobbying, the munitions industry, and rail-

road reorganization and finance. Out of these investigations came much of the New Deal legislation that changed
the shape of the national landscape. Especially notable was
the stock exchange investigation by the Senate Committee on Banking and Currency, which resembled the
"Money Trust" investigation twenty years before. This
inquiry, now known as the Pecora investigation after its
chief counsel Ferdinand Pecora, commenced at a time
(1933) when bank failures wrenched the nation, unem-
ployment was catastrophic, and the bread lines were end-
less. Interest in the committee's proceedings was intense as
the financiers and moguls of Wall Street trudged, often
unwillingly, to the Capitol to describe sophisticated manip-
ulations of the stock market and to tell how the wealthy
and the privileged (including some prominent political
figures) had prospered while the less influential suffered.
The stock exchange investigations eventually produced
the Banking Acts of 1933 and 1935, the Securities Act of
1933, the Securities Exchange Act of 1934, and the Public
Utility Holding Company Act of 1935. But significant legislation was not the only result of the New Deal inquiries.
The investigations demonstrated how effective a congressional probe could be not only in ferreting out information needed for legislative reform but also in mobilizing
public opinion to support a desired objective.

Starting in 1938 and running well past midcentury
was the loyalty investigations era. Three committees of
Congress—the House Committee on Un-American Activities, the Subcommittee on Internal Security of the Senate
Judiciary Committee, and the Subcommittee on Investigations of the Senate Committee on Government Operations under the chairmanship of Senator Joseph McCarthy
—ventured forth to discover the extent of Communist
activity and influence in American life. Their investigations, often conducted with methods now held in disrepute, were partially intended to spotlight subversives in
the government—particularly in the State Department and
the Army. But the inquiries also ranged beyond the

government, seeking out supposed Communist activities in private institutions: the churches, universities, tax-free foundations, the press. These investigations are chiefly memorable not for the number of subversives uncovered or the laws that resulted from their disclosures but for the disregard of individual rights and fundamental principles of fairness displayed by certain committee members and their staff. Senator McCarthy was eventually censured by the full Senate for his conduct, and calls for reform of the legislative investigatory process abounded. It is interesting to recall at this stage of history that Richard Nixon first came to national prominence in 1948 through his participation in the House Un-American Activities Committee's investigation of Alger Hiss.

Other congressional investigations of the 1940's and 1950's were more laudable. The World War II Senate Special Committee to Investigate the National Defense Program—called the Truman committee after its first chairman, Senator Harry S. Truman of Missouri—was one of the country's most effective investigating panels. In 1941 it began a series of studies into the state of the nation's preparedness for war, including investigations of the construction of training camps, the awarding of war contracts, shortages of critical war materials, the quality of materials supplied under defense contracts, and the various frauds perpetrated by contractors and others. The Truman committee was fully aware of the abuses of the joint committee that had scrutinized the conduct of the Civil War and thus carefully refrained from making judgments on military policy or operations. It sought cooperation, not confrontation, with the executive branch, and many of its suggestions concerning the national defense program were adopted.

A carefully prepared and highly revealing inquiry was the 1950–51 investigation by the Senate Special Committee to Investigate Organized Crime in Interstate Commerce. Through the medium of television this investigation, initially under the leadership of Senator Estes Kefauver of Tennessee, displayed to the public the sordid activities of racketeers, gamblers, narcotics pushers, and others of that ilk. High-level state and local government officials, as well as many gangland figures (such as crime syndicate chieftain Frank Costello), were called to testify before the committee. The committee's final report warned of shocking corruption in local government, and its hearings resulted in numerous local indictments.*

Another inquiry uncovering substantial corruption was the 1957–59 investigation of the Senate Select Committee on Improper Activities in the Labor or Management Field chaired by Senator John McClellan. This investigation was extraordinarily active. In two years the committee heard 1,726 witnesses, whose testimony consumed 46,150 pages, and its staff filed 19,000 investigative field reports. The investigation led to the passage of the 1959 Labor-Management Reporting and Disclosure Act, commonly known as the Landrum-Griffin Act, whose purpose is to prevent corruption and maladministration in internal union affairs.

In 1973–74 the Watergate investigations dominated the nation's attention. The task was begun by the Senate Select Committee on Presidential Campaign Activities, otherwise known as the Watergate committee or the Ervin committee after its chairman, Sam J. Ervin, of North Carolina. Later came the inquiry of the Judiciary Committee of the House of Representatives into the possible impeachment of President Nixon.

The Ervin committee was established by a unanimous vote of the Senate after the January 1973 trial of the initial seven men charged with burglarizing the Democratic National Committee headquarters at the Watergate office building failed to dispel questions regarding the actual scope of the affair. Before the Ervin committee's examinations were finished, significant facts had surfaced relating

* An excellent history of congressional investigations until 1955 is Telford Taylor's *Grand Inquest* (Simon and Schuster, 1955). See also *Congressional Quarterly Guide to the United States Congress*, 1971, pp. 245–62.

to the involvement of senior officials in the government and the President's reelection campaign in both the burglary and the cover-up that followed. The committee also uncovered important evidence relating to illegal campaign contributions, campaign dirty tricks, and the abuse of federal resources for political purposes. But the committee's activities were not limited to an investigation of the President's campaign; the campaigns of prominent Democrats who had sought the Presidency were also scrutinized, and certain abuses (albeit of far lesser magnitude) were found. The Ervin committee also proposed significant legislative reforms to prevent repetition of the wrongdoing revealed. (Unfortunately, most of its recommendations, have not yet been enacted into law.) The House Judiciary Committee, building on the evidence supplied by the Ervin committee and the special prosecutor appointed for Watergate matters, developed a compelling case for impeachment. After weeks of hearings, it sent an impeachment resolution to the floor of the House. Eventually the President, as the evidence mounted and his congressional support waned, was forced to resign.

The investigations currently receiving the most headlines are those conducted by select Senate and House panels into the nation's intelligence agencies. These inquiries were prompted by a spate of stories alleging, among other things, that the CIA plotted the assassination of several foreign leaders and engaged in illegal domestic surveillance, and that the FBI spied on the activities of prominent congressmen. At this writing the investigations are still in process, but the committees evidently intend a broad look at government intelligence operations to determine whether substantial revisions in the law are necessary.

Even this limited and selective historical review suggests several truths. The first is that Congress's investigatory power is immense and carries with it the potential for immense good. Without vigorous exercise of Congress's investigatory powers in the past, egregious corruption in our government and other serious shortcomings in our society might have gone undetected. Without conscientious probing by Congress, vital legislation would not now be on the books.

On the other hand, the investigatory powers of Congress can be greatly abused. Witnesses can be embarrassed, harassed, and hounded. Businesses can be disrupted. Individuals and businesses can be saddled with huge expenses, not the least of which is the payment of fees to high-priced Washington lawyers supposedly steeped in the wisdom and lore of "the Hill." Congress often can compel the production of voluminous records that touch not only the occupations but also the private affairs of those involved. Particularly with television there is the potential to expose the intimate details of an individual's professional and personal life to public scrutiny and to subject him, justly or unjustly, to blame and humiliation.

Because of the twin potential for great benefit and great harm inherent in the investigatory process, it is imperative that all participants in that process understand both the legitimate powers to conduct legislative inquiries which Congress possesses and the rights to resist overzealous congressional probing that belong to individuals under scrutiny. This book seeks to aid in that understanding. The practical and legal problems discussed here are those that pertain to many congressional investigations. For example: What is the scope of Congress's subpoena power? What prerogatives does Congress have to confer immunity from prosecution on a witness in order to gain his testimony despite the assertion of his privilege against self-incrimination? What powers does Congress have to punish those who place themselves in contempt of its processes or who dissemble or lie? What constitutional protections are available to individuals to fend off overreaching Congressional investigations? What procedural rights are allowed witnesses who must appear at congressional hearings? How deeply can Congress probe into criminal conduct, especially where federal or state prosecutors are inquiring into the same circumstances? What is the scope of Congress's "informing function," that is, the right of Congress to inform the people of corruption and waste in their government? Can this informing function conflict with the preservation of fair trials, and if so, what remedies are available? What right does Congress have to obtain information and materials from the executive branch? How thick a cloak of secrecy over the executive branch can the President draw by invocation of the doctrine of executive privilege? How should disputes between the executive branch and Congress over access to executive information be resolved? What can be done about the problem of leaks of confidential information by congressmen and their staffs? What restrictions should be placed on the media's coverage of legislative investigations? What is the scope of congressional protection from suit under the speech or debate clause of the United States Constitution and related doctrines? When can an individual abused by the investigatory process gain protection of his rights by the courts?

These are not theoretical problems suitable only for academic discussion in the murky pages of some law review article. Rather, they are live concerns which have permeated investigations throughout the history of Congress. Today, however, the perspective in which these questions are viewed is somewhat different from that in the past. In the 1950's the concern was with avaricious legislative committees which attempted to establish hegemony over considerable chunks of executive domain and showed unconscionable disdain for individual rights and the fundamentals of fairness. Now the principal concern is that the Congress is too weak, that the executive, with extraordinary assertions of executive privilege, has blocked the Congress from exercising its legitimate oversight functions. However, despite the change of context, the basic questions remain.

All the issues outlined above arose—some on an almost daily basis—during the Senate Watergate committee's investigations. The problems were also the subject of numerous courtroom battles in which the committee became involved which constituted a major, but largely unpublicized, aspect of its activities. During its short life span the Ervin committee was in court on over sixty separate matters—far more than the normal congressional committee for a comparable period. Some of these matters were routine, but others involved complex, extended litigation.

These litigations are significant for several reasons. They concerned a sizable portion of the activities of a historic committee. They intimately involved some of the major figures on the national scene—President Nixon, Senators Sam Ervin and Howard Baker, Special Prosecutors Archibald Cox and Leon Jaworski, Judges John Sirica and Gerhard Gesell, Watergate conspirators John Dean and Jeb Stuart Magruder—as well as certain intriguing fringe characters of history, such as Rabbi Baruch Korff, Howard Hughes, and Charles "Bebe" Rebozo. Most important for our purposes, however, these litigations raised the basic issues that accompany most congressional investigations.

This book is not simply a rehash of the Ervin committee's litigations and investigations: the discussions that follow will deal generally with the fundamental issues arising in many congressional investigations and will draw heavily on the experiences of other prominent investigatory committees. However, because the Ervin committee's major litigations do provide concrete examples of recent vintage that illustrate the problems faced in legislative investigations, they will serve as a convenient springboard for discussing the issues at hand.

Before continuing, however, it is only fair briefly to identify the point of view from which this study proceeds. It is a perspective which, no doubt, is colored by my experience on the Ervin committee.

Our system of government, it seems to me, demands continual, vigorous congressional investigation and oversight of the executive branch and other segments of our society where there is a legitimate federal interest. Only by constant scrutiny can the accreted powers of a proliferating executive branch be kept within proper bounds. One would have to be blind to the lessons of Watergate not to realize that Congress must scrupulously oversee the affairs of the executive branch, including its administration of criminal laws. This oversight function is implicit in our tripartite system of government, for without it Congress cannot properly meet its law-making and informing responsibilities. And only by its steadfast exercise can the confidence of the people in our system of government be maintained. Thus neither the executive nor the courts should erect undue obstacles that impede this function. In particular, application of the doctrine of executive privilege as it pertains to Congress should be limited.

Congress, however, must exercise its oversight function judiciously. It should not attempt to run roughshod over legitimate executive prerogatives. It must carefully protect the basic rights of those it scrutinizes, and not subject individuals under investigation to harassment and needless embarrassment. More particularly, congressmen and their staffs must refrain from leaking material to the press that could injure reputations or damage the effectiveness of the investigation. A vigorous investigatory role by Congress will be accepted by the public and the courts only when Congress demonstrates that it can perform this task with prudence, fairness, and integrity.

These observations may appear to some as truisms. But the history of congressional investigations shows that the basic precepts which should govern legislative inquiries are often not followed. Indeed, as we shall see, certain members of the Watergate committee and its staff were not always guiltless in their conduct of the committee's investigations.

·II·
The Ervin Committee and the Courts

The Ervin committee litigations involved the three major areas of concern that confront congressional investigating committees—their relations with the courts, with the executive branch, and with witnesses and others affected by committee inquiries. These cases were in fact remarkable for the range of issues they raised. Five of the committee's major suits—its quarrel with Special Prosecutor Cox, its complex litigation with President Nixon, and its struggles with Rabbi Baruch Korff, the Howard Hughes empire, and Charles "Bebe" Rebozo—are preliminarily reviewed in this chapter. These lawsuits provide specific factual contexts for the general discussion in later chapters of the basic issues relating to congressional investigations.

The Confrontation with the Special Prosecutor

In retrospect, the Select Committee's first major litigation —its bout with Special Prosecutor Cox—was perhaps its most important. It was this litigation that allowed the Select Committee to present on television the testimony of two principal Watergate conspirators, John Dean and Jeb Stuart Magruder. The public was thus given its first full-scale view of the scope of the plot to break into and bug the headquarters of the Democratic National Committee and of the subsequent cover-up to conceal the true participants in that plot—a cover-up that involved the President of the United States.

A little history will put this case into proper perspective. On March 23, 1973, Judge John Sirica, then chief judge of the United States District Court for the District of Columbia, read aloud in court a letter received from James McCord, one of the seven men convicted of burglarizing the DNC headquarters. The letter charged that there had been perjury at the trial and a cover-up of the involvement of persons of high rank in the break-in. (The prosecution's theory at the trial had been that George Gordon Liddy, former general counsel to the Finance Committee to Re-elect the President, was the mastermind of the break-in and the highest government or campaign official involved.) McCord's letter, however, named no names.

McCord soon began to provide names to the Ervin committee. He said Liddy had told him that Attorney General John Mitchell, Counsel to the President John Dean, and Deputy Campaign Director Jeb Magruder had participated in planning the DNC operation. Through that ubiquitous device known as the "leak"—a device previously not unknown on Capitol Hill but practiced with special relish by some committee members and staff—this information soon became public.*

* The practice of leaking and its legal and practical ramifications are explored in Chapter IX.

The pressure was thus on Dean and Magruder and they began to break. Both made overtures to the prosecutors in early April. And both, initially through their attorneys, indicated to the Ervin committee that they were willing to talk. But both wanted immunity from prosecution.

Under the Fifth Amendment to the Constitution, a witness before a congressional committee whose testimony would tend to incriminate him can refuse to testify. However, by a statutory procedure a congressional committee may obtain a court order allowing the committee to force a witness to testify after he is given immunity from the use of his testimony, or the fruits of his testimony, against him in any subsequent criminal proceeding.* A congressional committee normally grants immunity to a witness only when convinced that his testimony will produce new and vital facts previously undisclosed by the investigation. Immunity is sometimes given, for example, to allow a witness to implicate figures of greater rank or authority.

It was this type of immunity that Dean and Magruder sought. There then began that peculiar type of sparring between an attorney representing a witness seeking immunity and committee staff. The lawyer attempts to persuade the staff that his client has significant evidence to contribute without revealing so much information that a waiver of the client's Fifth Amendment rights might be effected. The staff, which has to convince its committee that an immunity order is required, seeks to dredge out all the information it can.

Both Dean and Magruder were represented by able, articulate Washington lawyers—Dean by Charles Shaffer, Magruder by James Bierbower. Shaffer—a dapper, rather dashing figure, as much thespian as attorney— made a particularly tantalizing presentation. He had the intriguing habit of using the first person singular when describing his client's potential testimony. Thus he would

* See Chapter III.

say: "I will testify that . . .; I will tell the Committee that . . ." Shaffer also had the skill to punctuate hours of innocuous, desultory conversation with just enough tidbits to keep his audience titillated. Toward the end of one lengthy conversation, for example, he dropped the startling fact that there never had been a "Dean Report." At a press conference on August 29, 1972, President Nixon had informed the nation that Dean had conducted a "complete investigation" of the Watergate affair. On the basis of this investigation and Dean's report to him, the President said, "I can state categorically that no one in the White House staff, no one in this administration, presently employed, was involved in this very bizarre incident." Dean, of course, later testified at public hearings that there was in fact no "Dean Report," and that, far from investigating the Watergate affair, he was engaged in trying to cover up its true nature by promoting perjury and arranging for payment of hush money and promises of executive clemency to ensure the silence of the original seven Watergate defendants. But when Shaffer first came to the committee in April, there was no public hint that the "Dean Report" was a presidential fabrication.

The staff (principally Chief Counsel Samuel Dash) later had the opportunity for long discussions with Dean before immunity was actually conferred. Upon staff recommendation the committee voted unanimously to seek an immunity order for both Dean and Magruder.

Applications to the court for immunity powers respecting Dean and Magruder were filed by the committee in May. Subsequently, on June 4, Special Prosecutor Cox wrote Senator Ervin imploring him to postpone the Committee's public hearings temporarily. "The continuation of hearings at this time," Cox argued, "would create grave danger that the full facts about the Watergate case and related matters will never come to light, and that many of those who are guilty of serious wrongdoing will never be brought to justice." Cox expressed considerable concern regarding "the danger that pretrial publicity will prevent fair trials from ever being held." He then continued, with his customary eloquence:

> There is much more to this question than whether one or two people go to jail. Confidence in our institutions is at stake. We must find a way both to expose the truth and to punish the wrongdoers. Failure to convict persons in high office shown guilty of crime—even as a consequence of Senate hearings—could well shatter public confidence in our governmental institutions, particularly confidence in our system of justice. At a time when the Nation's concern about crime has focused attention on our system of justice, it would be discriminatory and therefore demoralizing for the powerful to go scot-free while ordinary citizens are sentenced to prison.

Predictably, the committee, by unanimous vote, rejected Cox's request for a temporary halt in its hearings. It was Senator Ervin's view that informing the nation immediately of the full parameters of the Watergate affair was the country's most pressing need.

Cox then, on June 6, made a bold move. The court had asked the committee and the special prosecutor to advise the court regarding its powers in ruling on a request for immunity. Cox responded by contending that the court could and should condition its order allowing the committee to grant immunity to Dean and Magruder on the requirement that live or recorded television and radio coverage of their testimony be barred. Cox again cited the "very serious danger" created by the Senate hearings "of widespread, pretrial publicity which might prevent bringing to justice those guilty of serious offenses in high government office." He then stated, "If the anticipated publicity is given to the testimony of these witnesses, 'the risk that the jury [that may be called upon to try them and others] will not, or cannot, follow instructions [to disregard the extra-judicial confessions] is so great, and the consequences of failure so vital * * * that the practical and human limitations of the jury system cannot be ignored.' "*

The committee's response, in its answering papers filed the next day, was essentially twofold: first, that the immunity statute did not allow the judge to condition a grant of authority to confer immunity on any requirement that television and radio be banished, even if he disagreed with the wisdom of broadcast hearings; second, that separation of powers principles proscribed the judge from tampering with the inner workings of a congressional panel and the conduct of its hearings. The committee, believing that fair criminal trials were in all events possible, also discounted Cox's doomsday predictions of prejudiced proceedings if broadcast coverage of Dean's and Magruder's testimonies was permitted.

Because of the unprecedented nature of Cox's position, we felt when we entered the courtroom on the morning of June 8 that Judge Sirica would reject the special prosecutor's request. Our confidence was bolstered when Carl Stern, NBC's sagacious lawyer-reporter, remarked that our brief "had blown them out of the water." The television and radio broadcasters naturally had a keen interest in airing the complete hearings, and on the morning of the argument, the three major networks and the Public Broadcasting System filed a joint amicus curiae (friend of the court) statement urging Judge Sirica not to ban their coverage. When we discovered that Cox was not at the hearing but had entrusted the task of argument to his assistant and Harvard colleague, Philip Heyman, our expectations of success were further increased. Heyman is a talented lawyer and law professor and his argument was certainly respectable, but Cox's absence was a signal to us and to the court that he placed little confidence in the position he had taken.

---

* Cox was quoting from *Bruton* v. *United States*, 391 U.S. 123, 135 (1968).

Sirica ruled for the committee.* His opinion is important not only for its holding regarding the immunity statute, but also because of its discussion respecting the relationship between the courts and legislative bodies. He had no power, said the judge, under the statute, to condition an immunity order on legislative exorcism of the broadcast media. Moreover, he ruled, the court had no inherent power to grant the special prosecutor's request. In attempting to preserve fair trials, he said, the court "could not go beyond administering its own affairs and attempt to regulate proceedings before a coordinate branch of government. . . . Decisional [court-made] law mandates a 'hands-off' policy on the court's part." However, troubled by the issues Cox raised, Sirica intimated that he "sympathize[d] with the Special Prosecutor's wish to avoid serious potential dangers to his mission." But he declined "to comment on the wisdom or unwisdom of granting immunity in this case or to express [his] opinion on the desirability or undesirability of implementing the Special Prosecutor's proposals," observing that, because the court should not interfere with legislative prerogatives, "to comment would be not only gratuitous but graceless." Cox did not appeal Sirica's ruling.

In hindsight, perhaps even Cox would agree that the televised testimony of Dean and Magruder produced far more good than harm.† It was the testimony of these two men that first helped the nation understand the extent of the Watergate affair and the moral rot in the White House. It was Dean's testimony that gave the first clue that the President might have taped his conversations. In large part it was the testimony of Dean and Magruder that sensitized the country to such degree that it reacted with outrage when the President dismissed Cox as special

---

* Application of United States Senate Select Committee on Presidential Campaign Activities, 361 F. Supp. 1271 (D.D.C. 1973).

† The final *Report* of the Special Prosecution Force issued in October 1975 admits that televising Dean's and Magruder's testimonies was beneficial to the country. See the *Report*, pp. 6–7.

prosecutor upon Cox's courageous refusal to agree to a spurious and unacceptable compromise of his lawsuit to obtain presidential tapes and documents. And that firing was the principal event that led to the instigation of impeachment proceedings by the House Judiciary Committee.

Broadcasting the testimony of Dean and Magruder was not the prime cause of Nixon's downfall, but it is fair to say that it promoted and hastened this outcome. And while the public testimony of Dean and Magruder did produce pretrial publicity, that publicity was submerged and probably rendered meaningless by the coverage of the extraordinary events that surrounded the release of the tapes and the impeachment proceedings. There is also no chance, as the special prosecutor feared, that the trials of Dean and Magruder will be prejudiced or harmed in any way by their testimony, for there will be no such trials—both have pleaded guilty to conspiracy to obstruct justice in the Watergate affair.

So rejoice, Mr. Cox, that you lost that early skirmish!

The President Is Sued

On Friday, July 13, 1973, Alexander Butterfield, under sharp questioning during closed session by Deputy Minority Counsel Donald Sanders, grudgingly revealed that for several years President Nixon had electronically recorded certain of his conversations. The following Monday Butterfield repeated his testimony to the full committee and, via television and radio, to the country. Some observers, including the highly respected columnist Joseph Kraft, contended that the Ervin committee blundered onto this critical piece of information. That conclusion is flatly wrong.

Butterfield (who, at the time he testified, was the administrator of the Federal Aviation Administration) had been a deputy assistant to President Nixon. In that capacity he had worked closely with H.R. Haldeman, once the President's White House chief of staff and a principal witness-to-come. The committee's staff, in preparation for Haldeman's testimony, interviewed everyone who had worked closely with him in the White House—except, of course, President Nixon, who demonstrated a marked disinclination to meet with the committee or its representatives. We referred to this procedure, which we also followed regarding other major witnesses, as a "satellite" operation. Butterfield was a Haldeman "satellite" and consequently was asked to an interview.

John Dean had told the committee that he had an inkling that his April 5, 1973, conversation with the President had been taped. Describing this meeting, Dean testified:

> The most interesting thing that happened during this conversation was, very near the end, he [the President] got up out of his chair, went behind his chair to the corner of the Executive Office Building and in a nearly inaudible tone said to me he was probably foolish to have discussed Hunt's clemency with Colson. . . .

This peculiar behavior led Dean to believe that the conversation was taped and that the President had attempted to keep his clemency remarks from being recorded. The President's lawyers later represented in court that the tape on the White House recording device had run out before this conversation occurred and consequently it was not recorded. If this is true, it is one of the small ironies of the Watergate affair that the President's whisper giving Dean the crucial clue was wasted.

After Dean's testimony it was clear that the question whether presidential conversations had been taped should be asked. In fact, several other witnesses before Butterfield had been queried about their knowledge of presidential taping systems. Butterfield, subjected to the crucible of intense examination, told the truth and admitted the existence of the recording devices.

The committee thus did not stumble onto this information. It is true, of course, that when Butterfield was scheduled for an interview the committee had no firm idea as to what he might say. But often a committee, although justifiably convinced that there is a condition demanding investigation, has scant notion about what specifics its inquiry will produce.* The task in these circumstances is to be thorough and explore all reasonable avenues that may lead to relevant information. Diligence may produce a Butterfield.

Acting on Butterfield's revelation the committee quickly requested access to relevant tape recordings. On July 23 the President, citing the need for confidentiality of presidential communications and papers, refused the committee's entreaty. His letter of rejection, however, could hardly have done more to whet the committee's interest. He wrote:

> If release of the tapes would settle the central questions at issue in the Watergate inquiries, then their disclosure might serve a substantial public interest that would have to be weighed very heavily against the negatives of disclosure.
>
> The fact is that the tapes would not finally settle the central issues before your Committee. Before their existence became publicly known, I personally listened to a number of them. The tapes are entirely consistent with what I know to be the truth and what I have stated to be the truth. However, as in any verbatim recording of informal conversations, they contain comments that persons with different perspectives and motivations would inevitably interpret in different ways. . . .

* The Supreme Court has recently stated: "The very nature of the investigative function—like any research—is that it takes the searchers up some 'blind alleys' and into nonproductive enterprises. To be a valid legislative inquiry there need be no predictable end result." *Eastland* v. *United States Servicemen's Fund,* 421 U.S. 491, 509 (1975).

The President by this time had repeatedly denied any complicity in a criminal conspiracy to cover up the true nature of the Watergate affair. We now know his statement that "The tapes are entirely consistent with what I know to be the truth and what I have stated to be the truth" was just another lie. At the time, however, it was the admission that the tapes contained "comments that persons with different perspectives and motivations would inevitably interpret in different ways" which drew the most attention, for this statement bore the strong suggestion that the tapes were incriminating. That subpoenas would issue after that declaration was ineluctable.

The two subpoenas served on the President on July 23 were history's first congressional subpoenas to the chief executive. The first subpoena called for the tape recordings of five specific conversations between John Dean and the President. The second sought various materials relating to the involvement of twenty-five named individuals —including John Dean, H.R. Haldeman, John Ehrlichman, John Mitchell, Charles Colson, Jeb Magruder, and Howard Hunt—in any criminal activities connected with the 1972 presidential election. On the same day Special Prosecutor Cox delivered a grand jury subpoena to the President asking for nine specific tape recordings (including four requested by the committee) and certain related documents.

The President's response to the committee was prompt. Again relying on the need for confidentiality of presidential communications and papers, he declined to honor the two subpoenas. Moreover, he said, the tapes were under his personal control and not obtainable from any subordinate. He had thrown down the gauntlet.

Several alternatives now faced the committee. It could have done nothing—the course taken by many congressional bodies in the past when their informal demands for evidence from the chief executive were denied. But after the committee had taken the extraordinary step of subpoenaing the President, that alternative would have been a clear sign of indecision, weakness, and defeat.

The committee could have instigated criminal contempt proceedings against the President.* Several difficulties, however, hampered this course. The full Senate probably would not have supported such an attempt against the President. Substantial legal authority suggests that a President cannot be criminally tried before he is impeached; Special Prosecutor Jaworski subsequently adopted this position and instructed the grand jury investigating the Watergate cover-up not to indict Mr. Nixon while he was President. Also, a criminal contempt proceeding would have been a prolonged affair and would not have assured the committee prompt access to the materials it wanted. Perhaps most important, a criminal proceeding in the summer of 1973, when public outrage against President Nixon was not yet full-blown, appeared an unseemly course to take. A majority of the public probably would have opposed this tactic.

The Senate has authority to dispatch its sergeant at arms to arrest and detain an individual who defies its process, but this alternative was obviously impractical. The sergeant at arms could not have reached the President, the public would have been incensed, and the full Senate, which must approve this procedure, would in all probability not have authorized its use.†

The only feasible alternative, therefore, was to sue, although this choice also had its hazards. The committee was aware of the pitfalls, but, on Senator Howard Baker's motion, it voted without dissent to institute suit.

* See Chapter III for a discussion of criminal contempt proceedings.

† See Chapter III, where this procedure is discussed in detail. During the House Judiciary Committee's impeachment investigation, California Congressman Don Edwards dismissed the use of this procedure to force evidence from Nixon, observing that "he's got the Army, the Navy, and Air Force and all we've got is Ken Harding [the House sergeant at arms]."

Before suit was brought, the committee sought the advice of several experts, including the late Alexander Bickel, Yale Law School's brilliant constitutional scholar. Bickel (with some prescience, as we shall see) advised the committee that the principal danger to maintenance of the suit was lack of jurisdiction—that is, that there was not statutory authority that would definitely ensure that a federal court would hear the committee's case. Bickel's recommendation was to seek passage of a new jurisdictional statute that would establish beyond doubt the committee's right to be in court. The suggestion had merit but was rejected; the committee was not certain that in the prevailing atmosphere Congress would pass such a bill, or that if the President vetoed it the veto could be overridden. In any event, if this legislative route were followed, considerable time would elapse before suit could be brought.

Several days hence an interview with Bickel appeared in *The New York Times* and other papers. Bickel told the *Times* that he had advised the committee of its jurisdictional difficulties and recommended that it seek a new jurisdictional statute. The President's lawyer Charles Alan Wright—not one to eschew twisting the knife— reported this event with some glee to Judge Sirica during a subsequent court proceeding in this case:

> Before going to the merits, as tempting as they are, it seems to me we have to consider the extraordinarily formidable jurisdictional obstacles that lie in the way of this unprecedented suit.
>
> Prior to the commencement of this action it was widely reported in the press that Mr. Dash and Senator Ervin had met with two distinguished academicians, Professor Bickel and Professor [Philip] Kurland, and they had been advised by Professor Bickel at least, [that] the only way the Senate could bring a suit was to get a special act of Congress authorized. They apparently concluded the contrary and we shall demonstrate that

they would have been better advised to follow Professor Bickel's advice.

Suit was filed on August 9, 1973. It was, as Wright later said, "unprecedented"; no congressional committee had ever sued the President to obtain evidence in his control. (Special Prosecutor Cox had moved even more quickly, initiating a court proceeding to enforce the grand jury's subpoena on July 26.) The committee's papers claimed that its subpoenas were lawful, and asserted that the President's refusal to comply with the subpoenas was illegal and could not "be excused or justified by resort to any Presidential power, prerogative or privilege." It was particularly inappropriate, the committee argued, to assert executive privilege to shield possible criminal activities by the President and his closest aides. And, the suit said, the supposed confidentiality of certain presidential communications at issue had already been breached by the President (whom our papers usually described as the "defendant President") when he revealed their contents and allowed his aides to testify regarding their nature. The committee contended that any privilege of confidentiality regarding these communications had been waived.

Several days after suit was filed, I received an irate letter from a woman in North Carolina who chastised me roundly for this misdeed and then, with rhetorical indignation, asked: "How dare you sue the President when he hasn't even been found guilty?" The reactions of the courts to the committee's suit were not this hostile—but almost. The reasons for this judicial reception may simply be those embodied in the various opinions this litigation produced. But there may have been unspoken grounds as well. Perhaps the suit rekindled memories of the legislative abuses of the McCarthy era where congressional committees improperly impinged upon executive prerogatives. Perhaps it was felt that the Ervin committee, in trying to get to the bottom of the Watergate affair, was encroaching on the preserve of the judicial system, which, of course, is chiefly responsible for the pursuit of criminal matters. The judicial animus may have been the product of a growing distaste and disdain among the judges for the Niagara of leaks that seemed to tumble almost daily from committee sources. Whatever the reason, judicial resistance to the committee's positions was pronounced.

The President responded to the committee's suit with a potpourri of defenses. Indeed, he raised most of the crux issues that pertain when Congress investigates criminal conduct in the executive branch. The President asserted that the tapes and other materials subpoenaed were protected from disclosure by the doctrines of executive privilege and separation of powers. Because the Constitution gives a President the exclusive, absolute power to decide whether to disclose presidential material, the President said, the issue before the court was not "justiciable," that is, the issue was a "political question" which the courts had no power to resolve. Moreover, he said, echoing Professor Bickel, the courts had no statutory jurisdiction to hear this case. In investigating criminal conduct, the President contended, the committee was in effect conducting a criminal trial, usurping the functions of the judiciary, and acting without valid legislative purpose. The Senate, he asserted, had not given the Select Committee authority to subpoena or sue the President. Other defenses were also raised, but these were the most significant.

It was the jurisdictional issue that struck a responsive chord in Judge Sirica. The committee had urged four statutory bases for jurisdiction, but Sirica, in an opinion* issued on October 17, rejected all four. He held that Congress had provided no statutory basis for this suit and thus the court had no jurisdiction to hear it. He wrote: "When it comes to jurisdiction of the federal courts, truly, to paraphrase the scripture, the Congress giveth, and the

---

* *Senate Select Committee on Presidential Campaign Activities* v. *Nixon*, 366 F. Supp. 51 (D.D.C. 1973).

Congress taketh away. . . . Job 1:21 (The Holy Bible)."
We will examine Judge Sirica's analysis later because it is
of substantial importance in considering how conflicts
over information between Congress and the executive
branch should be resolved.* Suffice it now to say that
despite Bickel's views, the committee found extraordinary
the judge's opinion that the federal courts had no authority to hear a case between Congress and the President
raising some of the major issues of the day, especially
since significant precedent allowed a contrary result.

Sirica's determination was particularly frustrating
because several weeks earlier the judge had ruled in favor
of the special prosecutor in his attempt to enforce the
grand jury's subpoena.† In language also applicable to
the committee's case, the judge had held that the President does not enjoy an absolute discretionary power to
withhold relevant evidence. He said that the final decision whether materials are protected by executive privilege rests with the court, not with the President: " 'The
laws of evidence do not excuse anyone because of the
office he holds.' "‡ The court, he indicated, could order
the President to comply with a lawfully issued subpoena
because the White House is not a sacrosanct "fourth
branch of government." Sirica also reaffirmed the principle that executive privilege cannot be used "as a cloak for
serious criminal wrongdoing. . . . If the interest served by
[the] privilege is abused or subverted, the claim of privilege fails." He ordered the material sought submitted to
him for private inspection in chambers so he could properly determine whether the President's claim should be
upheld.

On October 12, five days before Sirica's opinion in the
committee's cause, the Court of Appeals, by a 5–2 vote,
affirmed the essence of his ruling in the special prose-

* See Chapter VI.
† *In re Subpoena to Nixon*, 360 F. Supp. 1 (D.D.C. 1973).
‡ Sirica was quoting from Chief Justice John Marshall's opinion in
United States v. *Burr*, 25 Fed. Cas. 30 (Case No. 14, 692 d) (1807).

cutor's litigation.* While declaring that presidential communications are "presumptively privileged," the court
held that the President has no absolute executive privilege and cannot deny access to all executive materials
merely by its assertion. "Support for this kind of mischief," it said, "simply cannot be spun from incantation of the doctrine of separation of powers." The court
then stated that "application of Executive privilege
depends on a weighing of the public interest protected
by the privilege against the public interests that would
be served by disclosure in a particular case." It ruled that
the President's presumption of privilege failed in this case
in the face of the "uniquely powerful showing" of need
made by the special prosecutor.

These rulings in the special prosecutor's case, however,
proved of no assistance to the committee when Sirica,
declining to reach the merits, dismissed the committee's
suit for want of jurisdiction. The committee promptly
appealed Sirica's ruling against it.

The stage was now set for some of the most remarkable
events in American history.

On Friday, October 19, President Nixon announced that
he would not seek Supreme Court review of the Court of
Appeals ruling in the special prosecutor's case. Although
"confident" that the high court would sustain his position, he said, he had concluded "that it is not in the
national interest to leave this matter unresolved for the
period that might be required for a review by the highest
court." Instead, he stated through Attorney General
Elliot Richardson that he had offered Special Prosecutor
Cox a "compromise"—"one that goes beyond what any
President in history has offered." The compromise, he
said, "would . . . have resolved any lingering thought that
the President himself might have been involved in a

---

* *Nixon v. Sirica,* 487 F.2d 700 (D.C. Cir. 1973).

Watergate cover-up." Pursuant to this compromise, the President declared, "there would be submitted to Judge Sirica, through a statement prepared by me personally from the subpoenaed tapes, a full disclosure of everything contained in those tapes that has any bearing on Watergate." The authenticity of this summary, he said, would be verified by Senator John Stennis.

The President then dropped one of those proverbial Washington "bombshells": "I am pleased to be able to say that Chairman Sam Ervin and Vice Chairman Howard Baker of the Senate Select Committee have agreed to this procedure and that at their request, and mine, Senator John Stennis has consented to listen to every requested tape and verify that the statement . . . is full and accurate."

Cox, however, refused to accept the deal. The President, therefore, directed him, "as an employee of the Executive Branch, to make no further attempts by judicial process to obtain tapes, notes, or memoranda of Presidential conversations." Cox, asserting that "Acceptance of these directions would . . . defeat the fair administration of criminal justice," declined to follow the President's order.

For this insubordination the President, on Saturday, October 20, ordered first Attorney General Elliot Richardson and then Deputy Attorney General William Ruckelshaus to fire Cox. Both refused and resigned their posts in protest. Subsequently, Solicitor General Robert Bork, who became Acting Attorney General upon the resignations of Richardson and Ruckelshaus, discharged Cox on the President's instruction. The position of special prosecutor was abolished and the FBI promptly sealed the offices of the Watergate special prosecution force as well as those formerly occupied by Richardson and Ruckelshaus. The nation thus had a new cause célèbre—"the Saturday Night Massacre."

These events produced what Alexander Haig, the President's chief of staff, depicted as a "firestorm." On the weekend of the Cox firing alone, a half million telegrams came to Congress, the overwhelming majority critical of the President's actions. By October 24, 84 members of the House of Representatives had introduced legislation dealing with impeachment. A total of 144 representatives and 59 senators authored or co-sponsored bills to create a truly independent office of special prosecutor.

In the face of such pressure the President was forced to back down. On October 23 Wright told a slightly incredulous Judge Sirica that the President "would comply in all respects" with the court orders in the special prosecutor's case. (Wright later learned, to his embarrassment, that the White House would not "comply in all respects" with the court orders because two of the conversations at issue, the White House said, had not been recorded and there was an unexplained eighteen-minute gap on the recording of another.) A new special prosecutor, Leon Jaworski, was appointed by the President on November 1. Jaworski was given the same independence purportedly afforded Cox, with the additional assurance that the President would not remove him without the agreement of a "substantial majority" of an eight-member congressional group which would include the majority and minority leaders of both houses and the chairmen and ranking minority members of the Senate and House Judiciary committees.

The actual role played by Senators Ervin and Baker in these events is the subject of some controversy. The President's statement implied that Ervin and Baker had agreed to a comprehensive deal by which both the special prosecutor's case and the committee's litigation would be dropped in exchange for "summaries," verified by Senator Stennis, of the tapes under subpoena. According to Ervin and Baker's account, this implication was grossly inaccurate. Their narration of the events surrounding the Stennis compromise suggests that the President's statement constituted a deliberate deception concerning their part in the matter.

On Friday, October 19, both senators were called to the White House from out-of-town engagements to meet with the President and two of his counsel. At that time, according to the senators, the President *unilaterally* offered certain materials to the committee. There was not even a tentative commitment by Ervin and Baker that in exchange the committee would forgo its suit. In fact, the senators understood that the committee was free to continue its litigation. Certainly, no understanding existed on their part that the President's dealings with the committee were in any way related to Cox's lawsuit. Moreover, Ervin and Baker claimed that the President had offered not mere "summaries" of the conversations in question but verbatim transcripts. Such transcripts or even summaries would have been far more helpful to the committee than to Cox, who, under the laws of evidence, needed the actual tapes—the best evidence available—for use in criminal proceedings. Whatever the nature of the President's offer, it was withdrawn after October 23, when Wright announced that the President would obey the court's commands to produce the tapes under grand jury subpoena to Cox.

There was strong feeling in Washington that Ervin and Baker had been used—that they had been cynically maneuvered into a position where it appeared they had approved an arrangement rejected by Cox. It was speculated that by securing the senators' acceptance the President was attempting to make the Cox rejection seem unreasonable and thus gain public support for firing him. Some observers felt that the firing of Cox, whose investigations were proving increasingly embarrassing and dangerous for the President and his aides and friends (e.g., "Bebe" Rebozo), was the design from the beginning. Committee member Lowell Weicker, never short on outrage, initially was openly critical of Ervin and Baker's role. "Rather than appearing wise and honorable," he declared on October 20, "last night's compromise looks like what it is—a deal between an evasive President and

an easily diverted Congress. I am glad the special prosecutor had no part of it. I will have no part of it."

―――――――

Judging that the mood of Congress and the country
had changed, the committee, with Ervin taking the lead,
decided to alter its litigation tactics. The committee and
staff were convinced that Sirica's jurisdictional ruling was
wrong in several respects and that the Court of Appeals
would reverse. Nevertheless, the committee, perceiving
that Congress would now be amenable, introduced a bill
to give the federal courts jurisdiction over the committee's suit.

The bill easily passed both houses and became law in
mid-December when the President failed to veto it.* He
did complain, however, that "The intent of this legislation is to circumvent the established judicial process by
making the court a vehicle for congressional actions not
envisaged in the Constitution," and his counsel later
referred to the new statute as "legislative legerdemain."
The committee also took advantage of the new mood in
Congress by introducing a Senate resolution declaring
that the committee was fully empowered by the Senate to
subpoena and sue the President, and that in so doing, it
was acting with valid legislative purpose and seeking
information vital to its legislative missions.† This resolution, unanimously passed on November 7, answered several objections to the committee's suit previously raised
by the President.

After enactment of these two measures, the committee, to expedite the matter, asked the appellate court
to keep the case and decide it on the merits. The court
declined to do so and remanded the matter to Sirica.
Sirica, already inundated with other Watergate matters,
transferred the case to Judge Gerhard Gesell. This move

* PL 93–190 (1973).
† S. Res. 194, 93d Cong., 1st Sess. (Nov. 7, 1973).

did not displease the committee because Gesell, a man of dominant intellect, had the courage to rule against the President if convinced the situation required it. As we soon discovered, he also had the fortitude to reject the committee's claims and to announce his own unique perceptions of controlling principles of law.

Gesell is known for moving the cases on his docket with alacrity, and his handling of the Ervin committee's case was consonant with his reputation. On January 25, 1974, less than three weeks after he received the matter from Sirica, Gesell issued three orders.* The first denied enforcement of the committee's subpoena that had sought all White House materials relating to the involvement of twenty-five individuals in criminal activities connected with the 1972 presidential campaign. This subpoena, said the judge, was too broad and unspecific to allow enforcement. Secondly, the judge ruled that the President's claim of executive privilege regarding the other subpoena for five specific tape recordings was too general, and requested the President to particularize his claims of privilege concerning each of those recordings. This request was in line with the Court of Appeals ruling in the special prosecutor's case; there the court had said that a blanket claim of privilege was insufficient in the face of a compelling need for production of the materials sought, and that the President must make a particular claim of privilege regarding each item he wished to protect. Finally, Gesell asked Special Prosecutor Jaworski to inform the court what the effect would be on pending or imminent criminal cases if he granted the subpoena for the five tape recordings.

Jaworski's response concerning the effect on Watergate prosecutions was much more restrained and less strident than Cox's contentions in his litigation with the Ervin committee about the adverse effect on upcoming trials of

* These orders are unreported. They are discussed in *Senate Select Committee on Presidential Campaign Activities* v. *Nixon*, 498 F. 2d 725, 728 (D.C. Cir. 1974).

the broadcast testimony of John Dean and Jeb Magruder. Jaworski did state that release of the tapes by the committee "would increase the risk that those indicted could contend with more force than presently available that widespread pretrial publicity prevents the Government from empaneling an unbiased jury for the trial of the offenses charged . . ." But, he added, "We are confident that notwithstanding prior publicity, if jurors are selected with the care required by the decisions in this Circuit, all defendants will receive a fair and prompt trial."

The President's reply was much less forthright. He declined to detail his claim of privilege regarding each of the tapes in issue—a result not surprising, since (with one minor exception) the President had been unable to suggest specific reasons in the special prosecutor's case why four of the same five tapes the committee sought were privileged. But, he said, "it is incumbent upon me to be sensitive to the possible adverse effects upon ongoing and forthcoming criminal proceedings should the contents of these subpoenaed conversations be made public at an inappropriate time. The dangers connected with excessive pretrial publicity are as well-known to this Court as they are to me. Consequently, my Constitutional mandate to see that the laws are faithfully executed requires my prohibiting the disclosures of any of these materials at this time and in this forum."

The hypocrisy of this statement was suffocating. The President and his counsel previously had essentially ignored the preservation of fair trials as a reason to avoid production of the tapes. Moreover, the President himself had made numerous statements about Watergate and allowed his aides to testify ad nauseum about the subject in a way that produced prolonged and sensational publicity. Plainly his pretrial publicity defense was an afterthought prompted only by Gesell's concerns. And shortly thereafter the President quickly forgot his proclaimed fears regarding prejudiced trials and made the transcripts of the five recordings available to the public when he perceived it was in his own best interest to do so.

Gesell's final opinion was issued on February 8.* He found that the tapes sought were relevant to the committee's functions. He ruled that the case did not involve a political question that the courts could not resolve. He held that the blanket assertion of executive privilege by the President was insufficient, and that because the President had declined to make specific his claims of privilege, no privilege based on confidentiality grounds could be sustained. But Gesell declined to enforce the committee's subpoenas in an opinion that is one of the most unusual in the history of relations between the courts and Congress. Echoing the special prosecutor, Gesell observed that "the risk exists that [pretrial publicity] would bolster contentions that unbiased juries cannot be impaneled for trial." "[T]he public interest," he said, "requires at this stage of affairs that priority be given to the requirements of orderly and fair judicial administration. * * * [S]urely the time has come to question whether it is in the public interest for the criminal investigative aspects of [the committee's] work to go forward in the blazing atmosphere of ex parte publicity directed to issues that are immediately and intimately related to pending criminal proceedings. . . . [T]he Court, when its equity jurisdiction is invoked, can and should exercise its discretion not to enforce a subpoena which would exacerbate the pretrial publicity in areas that are specifically identified with pending criminal charges." Judge Gesell's ruling thus amounted to a subjugation of legislative need to his view of the requirements of the criminal process. The committee, regarding Gesell's ruling as a dangerous intrusion on legislative prerogatives, determined to appeal.†

* *Senate Select Committee on Presidential Campaign Activities* v. *Nixon*, 370 F. Supp. 521 (D.D.C. 1974).

† There was more to Gesell's opinion and it warrants extended discussion, but that must wait until later. See Chapters IV and V.

Between Gesell's ruling and the Court of Appeals opinion several events of historical magnitude occurred that significantly shaped the appellate court's eventual decision. On March 1 the Watergate grand jury indicted seven men—H.R. Haldeman, John Ehrlichman, John Mitchell, Charles Colson, Robert Mardian, Gordon Strachan, and Kenneth Parkinson—for their alleged role in the Watergate cover-up. The grand jury also submitted a report to Judge Sirica dealing with President Nixon's involvement in Watergate, which included copies of four of the five tapes at issue in the committee's suit, and strongly recommended to the judge that he forward the report to the House Judiciary Committee, which was studying the President's possible impeachment. After litigation on the matter, Sirica ordered the report transmitted to the House. Subsequently the President, perhaps hoping to salvage some vestige of favorable public opinion, sent to the House duplicates of all materials he had previously surrendered to the special prosecutor, including copies of the five tapes the committee sought. Then, on April 30, the President released to the nation edited transcripts of forty-nine presidential conversations, including his versions of the five conversations under committee subpoena.

The committee in the appeals court contended that at this stage any argument that the actual tapes should be withheld from it for reasons of confidentiality or to protect fair trials was wholly untenable. No confidentiality was left to preserve, the committee said, and release of the tapes to the committee would not create a danger of *additional* prejudice to criminal defendants. To claim now that the tapes were privileged on any theory, the committee urged, "would be to wink at history."

The Court of Appeals' reaction to these events differed. On May 2 it issued an order requesting the committee to state whether, after these occurrences, "it has a present sense of need for the materials subpoenaed." The committee was thus caught in a dilemma. The tocsin had sounded: it was fairly clear from the tenor of the court's order that the court was now extremely dubious about the committee's need for the actual recordings. The committee, however, could now accept the transcripts as substantial compliance with its subpoenas and walk away claiming victory. This, after defeats at the hands of Sirica and Gesell, was not an unappealing option. But this course might severely undercut the position of the House Judiciary Committee in its impeachment inquiry. That committee had issued certain subpoenas to the President which had been answered only by the provision of edited transcripts. The House committee, which had a *judicial* function to perform, needed the best evidence available—the actual recordings. If the Ervin committee accepted transcripts, the President could lambast the House committee as unreasonable for failing to follow suit. The President had employed this trick before—the first special prosecutor, Cox, had been branded unreasonable and insubordinate for refusing to agree to the Stennis compromise for "summaries" of tape recordings, which, the President declared, Senators Ervin and Baker had accepted. For this reason, and since it was considered unwise to allow Gesell's ruling to stand as a possible precedent for the future, the committee decided to press its appeal.

The committee told the court it needed the actual recordings because the presidential versions of the conversations appeared "neither complete nor accurate." "The Committee," it argued, "should not have to perform its legislative missions on the basis of transcripts that are suspect." The umbrage the committee's statements roused in the President's counsel (James St. Clair, Charles Alan Wright, et al.) exuded from their written response: "Counsel for the [President] take the strongest possible exception to the tone and substance of [the] gratuitous statement . . . that the 'transcripts . . . are suspect.' " "[T]he Committee," they said, "has been provided with a complete and accurate account of all Watergate-related portions of privileged Presidential conversations sought by its subpoena." Quoting the President's April 30 statement that "as far as what the President personally knew and did with regard to Watergate and the coverup is concerned, these materials—together with those already made available—will tell it all," they asserted that "All the factual material concerning the President's discussions with his aides, of the events commonly called Watergate, are presented in the published transcripts."

These representations, events have proved, were essentially inaccurate. The nation now knows that the transcripts released on April 30 were not "complete and accurate," that they did not, in the President's words, "tell it all." There is now in the public domain, for example, a June 23, 1972, recording between the President and H.R. Haldeman that demonstrates conclusively the President's early knowledge of and participation in the Watergate cover-up. This recording, although its existence was well known, apparently had not been heard by the President's lawyers when they made their statements to the court. It is an interesting question, somewhat beyond the scope of this book, whether attorneys for any client—the President included—should, as officers of the court, make serious representations to a court about the state of vital evidence in their clients' possession without having personally examined that evidence.

Attorney General William Saxbe, in a friend-of-the-court brief not solicited by the court, supported the President's general position on appeal. This brief was unremarkable and added little to the discussion of the issues before the court. What was remarkable, however, was that he filed it at all. Saxbe had been a member of the Senate when, in November 1973, it passed without dissent a resolution putting its full support behind the committee's suit against the President. More significantly, however, in the confirmation hearing regarding his nomination as Attorney General, Saxbe in essence had pledged to let Special Prosecutor Jaworski handle Watergate issues. (Jaworski, in fact, at the court's request, submitted a friend-of-the-court brief in which he assumed essentially the same position he had ventured to Judge Gesell.) Saxbe's entry onto the Watergate scene brought the barbed charge from Senator Ervin that Saxbe had abandoned fidelity to his earlier representations. "The Attorney General," Ervin said, "has violated his solemn agreement . . . that he would leave all matters related to Watergate to . . . Jaworski."

Saxbe countered with the assertion that he was not promoting the President's position on the merits of the case, but was concerned only with "institutional issues" regarding the relations among Congress, the executive, and the courts. Saxbe's retort, however, was dissembling designed to extricate himself from an embarrassing situation (not the only one his loquacity has landed him in) because he had clearly urged adoption of the President's contentions in the immediate case. For example, he had asserted that "the district court . . . properly recognized that [the need to prevent unfair pretrial publicity] constituted a basis for refusing to enforce the subpoena of the Committee" and that "the interest of the President in protecting the confidentiality of presidential communications in this case . . . outweighs the needs of the Committee."

The Court of Appeals decision came on May 23, 1974, less than a month and a half before the committee ended its investigations.* The committee, which from the beginning had sought expedition of its litigation, had to struggle to achieve an opinion by even that late date. The committee's request to expedite argument on the case by two weeks had been granted only after it filed a motion to that end signed by all seven senators on the committee in addition to staff counsel. Two of seven Court of Appeals judges dissented from even that meager beneficence.

The Court of Appeals affirmed Judge Gesell but not for the reasons he had posited. The court began by reiterating that presidential communications are "presumptively privileged." But then a new wrinkle. This presump-

* *Senate Select Committee on Presidential Campaign Activities* v. *Nixon,* 498 F. 2d 725 (D.C. Cir. 1974).

tion, the court said, can be vitiated only by a strong showing of need by the institution of government seeking presidential materials—"a showing that the responsibilities of that institution cannot responsibly be fulfilled without access to records of the President's deliberations." It apparently had not occurred to Judge Gesell, nor to President's counsel before appellate argument, that the only way to dispel the presumption of confidentiality was to come forth with a demonstration of such substantial need. The committee had argued that the presumption was removed because the confidentiality of the conversations had been forfeited and because there was a prima facie case that the materials sought concerned the criminal involvement of the President and his closest aides.

Largely because of events that had transpired since the District Court's ruling, the appellate court said, the committee could not make this strong showing of need. Because the House Judiciary Committee already had copies of the five tapes, the court ruled that the Ervin committee did not need these tapes to fulfill whatever informing or oversight function the Congress as an entity might have. The court also declared that the tapes were not "critical" to the committee's performance of its lawmaking function. As a general matter, the court stated, Congress requires less information about past events to legislate than does a grand jury to indict. And, in the peculiar circumstances of this case, the court said, the committee had no critical need for the tapes, since partial transcripts of the five conversations had already been made public and the likelihood was that the House's factual finding in the impeachment inquiry would soon be released.

Because the committee's tenure was waning and because the factual posture of the case did not now portend a favorable ruling, the committee determined not to seek review of this decision in the Supreme Court. The Court of Appeals opinion, therefore, stands as the most authoritative decision on congressional requests for evidence from the President. We shall return to it later to explore its full ramifications and to consider the effect on its teachings of a later executive privilege ruling by the Supreme Court concerning a request for still more presidential tapes by Special Prosecutor Jaworski.*

The Ervin Committee as Defendant

The Ervin committee was the target of a number of lawsuits brought by individuals and organizations vexed with the committee's proceedings and procedures. Three of these, because of the variety of issues raised, are particularly relevant. The litigation initiated by Rabbi Baruch Korff and his National Citizens Committee for Fairness to the Presidency attempted to enjoin further *public* hearings by the committee. The suit brought by the Howard Hughes empire sought the converse; the plaintiffs contended that their interrogation at *private* or executive sessions should be prohibited. The litigation instituted by Charles "Bebe" Rebozo and his interests attempted to interdict *all* further investigations into his affairs and to prevent the initiation of contempt proceedings against him.†

President Nixon reportedly told Rabbi Korff in the spring of 1974 that "you are our greatest advocate." The rabbi was an improbable defender of the President. Most of Nixon's men—the Deans, Haldemans, Magruders—are clean-cut, well attired, urbane. They appear, on the surface, as American as the flag. Korff is different. Born in the Soviet Ukraine, he lived in Poland before coming to America and his accent still bears the traces of his heritage. He is a small, graying man of sixty, more rumpled than natty. His appearance suggests meekness and reserve.

His demeanor, however, belies the intensity of his pas-

* See Chapter VI.
† The opinions and orders in these three cases are unreported.

sions and the vigor of his dedication to his causes. During the Nazi regime he was instrumental in the escape of many Jews from Germany. After the war, *Time* magazine reported, he was involved with the so-called Stern gang, a terrorist organization bent on ousting Britain from Palestine. He was arrested by the French in 1947 for participation in a bizarre scheme to bombard London with leaflets advocating the independence of Israel.

The rabbi demonstrated a remarkable capacity to spew vitriol toward those he believed to be unfair to the President. On July 29, 1973, he began to place a series of advertisements in prominent newspapers castigating the press and Congress for what he felt were unwarranted attacks on the President. In his initial screed in *The New York Times* he branded the Ervin committee as "hanging judges . . . fostering a vigilante atmosphere." Later ads did not raise the level of discourse. In a September 19 open letter to the President's daughter Julie Eisenhower, he labeled her father's opponents as "purveyors of political pornography" who were guilty of "character assassination." He subsequently said he regarded Nixon as a man who had been "vilified, savaged, brutalized, whose blood has been sapped by vampires."

Despite his extravagant rhetoric, the rabbi's campaign to support the President was rather successful. His first ad, paid for by money he had saved for a Martha's Vineyard vacation with his wife, listed only seventeen other co-sponsors, including a housewife, a jeweler, a student, and a retired cab driver. In June 1974, however, he claimed a membership of two million for his Fairness committee, which, he said, was growing at a rate of twenty-five thousand a week. He had raised around $1 million from his advertisements, he declared, including $25,000 from the Teamsters Union.

The rabbi's lawsuit to block the Ervin committee's public hearings, brought in September 1973, continued the language of his advertisements. The charging papers said that the committee, through televised proceedings conducted with "considerable attendant theatrics" and "histrionic questioning," had "deliberately and inequitably disrupted the domestic tranquility of the United States of America by undermining the confidence of citizens of the United States in the integrity of the administration of the Department of Justice and the Judiciary of the Government of the United States of America, to the damage of all citizens of the United States of America . . ." (The suit, in fact, was brought as a class action on behalf of all the citizens of America; this Gargantuan class presumably included both President Nixon and Sam Ervin.) The committee's actions were illegal, the suit complained (paralleling previous claims by the rabbi's chosen ward, Mr. Nixon) because in investigating criminal conduct the committee was exceeding its legislative authority and usurping the functions of the judiciary. Moreover, the suit said, individuals affected by the televised hearings were being denied constitutional protections because: (1) witnesses were allowed to give public hearsay testimony about criminal matters—that is, to testify concerning facts told them by others about which the witnesses had no personal knowledge; (2) prior notice was not given to individuals who would be implicated in criminal conduct by the public testimony of others before the committee; (3) persons publicly accused of criminal conduct were not allowed to confront and cross-examine their accusers; (4) the televised proceedings denied potential defendants a prompt trial by an impartial jury.

Certain of the factual allegations made by the rabbi were correct. The committee did accept hearsay testimony. Those accused of criminal conduct at public session were not always aware that such accusations would be made. An individual adversely affected by public testimony was not given the right to cross-examine the offending witness. Nonetheless, the rabbi's lawsuit came to no avail, as we shall see momentarily.

The other two major lawsuits against the committee resulted from its inquiries into a $100,000 contribution by Howard Hughes, the eccentric tycoon, to Charles "Bebe" Rebozo for President Nixon's 1972 reelection campaign. This investigation was both effective and controversial. It was effective because it raised the clear possibility, contrary to Rebozo's claim that the $100,000 was returned untouched to Hughes after the 1972 election, that some of this money had actually been spent by Rebozo for the President's *personal* benefit. It was controversial because it was conducted in an aggressive manner and was plagued by a series of leaks of confidential information uncovered by the probe.

The first of the lawsuits spawned by this investigation was brought in November 1973 by the Summa Corporation and five of its employees. The Summa Corporation is the successor to the Hughes Tool Company; Howard Hughes owns 100 percent of its stock. The suit sought to block private or executive-session interrogation of Summa's employees. It also sought to stop the initiation of contempt proceedings against Summa officials who refused to testify in private session. In addition to the committee, the suit named as defendants Chief Counsel Sam Dash and Terry Lenzer, the assistant chief counsel in charge of the investigation. The Hughes lawyer was Summa's general counsel, Chester A. Davis, a voluble and volatile man formerly indicted along with Hughes and others by a Las Vegas grand jury for stock fraud.*

The spur to the suit was the leaks from the committee. Various Summa employees had given information in private interviews to committee staff. Afterwards what they considered inaccurate accounts of their sessions were reported in the press. "Following plaintiffs' voluntary statements to the staff of the defendant Committee," the suit stated, "stories appeared in the press and other media containing incomplete, distorted and speculative accounts

---

* The indictment against Davis and the other defendants has been dismissed, but the government is appealing this ruling.

of the information obtained from the plaintiffs by the staff of the defendant Committee." "I believe," said an indignant Chester Davis "that . . . public hearings are imperative in view of the numerous and prejudicial 'leaks' to the news media which have repeatedly followed the giving of testimony to the Committee in its 'executive sessions' which are closed to the public and press." To Davis, the committee's private sessions were no better than Star Chamber proceedings.

Davis's theories for his suit were several. He contended that the plaintiffs had a due process right to an open hearing to protect themselves against the prejudicial publicity that sprang from the leaks from the committee. He also asserted that his clients had a First Amendment free speech right to give their testimony in public session. His free speech argument, in particular, was lacking in substance. As I contended to the court for the committee, hopefully with some force: "As Your Honor knows, there are plenty of newsmen and plenty of cameras right outside the courthouse that I imagine would be available for Mr. Davis if he wants to go out there and give his full story about the matters we are inquiring into." Indeed, while arguing his cause, Davis displayed the interesting mannerism of turning from the bench to face the members of the press corps assembled in the courtroom.

Davis's best argument was statutory. At that time a provision of the federal code declared:

> Each hearing conducted by each standing, select, or special committee of the Senate (except the Committee on Appropriations) shall be open to the public except when the committee determines that the testimony to be taken at that hearing may relate to a matter of national security, may tend to reflect adversely on the character or reputation of the witness or any other individual, or may divulge matters deemed confidential under other provisions of law or Government regulation . . .*

* 2 U.S.C. 190–a–1 (b) (1970), now replaced by Senate Standing Rule xxv, par. 7 (b).

The committee had not made a determination for private hearings in regard to the Hughes-Rebozo investigation. Neither had it done so concerning any of its other inquiries, although all were initially pursued in private sessions. Davis had caught the committee amiss, much to its embarrassment.

But the committee had a remedy. It promptly passed a resolution stating that the Hughes-Rebozo investigation, which was probing possible criminal conduct, was expected to produce information that might defame certain individuals and might relate to a matter of national security. The purported national security matter concerned the electronic surveillance, allegedly at the President's behest, of his brother Donald Nixon because of the latter's business relationship with a one-time Hughes employee. The committee was investigating this same relationship, but the White House had instructed John Ehrlichman and H.R. Haldeman not to discuss the matter on grounds of national security. The ever-incensed Davis denounced the committee's resolution in court as a "sham" and "a fraud on the public." The committee, with some restraint, dismissed these charges as "unsupported, imprudent advocacy."

As can be surmised from this discussion, there was considerable animosity between the Hughes forces and those members of the Ervin committee's staff conducting the Hughes-Rebozo investigation. But that animosity pales when compared to the enmity between those investigators and Rebozo and his lawyers, most particularly William Snow Frates, whose booming sonorous voice was later heard at the Watergate conspiracy trial, where he represented John Ehrlichman.

In April 1974 the investigation of Rebozo had been under way for around eight months. The staff had subjected Rebozo and the Key Biscayne Bank and Trust Company, of which Rebozo is president and chairman of the board, to rigorous examination. Rebozo and the bank had responded to several subpoenas and Rebozo had been intensively interrogated. But in April the staff, hot on the trail of new leads concerning possible expenditures of the $100,000, persuaded Senator Ervin to issue additional subpoenas to Rebozo and his bank. These subpoenas touched off the lawsuit against the committee; the suit sought to quash the subpoenas, stop all further investigation of Rebozo and the bank, and enjoin the initiation of contempt proceedings against Rebozo for failure to honor the committee's subpoenas. It also asked damages from the committee for past harassment.

The language of the charging papers was worthy of Rabbi Korff. The staff, they said, was conducting an "exploratory witch hunt" which amounted to "a partisan vendetta against a friend of the President." In fact, the suit said, one staff member had stated that the purpose of the investigation "was 'getting the whole damn crowd' for the alleged laundering of funds by the Plaintiffs in connection with campaign contributions during the Presidential elections of 1972, thereby indicating that the purpose of the investigation was not a legislative one but rather prosecutorial in nature."

Two aspects of the investigation particularly irked Rebozo. The first was the extraordinary thoroughness of the inquiry, which had probed deeply into his private and business affairs in an effort to determine what use had been made of the $100,000 Hughes contribution. On several occasions the investigators had even subpoenaed records of concerns doing business with Rebozo to ascertain the extent of his expenditures. This activity, which Rebozo described as a "deluge of subpoenas," led him to make the following complaint: ". . . [T]he Committee's investigations now seek to humiliate and embarrass the Plaintiff by new subpoenas to every other type of business with which Plaintiff Rebozo has dealt. They have subpoenaed the records of such diverse businesses as Plaintiff Rebozo's grocer, a Miami department store and the public utility which furnishes water to the Plaintiffs." The subpoenas issued to him personally, he claimed, were "being used as a bludgeon by irresponsible members of the Committee staff who are engaged in a harassing witch hunt . . ."

But the feature of the probe that rankled Rebozo the most was the regular flow of leaks from the investigation that appeared in the press. His papers variously declared: "The Committee's agents . . . determined that they would use the auspices and color of authority of The Committee in order to conduct an investigation and simultaneously reveal to the media their personal belief as to the activities to the Plaintiffs so as to create an inflammatory public atmosphere and thereby impede and otherwise adversely affect the deliberations of various judicial and legislative bodies . . ." "(A)gents of The Committee willfully and maliciously disclosed and caused to be published by the news media false and inaccurate accounts of information given by Plaintiff Rebozo . . ." "The Committee investigators . . . [employed an] invariable method of attack on Plaintiff Rebozo by disseminating their prevarications to the media."

Frates proffered a variety of legal theories which, he contended, entitled Rebozo to relief. The outstanding subpoenas, he said, were not supported by valid legislative purpose and were "so broad as to constitute an unreasonable search and seizure in violation of the Fourth Amendment." The leaks, he claimed, not only violated the committee's own rules but also transgressed specific provisions of the federal criminal code. Moreover, Frates argued, "The undue publication of private testimony has denied Mr. Rebozo the rudiments of due process and the elemental protections necessary for a fair hearing. The true facts and the public exoneration of Mr. Rebozo has (*sic*) been irrevocably obliterated and smothered by a group whose designated purpose was to investigate to safeguard the process of government."

The committee came to the defense of its staff. In papers filed with the court, it said: "[Plaintiffs'] documents make scurrilous and irresponsible charges against the Committee and its staff which the Committee takes this opportunity to reject . . . This suit is most properly viewed as an attempt to divert public attention from the legitimate role of this Committee." Despite the committee's protestations, this might have been a difficult lawsuit to defend on the merits. There was concern that a judge might rule that the subpoenas to Rebozo were too indiscriminate. More significantly, however, the leak charge would have been exceedingly embarrassing to confront directly. There was no disputing that—whatever the sources, detailed supposedly confidential information concerning the Rebozo investigation had appeared in the media at frequent intervals.

The committee's defense against all three suits was successful. But none of these cases resulted in a final decision on the merits of the specific issues raised by the plaintiffs. In all three the committee convinced the court that technical legal obstacles prevented the relief plaintiffs sought.

District Judge June Green dismissed Rabbi Korff's suit on two grounds. First, she said, the rabbi and the members of his committee had no standing to sue—that is, they had no legally recognizable injury because they would not be called before the committee to testify or otherwise be affected in any substantial manner by its proceedings. Furthermore, she ruled, the speech or debate clause found in Article I of the United States Constitution protects congressmen from a suit of this nature. That clause provides, rather ambiguously, that "for any Speech or Debate in either House, [a Congressman] shall not be questioned in any other Place."* Our argument in this regard was that the clause safeguards senators from suits growing out of the exercise of their legislative duties and that clearly the conduct of committee hearings was a legislative act protected from court challenge.

* United States Constitution, Art. I, Sec. 6, Cl. 1. We shall examine the clause in considerable depth in Chapter X.

Undaunted, Rabbi Korff immediately took his case to the Court of Appeals and then the Supreme Court. Both courts refused to enter an injunction against the committee pending appeal of the case. The Supreme Court's ruling was by Chief Justice Warren Burger. The public hearings continued.

Rabbi Korff personally participated in the lengthy argument before Judge Green. In a deferential and courtly manner he approached the lectern to state, "While I am at this pulpit for a moment, Your Honor, I want to point out that I look upon any court as a sanctuary and when I am here I feel as if I am in a sanctuary." It was reported that Korff, after Judge Green ruled against him, paraded the halls of the courthouse contending he had not received a fair hearing. While the rabbi may equate courtrooms and sanctuaries, he apparently believes he receives more attention from the Almighty than the judiciary.

The committee was victorious in the Hughes and Rebozo suits for different reasons. Judge Aubrey Robinson denied the Hughes request for an injunction and dismissed the case principally because he thought it would be premature to review the committee's action at that juncture. Examination of the committee's conduct should come, he observed, only in a criminal contempt proceeding initiated by the committee, if that circumstance should eventuate. He made plain his view that a court should not lightly interfere with the conduct of legislative investigations.*

Judge John Smith's reasons for denying Rebozo's request for an injunction were in part similar. A contempt proceeding, not a civil suit, he indicated, was the correct place to review the actions of the committee and its staff. And because the suit was not finally heard until after the committee's investigatory powers lapsed, Judge

* The Court of Appeals rejected Davis's attempt to enjoin the committee while appeal was pending. After the committee's investigatory powers expired, the Court of Appeals dismissed the appeal as moot.

Smith ruled that the portion of the suit seeking to restrain the committee's investigation was moot.

After Watergate, there may be few tears shed for Rabbi Korff, Howard Hughes, and Bebe Rebozo. Indeed, after all the publicity—much of it negative—that has surrounded these persons, some may be inclined to view them more as caricatures than flesh-and-blood people with legitimate problems. Because of these factors and because definitive rulings on some of the issues raised in their lawsuits were not reached, there may be a tendency to dismiss these suits as unimportant. That notion should be disabused. The problems raised in these suits—what rights witnesses have to open (or closed) hearings; what standards of due process apply to televised proceedings; what safeguards are available against legislative harassment; what can an individual under investigation do about prejudicial leaks; when can an individual secure court review of his complaints against the Congress—are among the crucial problems faced by those subjected to legislative scrutiny in the media age. They are problems we will deal with again in due course.

·III·
The Congressional Tools

"The power of Congress to conduct investigations," Chief Justice Earl Warren observed, "is inherent in the legislative process." And, he continued:

> That power is broad. It encompasses inquiries concerning the administration of existing laws as well as proposed or possibly needed statutes. It includes surveys of defects in our social, economic or political system for the purpose of enabling the Congress to remedy them. It comprehends probes into departments of the Federal Government to expose corruption, inefficiency or waste.*

Justice John Harlan's formulation is comparable. Observing that historically Congress has inquired into a

---

* *Watkins v. United States*, 354 U.S. 178, 187 (1957).

wide range of national interests to determine whether or
not to legislate or appropriate from the national purse, he
declared in a prominent opinion that "the scope of the
power of inquiry, in short, is as penetrating and far-
reaching as the potential power to enact and appropriate
under the Constitution."*

Congress normally investigates through committees.
Investigations generally begin in one of two ways. A standing committee with jurisdiction over a certain area will
start on its own to probe an aspect of its domain. Or a
house by resolution will entrust a particular inquiry to a
select, special, or standing committee.

To exercise its expansive powers of inquiry, Congress
(and its committees where authority is properly delegated) has several tools. It has the power to subpoena
witnesses and materials. It can administer oaths to witnesses who then face the threat of prosecution for perjury.
It can grant partial immunity from prosecution to witnesses who refuse to testify or produce materials because
of their Fifth Amendment privilege against self-
incrimination. It can initiate contempt proceedings against
those who defy its subpoenas and commands. And it can
instigate suit to achieve compliance with its subpoenas
and lawful orders.

This chapter examines these congressional tools. Later
chapters will deal with the restrictions on their use
imposed by the Constitution, statutes, congressional rules,
and court decisions.

The Subpoena Power

No express constitutional provision gives the houses of
Congress authority to issue subpoenas. But none is needed.
The Constitution grants "legislative powers" to the Con-
gress.† Implicit in this grant is the authority to mandate

---

* *Barenblatt* v. *United States*, 360 U.S. 109, 111 (1959).
† United States Constitution, Art. I, Secs. 1, 8.

the production of information by subpoena. The Supreme Court has said that "the power of inquiry—with process to enforce it—it is an essential and appropriate auxiliary to the legislative function,"* and on another occasion has remarked, "The issuance of a subpoena pursuant to an authorized investigation is . . . an indispensable ingredient of lawmaking."†

The reasons supporting an implied subpoena power are not difficult to surmise. Again to quote the Supreme Court:

> A legislative body cannot legislate wisely or effectively in the absence of information respecting the conditions which the legislation is intended to affect or change; and where the legislative body does not itself possess the requisite information—which not infrequently is true— recourse must be had to others who do possess it. Experience has taught that mere requests for such information often are unavailing, and also that information which is volunteered is not always accurate or complete; so some means of compulsion are essential to obtain what is needed. All this was true before and when the Constitution was framed and adopted. In that period the power of inquiry—with enforcing process—was regarded and employed as a necessary and appropriate attribute of the power to legislate—indeed, was treated as inhering in it. Thus there is ample warrant for thinking, as we do, that the constitutional provisions which commit the legislative function to the two houses are intended to include this attribute to the end that the function may be effectively exercised.‡

An ancient maxim in Anglo-American jurisprudence declares that "the public has a right to every man's evi-

* *McGrain* v. *Daugherty*, 273 U.S. 135, 174 (1927). See also *In re Chapman*, 166 U.S. 661, 671 (1897).

† *Eastland* v. *United States Servicemen's Fund*, 421 U.S. 491, 505 (1975).

‡ *McGrain* v. *Daugherty*, 273 U.S. 135, 175 (1927). See also, *Eastland* v. *United States Servicemen's Fund*, 421 U.S. 491, 504–5 (1975).

dence." This principle is reflected, for example, in a venerable statement by Jeremy Bentham in his 1827 "Draught for the Organisation of Judicial Establishments": "Were the Prince of Wales, the Archbishop of Canterbury, and the Lord High Chancellor, to be passing by in the same coach while a chimney-sweeper and a barrow-woman were in dispute about a halfpennyworth of apples, and the chimney-sweeper or the barrow-woman were to think proper to call upon them for their evidence, could they refuse it? No, most certainly."*

This fundamental proposition, the Supreme Court has indicated, is as applicable to subpoenas issued by Congress as to those issued by the courts.† The reasons for this were aptly stated by Circuit Judge George E. MacKinnon in his dissent in Special Prosecutor Cox's case against President Nixon. Judge MacKinnon observed that although congressional and judicial subpoenas have different purposes, a congressional subpoena "carries at least as much weight as a judicial subpoena." Elaborating further, he remarked:

> Congressional subpoenas seek information in aid of the power to legislate for the entire nation while judicial subpoenas seek information in aid of the power to adjudicate controversies between individual litigants in a single civil or criminal case. A grand jury subpoena seeks facts to determine whether there is probable cause that a criminal law has been violated by a few people in a particular instance. A congressional subpoena seeks facts which become the basis for legislation that directly affects over 200 million people. Thus, both congressional and judicial subpoenas serve vital interests, and one interest is no more vital than the other.‡

* J. Bowring, ed., *The Works of Jeremy Bentham*, (Simpkin, Marshall & Co., 1843), Vol. IV, pp. 320–21.

† See *United States* v. *Bryan*, 339 U.S. 323, 331 (1950).

‡ *Nixon* v. *Sirica*, 487 F.2d 700, 737 (D.C. Cir. 1973).

Because of the "vital interests" served by congressional inquiries, it is now recognized that all citizens have the duty to cooperate with Congress's efforts to obtain the information it requires. "It is their unremitting obligation," the Supreme Court has declared, "to respond to subpoenas, to respect the dignity of Congress and its committees and to testify fully with respect to matters within the province of proper investigation."*

The subpoena power belongs to each house of Congress. Before a congressional committee can issue subpoenas, that prerogative must be delegated to it by its parent body. By the Legislative Reorganization Act of 1946, subpoena power was delegated to all Senate standing committees.† However, no provision in the Act granted similar power to all House standing committees. Speaker Sam Rayburn of Texas and Minority Leader Joseph W. Martin of Massachusetts blocked general subpoena rights for House committees fearing that such authority would give them excessive latitude and tempt their members to engage in partisan, sensational investigations. But the House Un-American Activities Committee was given subpoena power by the Act.‡ In 1947 and 1953 the House amended its Standing Rules to grant subpoena power to the House Government Operations Committee and the House Appropriations Committee, and at the beginning of each Congress, it has routinely granted the authority to subpoena to other House committees that specified a need for that power. Moreover, starting with the Ninety-fourth Congress, which was seated in January 1975, all House standing committees, pursuant to just revised Standing Rules, have full subpoena authority.§ Once the Senate or House has awarded subpoena power to a committee, sub-

---

* *Watkins* v. *United States,* 354 U.S. 178, 187–88 (1957).

† See 2 U.S.C. 190b (a) (1970).

‡ This committee's name was later changed to the House Internal Security Committee. It has now been demoted to a subcommittee of the House Judiciary Committee.

§ See Rule XI 2 (m) (2) (A).

poenas served by that committee are treated as if issued by its parent, a proper result since committees are the eyes and ears of Congress.*

The revised House Rules provide that a House committee may issue subpoenas "only when authorized by a majority of the members of the committee." Senate committees, however, normally have freedom to determine what authorization is necessary for the issuance of subpoenas.† The Ervin committee Rules of Procedure stated that subpoenas could be authorized by the chairman, vice chairman or a majority of the committee. Important subpoenas, such as those to the President, were served only upon a vote of a majority of the committee.

Because the Ervin committee was a select, not a standing, committee it was necessary for the Senate to delegate subpoena power to it. The Senate took this step in the committee's enabling resolution—Senate Resolution 60. The scope of the committee's subpoena power under this resolution became an issue in its suit against President Nixon. Senate Resolution 60 granted authority to the committee to subpoena "any . . . officer . . . of the executive branch of the United States Government," but Mr. Nixon's lawyers nonetheless claimed that the resolution did not confer power to subpoena him. They asserted, with considerable hyperbole, that "it is beyond belief that any member of the Senate, when voting to authorize the Select Committee to direct subpoenas to an 'officer,' had any thought that he was voting to empower the Committee to take the unprecedented and unauthorized action that has led to the present litigation." For authority the Presi-

---

* *McGrain* v. *Daugherty*, 273 U.S. 135, 158 (1927); *Watkins* v. *United States*, 354 U.S. 178, 200–01 (1957); *Eastland* v. *United States Servicemen's Fund*, 421 U.S. 491, 505 (1975).

† See 2 U.S.C. 190a–2, 190b(a) (1970). The requirements of an enabling resolution may place limitations on how subpoenas can be authorized. The resolution, for example, may require that subpoenas be authorized by the full committee, not just by its chairman. See *Shelton* v. *United States*, 327 F.2d (601) (D.C. Cir 1963); *Liveright* v. *United States*, 347 F.2d 473 (D.C. Cir. 1965).

dent cited the views of Yale Law School professor Charles
L. Black, who, with direct reference to Senate Resolution
60, had written:

> Perhaps a lexicographically programmed computer
> might print out the judgment that the President is an
> "officer" or "employee" of the executive branch. But
> that is not the way we construe statutes. Is it not per-
> fectly plain that such language is entirely inapt, as a
> matter of usage, to designate the President of the
> United States?*

The committee had always thought that its authority
to subpoena the President under the enabling resolution
was rather clear. The President was clearly an "officer" of
the executive branch and the committee had been specifically established to investigate the conduct of 1972 presidential candidates, including the President.† But why
leave the matter to chance? After the Saturday Night
Massacre and the resultant public outrage, the Senate was
sufficiently traumatized to support any reasonable request
by the committee. Consequently, the committee, in
November 1973, introduced Senate Resolution 194.‡ This
resolution, unanimously passed by the full Senate, stated
that it was "the sense of the Senate" that the subpoenas
to the President were "fully authorized" by Senate Resolution 60. Senate Resolution 194 went on to proclaim that
the full Senate "approves and ratifies" the committee's
subpoenas. The President's rather extreme speculation as
to senatorial intention thus proved inaccurate, and the
issue of authority to subpoena the President under the
enabling resolution passed from the case.

* See *Congressional Record*, E 5321 (daily ed., August 1, 1973).
† In March 1974, District Judge William B. Jones wrote, "That
[the Ervin committee] has authority to direct subpoenas to the
President . . . is evident from [the resolution] which established the
committee and granted it authority to issue subpoenas." *Nader* v.
Butz, 372 F. Supp. 175, 177 (D.D.C. 1974). In this case, Judge Jones
refused to lift a protective order denying materials to the committee.
‡ 93rd Cong., 1st Sess., Nov. 7, 1973.

Many Congressional committees proceed informally in obtaining information, preferring to secure needed evidence by request rather than by subpoena. But the subpoena power has been employed throughout Congress's history. The House first approved the use of subpoenas in 1792 for a select committee investigation of General St. Clair's defeat by Indians on the Ohio frontier. Another early authorization of subpoena power by the House came in 1794, when a special House committee was given that tool to inquire into the possible impeachment of Senator William Blount, of Tennessee, who was accused of conspiring with the British in their attempt to assume control of Louisiana and Spanish Florida. The first standing committee of the House to receive such authority was the House Committee on Manufactures for its 1828 investigation of tariffs. An early grant of subpoena power by the Senate occurred in 1818 respecting the inquiry into Andrew Jackson's Seminole campaign.

At times the use of the subpoena power by Congress has been abundant. During 1957–59, Senator John McClellan's Select Committee on Improper Activities in the Labor or Management Field served more than eight thousand subpoenas. Between 1965 and 1974, the House Banking and Currency Committee issued over three hundred. Its chairman, Wright Patman of Texas, failed in October 1973 to persuade the committee to subpoena Nixon aides to explore the Watergate affair, but the Ervin committee, during its eighteen-month investigation, served hundreds of subpoenas in furtherance of its Watergate inquiries.

The most celebrated of the Ervin committee's subpoenas were those issued to President Nixon. The two subpoenas served on July 23, 1973—the subjects of the committee's suit against the President—have already been discussed. However, on December 19, 1973, three other subpoenas were transmitted to the President. By then the new jurisdictional statute allowing the committee to sue in federal court to enforce its subpoenas was in effect. It heartened some committee members and staff into believing that they could now obtain substantial evidence from the President.

The December subpoenas, in my judgment, were grossly excessive. One subpoena called for the tape recordings of 477 specific presidential conversations. Another demanded 37 categories of documents including (1) "all records . . . of any compensation to Richard M. Nixon maintained by Rose Mary Woods," the President's personal secretary; (2) " 'President Richard Nixon's Daily Diary' for January 1, 1970, to December 19, 1973"; and (3) "any memoranda or reports on Donald A. Nixon, F. Donald Nixon or Edward Nixon or their activities." Certain staff members had recommended vastly reduced subpoenas and had vigorously opposed portions of those actually issued, but we were overruled. We did succeed, however, in excising several demands, including one for all communications between President Nixon and his brothers.

The three subpoenas provoked howls of protest not only from the White House, which called the subpoenas "incredible" and refused compliance, but also from others. Vice President Gerald Ford labeled the subpoenas a "scattergun approach," and Attorney General designate William Saxbe attacked them as a "fishing expedition." The committee was similarly excoriated by certain elements in the press. Senator Baker complained that he had not been apprised of the subpoenas before their service and stated he thought they were a mistake and should be reconsidered.*

In defense of those who supported the subpoenas, it should be said that a justification of some sort could be mounted for all the specific materials demanded. There was *eminent* warrant for some materials subpoenaed; for example, the committee subpoenaed the June 23, 1973, Nixon-Haldeman tape, which depicted the President's

---

* The committee members present at a December 18 executive session had voted the subpoenas after having been informed in general terms of their contents.

early participation in the cover-up and whose revelation was the final blow leading to his resignation. The House Judiciary Committee and the special prosecutor eventually subpoenaed many of the tapes called for in the December subpoenas.

However, in October 1973 the Court of Appeals in dealing with Special Prosecutor Cox's case against the President had said that presidential communications are "presumptively privileged" and had disallowed the President's claim of privilege solely because of the "uniquely powerful showing" of need by the grand jury for the tapes subpoenaed.* The Ervin committee could not make such a rigorous demonstration in regard to many of the requests in the three subpoenas. Moreover, by the time they were issued, the brunt of the Watergate inquiry was shifting to the special prosecutor and the House Judiciary Committee. To borrow Senator Herman Talmadge's folksy metaphor, "The train had passed our station." Issuance of blunderbuss subpoenas suggested to some that the committee, enjoying its unprecedented publicity, wanted to monopolize the limelight.

The December subpoenas, it seems fair to speculate, also harmed the committee's chances in its suit for enforcement of the first two subpoenas. The later subpoenas were not involved in that lawsuit, but their issuance portrayed the committee as overreaching and perhaps made the courts chary of affixing their judicial imprimatur to the earlier demands. In his opinion refusing to enforce the committee's subpoena for five tapes, Judge Gesell observed: "This is, moreover, in the nature of a test case and should the Committee prevail, numerous additional demands might well be made . . . A sweeping subpoena seeking some 500 items has apparently been served on the President . . ."†

On the whole, however, the committee's use of the sub-

---

* *Nixon v. Sirica*, 487 F. 2d 700, 717 (D.C. Cir. 1973).

† *Senate Select Committee on Presidential Campaign Activities* v. *Nixon*, 370 F. Supp. 521, 523 and n. 2 (D.D.C. 1974).

poena power was exceptionally effective. An early subpoena to Jeb Magruder's secretary, for example, produced
Magruder's diary, which corroborated James McCord's
hearsay testimony concerning Magruder's meetings with
Mitchell, Dean, and Liddy where "Gemstone" bugging
plans were discussed. A subpoena to Charles Colson's
secretary revealed a memorandum from Colson to Haldeman indicating that perjury regarding the ITT affair had
been committed at the Senate hearings on the confirmation of Richard Kleindienst as Attorney General. A
subpoena opening the files of the Committee to Re-elect
the President allowed committee investigators to uncover
numerous documents relating to the "Responsiveness Program," an incredible White House scheme devised by
Frederick Malek, a special assistant to President Nixon,
which had as its goal the harnessing of the vast resources
of the executive branch to reelect the President.

One of the most fascinating pieces of evidence garnered
by committee subpoenas was the $100,000 in $100 bills
that "Bebe" Rebozo had returned to Howard Hughes
after the 1972 campaign. An examination of the serial
and series numbers on the $100,000 demonstrated that the
bills probably were *not* the same ones given Rebozo several years earlier by Hughes as a contribution to President Nixon's 1972 campaign, as Rebozo had asserted.
(Actually, $100,*100* was returned to Hughes, raising the
obvious question whether, in assembling a new collection
of bills, an additional $100 had been inadvertently
added.) Hughes's lawyer, the garrulous Chester Davis,
presented the money to the committee at executive session: after prolonged protestations he produced two seem-
ingly innocuous manila envelopes and, with considerable panache, dumped the one thousand and one $100
bills on Senator Ervin's desk.

Senator Ervin, who had not expected Davis to deliver
the money, was startled. In many respects the senator is
one of the most sophisticated men in public life. He is a
keen constitutional scholar and is acutely aware of the

subtleties and abstruse interplays of political manuverings on the Hill. But he is also, as he has professed many times and as the title of his biography proclaims, "a country lawyer." I doubt if he (or anyone else on the committee or its staff) had ever seen $100,100 in cash. When the money hit his desk his famous eyebrows commenced a St. Vitus' dance. He promptly summoned a squad of Capitol Hill policemen to guard the cash. Then he ordered the immediate manual copying of the bills' serial and series numbers so the money could be quickly returned to Davis. This process, it soon appeared, was too time-consuming. Several staff members were therefore dispatched, under guard, to the committee's offices to photocopy the bills. But in the exigencies of the moment, we forgot the federal law declaring it criminal to make a facsimile of United States currency. This oversight was brought home shortly when the Secret Service, which has responsibility in such matters, called a staff member to inquire about the apparent violation. This episode must have produced some wry humor within the Service, for the committee had recently investigated the Service's role in handling President Nixon's tapes. The Secret Service eventually dropped the matter, but the incident had been chagrining.*

The Power to Take Testimony

A congressional committee can gain the testimony of witnesses in several ways. It can request a witness to come before it to give testimony under oath. Often this "request" comes in the form of a subpoena *ad testificundum*—that is, a subpoena for testimony—which can be ignored only upon pain of contempt.† Testimony taken under oath is recorded verbatim.

---

* It appears that no prosecution of committee members or staff could have been sustained because of the protections afforded by the speech or debate clause of the Constitution. See Chapter X.

† A subpoena *ad testificundum* should be distinguished from a subpoena *duces tecum*, which is a subpoena for the production of physical items.

A committee may also ask an individual to appear informally before it or its staff to answer questions on an unsworn basis. Statements taken in this fashion are sometimes transcribed verbatim, but often only summaries are prepared. This informal method of receiving evidence is more common. Especially in a far-flung investigation where witnesses in scattered areas of the country are interviewed, it is often inconvenient or impossible for a congressman to attend every staff interview to swear the witness. The Ervin committee examined sixty-three persons under oath in public sessions and around two hundred sworn witnesses in executive sessions, but its staff questioned many more individuals on an informal basis across the nation.

TESTIMONY UNDER OATH

Each member of a congressional investigating committee may, by statute, administer oaths to witnesses appearing before it.* Congress first passed a law in 1798 allowing certain members to swear witnesses. Before that enactment, doubt existed that congressmen had this power, and the often inconvenient practice of requesting federal judges to swear congressional witnesses was followed.

A witness properly sworn must testify truthfully or be subject to prosecution for perjury. Prosecutions for perjury before Congress can be brought under two statutes: the general federal perjury statute and the perjury provisions of the District of Columbia code. The statutes are essentially the same except for the penalties provided for violation. Both require that a proper oath be administered and that the perjury be "willfully" done, i.e., intentionally and not by inadvertence. Both require that the perjury involve a "material matter," that is, that the false testimony not be concerned with some incidental or irrelevant

* See 2 U.S.C. 191 (1970); *United States* v. *Norris*, 300 U.S. 564 (1937); *Sinclair* v. *United States*, 279 U.S. 263, 291 (1929).

issue. And both demand that the perjury be committed before a "competent tribunal."*

This last-mentioned requirement is sometimes a snag to perjury convictions. In the late 1940's the government attempted to prosecute one Harold Roland Christoffel under the District of Columbia statute for his testimony before the House Committee on Education and Labor where he denied under oath that he was a Communist or that he endorsed, supported, or participated in Communist programs. Christoffel argued that his conviction should be reversed because when the perjurious statements were issued, the committee was not a "competent tribunal." His contention was that a quorum of the committee was not present when the offending statements were made, and thus the committee was incompetent to take his testimony. Under the rules governing the committee at that time a quorum was thirteen of the committee's twenty-five members. The trial judge was in error, Christoffel said, in charging the jury that it need only find that a quorum was present when the committee *convened*. The Supreme Court, by a 5–4 vote, agreed with Christoffel and reversed his conviction.† Conse-

---

* See 18 U.S.C. 1621 (1970) and D.C. Code Sec. 22–2501. The federal statute prescribes a maximum penalty of a $2,000 fine, five years' imprisonment, or both. The penalty under the District of Columbia statute is imprisonment for a minimum of two years and a maximum of ten years. For a general discussion of the requirements for a perjury conviction, see the annotation, Perjury Committed by False Testimony before a Congressional Committee, 98 L. Ed. 98 (1955) Some courts have indicated that a statement is "material" only if it could affect the course of a congressional investigation or influence a panel's final conclusions. E.g., *United States* v. *Makris*, 483 F. 2d 1082, 1088 (5th Cir. 1973) *cert. denied*, 415 U.S. 914 (1974). *United States* v. *Moran*, 194 F. 2d 623, 626 (2d Cir. 1952) *cert. denied* 343 U.S. 965 (1952); *United States* v. *Icardi*, 140 F. Supp. 383, 388–89 (D.D.C. 1956). But other cases at least suggest that a statement is material simply if it concerns a matter pertinent to a committee's legitimate inquiries. E.g., *United States* v. *Norris*, 300 U.S. 564, 573 (1937); *Sinclair* v. *United States*, 279 U.S. 263, 298 (1929).

† *Christoffel* v. *United States*, 338 U.S. 84 (1949). See also *United States* v. *Icardi*, 140 F. Supp. 383 (D.D.C. 1956). Compare *United States* v. *Bryan*, 339 U.S. 323 (1950).

quently, the law now is that in order to convict for perjury, the government must prove that a quorum existed when the statements under challenge were uttered.

This case presents no serious problem where at least some congressmen are available to take testimony. The Constitution states that "Each House may determine the Rules of its Proceedings,"* and each house, or its committees when the power is properly delegated to them, can therefore prescribe the number of committee members which constitutes a quorum. Under the 1975 House Rules, a quorum for the taking of testimony is two committee members.† By the Senate Rules, a quorum for testimony before a *standing* committee is whatever number the committee determines.‡ A Senate select or special committee is empowered by statute to adopt its own rules and therefore can also fix the number required for a quorum unless its authorizing resolution specifies otherwise.§ The Ervin committee, by its Rules of Procedure, provided that one member constituted a quorum for testimony. Thus, perjurious testimony delivered while any member was present was susceptible to successful prosecution.¶

The trouble comes when legislators are not available for the duration of a witness's testimony. The public sessions of the Ervin committee did not proceed without a senator present, but a great many hours of executive-session testimony under oath were received with all committee members absent. Given the other demands on their time, it was simply impossible for a senator to be available during every minute of sworn testimony.

It makes little sense to exempt a witness before Con-

---

* United States Constitution, Art. I, Sec. 5, Cl. 2.
† See Rule XI 2(h).
‡ See Rule XXV 5(b).
§ See 2 U.S.C. 190a–2 (1970).
¶ See *United States* v. *Moran*, 194 F. 2d 623 (2d Cir. 1952) *cert. denied*, 343 U.S. 965 (1952).

gress from perjury prosecution because no congressman is present when he lies. A witness who falsifies during grand jury testimony can be prosecuted even though no judge is present when the perjurious testimony is given. Similarly, a prevaricating witness in a civil deposition conducted without a judge is subject to criminal penalties. The Ervin committee recommended that the federal code be amended to allow prosecution for statements made when no congressman is present. However, because the Constitution gives each house the authority to fix its own rules, it may be that each house, by appropriate rule changes, could effect the same result. Each house could provide that a quorum for taking testimony is one congressman and that the quorum is not vitiated if the member leaves after swearing the witness. Thus, if the witness is properly sworn, the tribunal apparently would be "competent" under the language of the relevant statutes even if the congressman subsequently departs. If this were the law, there would be no potential for significant abuse: a witness who believes he is being harassed or that the committee staff is propounding irrelevant questions could still decline to testify until ordered to do so by a congressman.

The Ervin committee proffered another sensible suggestion. Under existing law, to gain a perjury conviction regarding statements made in proceedings before or ancillary to a U.S. court or grand jury, the prosecution must prove only that the defendant made two "irreconcilably contradictory [material] declarations" during any such proceedings.* Pursuant to this statute, for example, it would suffice for conviction to demonstrate that a witness said one thing under oath during grand jury testimony but the contrary during sworn testimony at a public trial; there is no need to introduce evidence proving that one of the statements actually is false. The Watergate commit-

---

* 18 U.S.C. 1623 (1970).

tee's recommendation is that similar protection be
extended to congressional proceedings. By its proposal,
conviction would result if testimony under oath before a
committee was diametrically opposed to the witness's
sworn testimony during another congressional or court
proceeding. As with court and grand jury related testimony, there would be no need to prove that either statement was actually false. At this writing, neither this suggestion nor the one discussed earlier regarding competent
tribunals has been adopted by Congress.

Historically, prosecutions for perjury before congressional committees have not been plentiful. One of the
most publicized concerned the 1950's prosecution of the
noted Far Eastern scholar Owen Lattimore. In 1950 Lattimore was chief of the United Nations Mission in Afghani-
stan when Senator Joseph McCarthy denounced him as
"one of the top Communist agents in this country." Lattimore promptly returned home to defend himself with
exceptional vigor and more than a modicum of truculence
against this calumny, and subsequently was vindicated
by a Senate Foreign Relations Subcommittee chaired by
Senator Millard Tydings of Maryland. The subcommittee
found that the charges against him were a "fraud and a
hoax perpetrated on the Senate of the United States and
the American people." However, Senator Tydings was
defeated in the fall of 1950—much to the satisfaction of
the McCarthy forces—and in 1951 the Internal Security
Subcommittee of the Senate Judiciary Committee, under
the leadership of Senator Pat McCarran of Nevada,
began again to investigate Lattimore in connection with
its inquiry into the Institute of Pacific Relations, with
which Lattimore had been affiliated.

The McCarran subcommittee's treatment of Lattimore
was no less than vicious. On the stand for twelve days,
Lattimore was constantly interrupted, badgered, and
harangued; he was denied the right to refresh his memory; his counsel was not allowed to object to improper

questions. McCarran, in particular, appeared engaged in a vendetta against Lattimore. During the confirmation hearing of Attorney General James P. McGranery, McCarran pried a promise from McGranery that, when confirmed, he would bring perjury charges against Lattimore for his testimony before the McCarran subcommittee.

The government indicted Lattimore on several counts, the chief one being that he had lied when he testified that he had "never been a sympathizer or any other kind of promoter of Communism or Communist interests." Lattimore's voluminous writings, the government said, contradicted these claims. Judge Luther Youngdahl (a former Republican governor of Minnesota who is still a sitting judge) dismissed this charge on the grounds that it was too vague to meet the requirement of the Sixth Amendment that the accused "be informed of the nature and cause of the accusation" against him in order that he might prepare a defense and be protected against subsequent prosecution for the same offense. Judge Youngdahl said, "It seems to the court that this charge is so nebulous and indefinite that a jury would have to engage in speculation in order to arrive at a verdict." It is difficult to quarrel with the judge's dismissal: how could Lattimore defend against the claim that he was a Communist "sympathizer" or "promoter" without any firm notion as to what these diffuse, shadowy terms were supposed to mean? The Court of Appeals sustained Judge Youngdahl's decision in this regard.*

Undeterred, the government reindicted Lattimore, contending he had lied when he denied he was a "follower of the Communist line" or had ever been "a promoter of Communist interest." Judge Youngdahl, after indignantly rejecting a spurious attempt by the government to disqualify him from hearing the case, again dismissed the

---

* *United States* v. *Lattimore*, 112 F. Supp. 507 (D.D.C. 1953), *affirmed in part, reversed in part.* 215 F. 2d 847 (D.C. Cir. 1954).

indictments for vagueness. He wrote: "To require defendant to go to trial for perjury under charges so formless and obscure would be unprecedented and would make a sham of the Sixth Amendment. . . ." Again the Court of Appeals, this time by a 4–4 vote, affirmed.* The government, bloodied by bringing a shoddy prosecution, dropped the case.†

The Ervin committee, though faced with fierce temptation, did not recommend to the special prosecutor that any specific individual be prosecuted for perjury. But several Watergate prosecutions did grow out of testimony before congressional bodies. John Mitchell and H.R. Haldeman were convicted for their testimony before the Ervin committee regarding the Watergate cover-up. Howard Edwin Reinecke, the former lieutenant governor of California, was convicted for lying to the Senate Judiciary Committee during Richard Kleindienst's confirmation hearing as Attorney General; Reinecke's testimony concerned the relationship between an aborted offer by an ITT subsidiary to help finance the Republican National Convention and the resolution of antitrust cases against ITT by John Mitchell's Justice Department. However, a Court of Appeals recently reversed the conviction for failure to prove a quorum. Kleindienst, under threat of a felony prosecution for perjury regarding the ITT affair, pleaded guilty to a misdemeanor charge, admitting that he had refused to answer fully and accurately certain questions put to him during his confirmation hearing.‡ Special Prosecutor Jaworski's deal with Mr. Kleindienst prompted three attorneys on Jaworski's staff to resign in

* *United States* v. *Lattimore*, 127 F. Supp. 405 (D.D.C. 1955) *affirmed*, 232 F. 2d 334 (D.C. Cir. 1955).

† For two exceptionally readable accounts of this episode, see Thurman Arnold's *Fair Fights and Foul* (Harcourt, Brace & World, 1965), pp. 214–27, and Alan Barth's *Government by Investigation* (Viking Press, 1955), pp. 95–111.

‡ The statute employed was 2 U.S.C. 192 (1970), a provision normally utilized to prosecute contempts of Congress.

protest. Kleindienst received a suspended sentence of thirty days' imprisonment and a $100 fine. The light sentence—which was coupled with lavish, unexpected praise for Kleindienst by the sentencing judge, George Hart— stood in stark contrast to the fate of the less prominent Watergate burglars who suffered many months in jail for their malefactions.

STATEMENTS NOT UNDER OATH

As remarked, most statements and representations made to Congress during its investigations are unsworn. In some circumstances, sanctions are also available to punish those who lie to Congress without submitting to an oath.

A federal statute declares that it is a felony willfully to make a false statement or representation regarding "any matter within the jurisdiction of any department or agency of the United States."* The maximum penalties for violation of this statute are harsh—a fine of $10,000 and imprisonment for five years. (The federal perjury statute, while allowing imprisonment for five years, carries only a maximum fine of $2,000.) There is little doubt that this statute applies to certain statements and representations made to Congress.

This proposition appears established by the case of *United States* v. *Bramblett.†* Bramblett was a former congressman who, while in office, had certified in writing to the House Disbursing Office that a certain woman was a clerk on his staff. The jury found that, whatever other services she may have performed, she had not functioned as an office employee.‡ Bramblett, however, argued to the

---

* 18 U.S.C. 1001 (1970).
† 348 U.S. 503 (1955).
‡ Bramblett and the woman were engaged in a kickback scheme. See *United States* v. *Brewster*, 408 U.S. 501, 522 n. 16 (1972).

Supreme Court that the House Disbursing Office was not a "department . . . of the United States" within the meaning of the statute and that consequently he could not be prosecuted under it. The Supreme Court rejected this contention and upheld the jury's verdict. After examining the statute's legislative history, the Court ruled that "the development, scope and purpose of the section shows that 'department,' as used in this context, was meant to describe the executive, legislative and judicial branches of the Government."

The Ervin committee, relying largely on the Bramblett case, considered this statute applicable to its investigations, and at times informed those under staff interrogation that their voluntary unsworn statements were covered by it. This conclusion, however, is open to question. In a recent decision regarding the prosecution of John Ehrlichman for various offenses relating to the burglary of the office of Daniel Ellsberg's psychiatrist, Judge Gerhard Gesell ruled that the statute does not apply to voluntary oral statements given to the Federal Bureau of Investigation.* His ground was that Congress "did not intend [the] statute to be applied to statements given to the FBI voluntarily and without oath or verbatim transcript." What bothered Gesell was the lack of safeguards for the person under interrogation: "There is no requirement of an oath, no strict rule of materiality, and no guarantee that the proceeding will be transcribed or reduced to memorandum." Without a transcript, the judge stated, it would be "nearly impossible" to determine if what the witness said was literally true and not just

---

* 379 F. Supp. 291 (1974). Judge Sirica also dismissed counts of lying to the FBI against Ehrlichman and Mitchell during the Watergate cover-up trial. (Order unreported.) And other courts, on a variety of theories, have held that the statute does not apply to statements given the FBI, e.g. *United States* v. *Lambert*, 470 F. 2d 354 (5th Cir. 1972); *Freedman* v. *United States*, 374 F. 2d 363 (8th Cir. 1967). Compare *United States* v. *Adler*, 380 F. 2d 917 (2d Cir. 1972), *cert. denied*, 380 U.S. 1006 (1972).

incomplete or misleading.* Furthermore, he said, such interviews occur "under extremely informal circumstances which do not sufficiently alert the person interviewed to the danger that false statements may lead to a felony conviction."

Many of the same observations apply to congressional committee staff investigations. There is no oath and usually no verbatim transcript, although a summary memorandum is often prepared. The interviews are informal, the witness attends voluntarily, not under compulsion of subpoena, and normally no warning is given that a false statement renders the witness liable to prosecution for a serious felony. In such circumstances it is possible that a court, despite the broad pronouncements of the *Bramblett* case, would hold that the statute is not applicable to voluntary, unsworn, oral statements to congressional investigators who, in many cases, are not as skillful as FBI agents in conducting and accurately recording informal interviews.

This discussion suggests that an overhaul of the statute is in order. The law should be amended to specify that certain procedures to protect individual rights must be followed before a conviction for false oral statements will stand. At a minimum the statute should require that an individual be warned before his interrogation that false statements will subject him to prosecution. It should specify that a prosecution for oral falsifications is only permissible if the misstatement is made to two or more representatives of the governmental department or agency concerned. Additionally, it should provide that the statement be reduced to writing in memorandum or transcript form within three working days of its utterance and verified within an additional three working days by at least two of the government officials present when the statement was made. The warning requirement might result in putting the lid on a witness's revelations, but this con-

---

* Compare *Bronston* v. *United States*, 409 U.S. 352 (1972).

sideration does not outweigh the need to protect those under interrogation from unjust prosecution. In any event, investigators, fearful that a warning would silence their witness, could elide the warning and thus forfeit the chance of future prosecution.*

Immunity Power

To get to the bottom (or the top) of many crimes, it is necessary to secure the testimony of one of the wrongdoers. The wrongdoer, however, has a privilege under the Fifth Amendment not to give testimony that would incriminate him. To circumvent this privilege the immunity concept was created. Under an immunity statute, a witness can be compelled to testify about crimes in which he may be implicated, but he is given concomitant protection from prosecution based on his testimony. Historically the immunity mechanism has been widely used—the Ervin committee, for example, conferred immunity on twenty-seven witnesses.

* There are other federal statutes that attempt to ensure the veracity of testimony and statements of witnesses before Congressional bodies. See, e.g.: (1) 18 U.S.C. 1622 (1970) and D.C. Code 22–2501, which proscribe subornation of perjury, that is, the procuring of another's perjury; (2) 18 U.S.C. 201 (h) (1970), which provides that it is unlawful to bribe a witness to influence his sworn testimony before a congressional body; (3) 18 U.S.C. 1505 (1970), which makes illegal the intimidation of congressional witnesses and the obstruction of congressional inquiries by threats or force or other corrupt means. Nixon's tax attorney, Frank Demarco, Jr., was indicted under this last provision for corruptly obstructing the inquiries of the Joint Committee on Internal Revenue Taxation into Nixon's tax returns by transmitting false documents to the committee; the trial judge, however, dismissed this case for prosecutorial misconduct when he discovered that the special prosecutor's office had withheld relevant documents from the defense. See further *Stein* v. *United States,* 337 F. 2d 14 (9th Cir. 1964), *cert. denied* 380 U.S. 907 (1965); *United States* v. *Presser,* 187 F. Supp. 64 (N.D. Ohio 1960), and 292 F. 2d 171 6th Cir. 1961), *affirmed by an equally divided* court, 371 U.S. 71 (1962). An argument could be made that this statute may be used to prosecute one who obstructs a congresssional inquiry by providing false and evasive oral answers. In addition to the Stein case, see *United States* v. *Alo,* 439 F. 2d 751 (2d Cir. 1971). Compare *United States* v. *Essex,* 407 F. 2d 214 (6th Cir. 1969).

The statute used by the Ervin committee, which was construed by Judge Sirica during the committee's conflict with Special Prosecutor Cox over broadcasting the testimony of John Dean and Jeb Magruder, is of recent genesis, having been enacted in 1970 as part of the Omnibus Crime Control Act.* Behind that statute is a curious history reaching back to eighteenth-century England. Shortly after the privilege against self-incrimination became firmly entrenched in English law, Parliament began to enact immunity statutes—or "indemnity" statutes in British parlance. Under these laws a witness could be forced to give self-incriminating testimony, but in return he would receive *total* immunity from prosecution concerning matters revealed in his testimony. An early Watergate-flavored instance of immunity legislation concerned the 1725 impeachment trial of Lord Chancellor Macclesfield, who was accused by the House of Commons of selling public offices and appointments. The specific charge was that certain masters of chancery had purchased their positions from the Lord Chancellor. In order to produce the testimony of these notables, who would incriminate themselves by testifying, Parliament passed a statute granting them full immunity from prosecution.

Following the British practice, certain colonial legislatures also passed various immunity laws in the eighteenth century. Congress first enacted federal immunity legislation in 1857.† This initial federal statute—an odd device—was enacted to force witnesses to testify before Congress in regard to bribery and corruption in the House of Representatives concerning the disposal of public lands. According to the statute, all a miscreant needed to do to obtain total immunity from prosecution for past misdeeds was to testify about his wrongdoings before a congressional committee. This statute obviously presented a boon

---

* The immunity provisions of that act are codified at 18 U.S.C. 6001–6005 (1970). Sirica's opinion is found at 361 F. Supp. 1270 (1973).

† See 11 Stat. 155 (1857).

for those more concerned about a jail cell than the stigma resulting from revelation of their shortcomings. For five years, rascals and scalawags of various stripes journeyed with celerity to Congress to confess and thus receive an "immunity bath" that cleansed them, if not of their sins, at least of legal culpability for crimes committed. As Alan Barth descriptively put it: "The investigating committees became, during the brief period the law was in force, a kind of bargain-basement confessional where easy absolution could be secured."*

Obviously Congress could not long allow this aberration to remain the law, and in 1862 it amended the statute.† The new act provided that a witness's actual testimony before Congress could not be used against him in a criminal prosecution. A witness, however, could still be prosecuted for matters testified about, and under the new law, information *derived from* a witness's testimony could be employed against him in subsequent criminal proceedings even though the testimony actually compelled could not.

In 1892 the Supreme Court declared unconstitutional a statute similar in all essential respects to the act of 1862 concerning testimony before Congress.‡ The Supreme Court ruled that statutes of this nature were invalid under the Fifth Amendment because they did not bar the use of the *fruits* of compelled testimony, as well as the actual testimony, in later criminal proceedings. To be constitutional, the Court said, the immunity statute must protect a witness to the same degree that the Fifth Amendment protects him. The Fifth Amendment, of course, offers complete protection from both the use of testimony and leads garnered from it because, under its safeguards, a witness does not have to testify at all about any matter that might incriminate him.

---

* Barth, *Government by Investigation*, p. 131.
† See 12 Stat. 333 (1862).
‡ *Counselman* v. *Hitchcock*, 142 U.S. 547 (1892).

There was, however, language in the 1892 opinion that reached beyond its actual holdings. At one point the Court had said, "In view of the constitutional provision, a statutory enactment, to be valid, must afford absolute immunity against prosecution for the offense to which the question relates." Because of this language, this case for many years was interpreted to mean that an immunity statute was constitutional only if a witness was given absolute, or "transactional," immunity concerning the matters revealed during his testimony.

Within three weeks of this decision, Congress began to amend various immunity provisions in the federal code so that they provided "transactional" instead of "use" immunity. But Congress neglected to alter the immunity provision relating to Congress—which was clearly unconstitutional—until 1954. The statute finally passed in 1954 was a product of the loyalty investigation era and was limited in that it allowed a house of Congress or a congressional committee to obtain a court order granting transactional immunity only to witnesses who would testify concerning "attempts to interfere with or endanger the national security or defense of the United States by treason, sabotage, espionage, or the overthrow of its government by force or violence."* Its enactment was castigated by civil libertarians who contended that the law's real purpose was to get behind the Fifth Amendment pleas of witnesses who had been queried about Communist affiliations and thus to pillory them further. It was, they contended, a device to promote legislative trials where public obloquy was the punishment. In practice, however, congressional use of this statute was sparse.

The view that the Constitution required transactional immunity persevered until 1964, when the Supreme Court, in a case dealing principally with another issue, indicated that use immunity would be lawful if the immunity statute interdicted the use of the fruits of the testi-

* See 68 Stat. 745 (1954).

mony in later criminal proceedings.* This decision sent
the statute makers back to the drafting board, and eventually the immunity provisions of the 1970 Omnibus Crime
Control Act were produced. At the time this statute was
passed, at least fifty separate immunity statutes were in
the federal code. The new law, which has separate sec-
tions relating to witnesses before courts and grand juries,
administrative agencies and Congress, is a use immunity
statute; it provides that "no testimony or other information compelled under the [court] order (or any information directly or indirectly derived from such testimony or
other information) may be used against the witness in
any criminal case, except a prosecution for perjury, giving
a false statement, or otherwise failing to comply with the
order." Those who had divined that the Supreme Court
would uphold the constitutionality of this type of use
immunity statute were shortly proven correct, for the
Court did so in a 1972 decision.†

The workings of the new statute should be of interest
even to laymen because the law protects the power of
Congress to immunize and receive evidence from a witness even if that result is bitterly opposed by the executive or judicial branch. When a witness has asserted, or it
appears that he will assert, his Fifth Amendment privilege before either house of Congress or a congressional
committee, the house or committee may apply to a federal
district court for an order allowing it to immunize the
witness. The application must show two things: first, that
the house by a majority vote or the committee by a two-
thirds vote approved the application; second, that ten
days before the application the Attorney General was

---

* *Murphy* v. *Waterfront Commission*, 378 U.S. 52, 79 (1964). The
court held that immunity conferred by one sovereign (a state) prevented another sovereign (the federal government) from using
compelled testimony, or information derived from it, in a later
criminal prosecution.

† *Kastigar* v. *United States*, 406 U.S. 441 (1972). Under the statute,
an individual can be forced to produce *physical* evidence, as well as
testimony, which would tend to incriminate him.

notified of the intent to apply for the immunity order. The Attorney General has the right to require the judge to wait an additional twenty days from the date of the application before the judge enters the immunity order. This provision, in effect, gives the Attorney General thirty days from notification of the intent to seek immunity to isolate all evidence in his possession which would serve as an independent basis for prosecution of the witness. This isolation of evidence is critically important because the Attorney General, in a subsequent prosecution, has the burden of establishing that leads derived from the witness's congressional testimony were not used to build the prosecution's case.*

The Attorney General, however, has no authority to block the immunity order. The initial drafters of the statute (the National Commission for the Reform of Federal Criminal Laws) vividly remembered the Teapot Dome era when Attorney General Harry Daugherty was investigated by a Senate select committee regarding corruption in his office. "[I]t would be virtually unthinkable," the drafters said, "to give the Attorney General the additional power of disapproval of conferment of immunity, because in a Teapot Dome-type Congressional investigation, the Attorney General himself would be the focus of the inquiry."† How prophetic that insight now seems after the Watergate inquiries, which centered in part on present and past Justice Department officials, including former Attorney General John Mitchell.

A federal court, as Judge Sirica ruled concerning the Dean/Magruder immunity requests, has no authority to deny an immunity application because it thinks immunity unwise. Additionally, as Sirica also held, the court has no prerogative to condition the allowance of immunity on a requirement that the Congressional unit involved ban the

---

* *Kastigar* v. *United States,* 406 U.S. 441, 460 (1972). See also *Murphy* v. *Waterfront Commission,* 378 U.S. 52, 79 n. 18 (1963).

† *Working Papers of the National Commission for the Reform of Federal Criminal Laws,* p. 1440 (1970).

broadcast media or otherwise alter its procedures. The court's role is only to determine that the procedural requirements—a proper vote and notification of the Attorney General—have been fulfilled. "[I]ts function," said the National Commission, "[is] a weak and paltry thing—ministerial, not discretionary in nature."* To give the court a choice in the matter, the National Commission felt, would allow it to usurp the discretionary constitutional power of a coordinate branch of government—the legislature—to decide what information it needs to fulfill its functions or how it will conduct its hearings, and thus would run afoul of the constitutional doctrine of separation of powers.

But Sirica, quoting the National Commission, did indicate that a court might deny an immunity request if (1) the investigation involved had no legitimate legislative purpose; (2) the investigation exceeded the committee's authorizing or enabling resolution; (3) the testimony sought was protected by some privilege; (4) the testimony desired was clearly irrelevant to the investigation. Sirica's speculations notwithstanding, whether a court actually may deny an immunity request if one of these circumstances is present remains an open issue. In any event, these considerations go to the general limitations on the scope of Congress's investigating power and are better discussed elsewhere in this book.†

One other matter of importance should be examined before we leave the immunity statute. The statute allows a witness's testimony to be used against him in a prosecution for perjury or issuing false statements. But what perjury and what false statements? Does the statute refer only to falsifications voiced during the compelled testimony or does it also relate to earlier deceptions? This issue was raised by David Young—a member of the "Plumbers" group responsible for burglarizing the office

* Ibid.
† Chapters IV, VI, and VII.

of Daniel Ellsberg's psychiatrist—during court proceedings on the Ervin committee's application for an immunity order regarding his testimony. Young had previously testified before a grand jury and made statements to the FBI concerning the Ellsberg break-in. He was fearful that, if his Senate testimony conflicted with his previous statements, he could be tried for those declarations. Young produced a recent case holding that the statute allowed use of immunized testimony in a prosecution for past statements and thus, in this respect, was unconstitutional, because the protection it afforded was not coextensive with that vouchsafed by the Fifth Amendment.*

This conclusion, Judge Sirica said in essence, was balderdash. He found it clear from the language of the statute and its legislative history that compelled testimony could be used solely in a prosecution relating to false statements or perjury uttered during the immunized testimony. The statute therefore, was not constitutionally infirm in this regard.† Sirica's opinion is unimpeachable, and the matter should now be considered settled.

The Contempt Power

Congress has two means to punish for contempt those who disregard its subpoenas or orders. The federal code contains a provision by which Congress can initiate criminal proceedings against persons who, under subpoena or order, refuse to produce materials or to testify. But Congress need not deliver defiances of its subpoenas and orders to prosecutorial authorities because it has its own self-help powers as a remedy. Either house may dispatch its sergeant at arms to arrest and imprison those who obstruct its legislative functions. This latter nonstatutory contempt power was the first established and is thus the first examined.

* *In re Baldinger* 356 F. Supp. 153 (C.D. Cal 1973).
† *Application of United States Senate Select Committee on Presidential Campaign Activities*, 361 F. Supp. 1282 (D.D.C. 1973).

SELF-HELP POWERS

With one exception, the Constitution contains no express grant of authority to Congress to deal with contempts against it. (The exception is that each house is empowered to remedy contempts committed by its own members.*) However, as with the authority to investigate and subpoena, the power to punish for contempt in appropriate circumstances is implied in the grant of legislative functions to the Congress.

The Supreme Court in 1821 confirmed this power in a landmark decision.† John Anderson had attempted to bribe a member of the House to gain his support for a land claim pending in Congress. The House, viewing this act as a flagrant endeavor to impede its processes, sent the sergeant at arms, Thomas Dunn, to arrest Anderson. Anderson was tried and convicted at the bar of the House, reprimanded by the Speaker of the House, Henry Clay, and released. Considerably miffed by the whole affair, Anderson then brought an action against Dunn for assault and battery and false arrest. The Supreme Court ruled against Anderson, holding that, despite the absence of an express constitutional provision, Congress had an implicit right to punish those who attempted to obstruct its functions by bribery. Finding that the Constitution gave Congress inherent power to redress contempts, the Court in a historic passage said, "There is not in the whole of that admirable instrument, a grant of powers which does not draw after it others, not expressed, but vital to their exercise . . ."

The reasons supporting this implied power are clear. The Congress must have a method to compel the production of evidence it needs to meet its legislative responsibilities. The authority to investigate and subpoena would be hollow without the right to punish those who choose not to respond. Moreover, Congress must have the authority to

---

* United States Constitution, Art. I, Sec. 5, Cl. 2.
† *Anderson* v. *Dunn*, 6 Wheat. (19 U.S.) 204 (1821).

interdict affirmative acts such as bribery that detrimentally affect the legislative process. As the Supreme Court said in a later case, Congress's implied contempt power "rests only upon the right of self-preservation, that is, the right to prevent acts which in and of themselves inherently obstruct or prevent the discharge of legislative duty or the refusal to do that which there is inherent legislative power to compel in order that legislative functions may be performed."*

The self-help contempt power had been exercised by Congress long before the Supreme Court's decision in John Anderson's case. The early Congress had as examples the use of inherent contempt powers by the House of Commons, the colonial legislatures, and the Continental Congress. The first employment of Congress's contempt powers—similar in circumstances to the Anderson matter —came in 1795, when Robert Randall and Charles Whitney were arrested by the House of Representatives for attempting to bribe certain members. Whitney was discharged before trial, but Randall was found guilty by the House, reprimanded by the Speaker, and committed to the custody of the sergeant at arms. He was released after seven days' confinement. The Senate's first contempt citation came in 1800, when William Duane was imprisoned for thirty days for libeling a senator. (As will be seen shortly, the legality of imprisonment for libeling a congressman is now in severe doubt.)

The first contempt citation by Congress for refusing to produce evidence occurred in 1812. Nathaniel Rounsavell, the editor of the Alexandria, Virginia, *Herald* was convicted for declining to answer questions put him by a House committee inquiring into leaks from a secret House session. Imprisoned for a day, Rounsavell was released after he informed the speaker that he was now willing to testify. The Senate's initial contempt citation to a contumacious witness involved the 1860 refusal of a summons

---

* *Marshall* v. *Gordon*, 243 U.S. 521, 542 (1917).

by Thaddeus Hyatt, who was called by a committee investigating John Brown's raid on Harper's Ferry. Hyatt, by a 44–10 vote, was jailed for over three months.

Other uses of the nonstatutory contempt power are noteworthy. In 1832 Sam Houston was arrested and tried by the House for assaulting Representative William Stanbery because of statements Stanbery had made during debate; Houston escaped with a reprimand. During the Credit Mobilier investigations the House in 1873 imprisoned Joseph B. Stewart, counsel for the Union Pacific Railroad, for refusing, on the basis of the attorney-client privilege, to answer a committee's questions concerning the railroad's affairs. Stewart was confined in a room in the Capitol, but the railroad, refusing to allow its champion to languish unattended, made sure he was royally supplied with sustenance while imprisoned. Remembering the Stewart affair, the House dealt differently with the next witness cited for contempt, R.B. Irvin, the Washington agent of the Pacific Mail Steamship Company, which was involved in corruption in the procurement of subsidies. Irvin was denied quarters in the Capitol, and instead was housed in the District of Columbia jail. Several years later Hallet Kilbourn, who refused to answer questions or produce documents concerning the failure of Jay Cooke's banking firm (a depository of federal funds), was imprisoned by the House in the District of Columbia jail. Kilbourn, like Joseph Stewart, had friends who fed him sumptuously and supplied him with vintage wines until an annoyed House forbade their generosity. But Kilbourn had the last laugh; in an important decision which we shall examine later, he was awarded a $20,000 judgment against the House sergeant at arms for false imprisonment.*

* *Kilbourn* v. *Thompson*, 103 U.S. 168 (1881). The Congress by a special appropriation paid the judgment. On these historical matters, see *Jurney* v. *MacCracken*, 294 U.S. 125 (1935), *Congressional Quarterly Guide to the United States Congress*, 1971, pp. 246–48, Telford Taylor, *Grand Inquest* (Simon and Schuster, 1955), pp. 45–

Numerous safeguards, constitutional and otherwise, protect individuals from unwarranted use of the self-help contempt power. Many of these are dealt with below when the general protections available to ward off congressional overreaching are discussed, but it is appropriate to mention here several limitations on the self-help power that relate, in a particularly intimate way, to its exercise. First, Congress does not enjoy general powers of punishment and can only penalize conduct that interferes with or obstructs its legislative duties. Congress, therefore, may not punish a libel against one of its members that does not impede the performance of legislative responsibilities.* A corollary to this principle is that Congress may not use its self-help power to redress the refusal to produce evidence concerning matters about which it has no legitimate legislative interest. Consequently the contempt remedy is not available to rectify the refusal of an individual to produce evidence relating solely to private affairs which in no way could be the subject of legislation.†

In applying sanctions for contempt, Congress may employ only "[t]he least possible power adequate to the end proposed . . . which is the power of imprisonment."‡ While Congress has implied power to jail individuals who ignore its process, it may not send them to the rack! Furthermore, the legislature may only imprison an intransigent witness or other obstructor of its functions during the session of Congress in which the contempt occurred.§

The courts have allowed individuals who view themselves abused by self-help powers to challenge the legis-

---

50. On contempt powers generally, see Carl Beck, *Contempt of Congress* (Hauser Press, 1959), and Ronald Goldfarb, *The Contempt Power* (Columbia University Press), 1963.

* *Marshall* v. *Gordon*, 243 U.S. 521 (1917).

† *Kilbourn* v. *Thompson*, 103 U.S. 168 (1881). As we shall see in Chapter IV, the holding of this case has been limited by later decisions.

‡ *Anderson* v. *Dunn*, 6 Wheat, (19 U.S.) 204, 231 (1821).

§ Id. at 231; *Marshall* v. *Gordon*, 243 U.S. 521, 542 (1917).

lature's actions in either a suit for damages against the sergeant at arms of the House involved or in a habeas corpus action.* In a habeas corpus action a federal court commands the legislature to bring the confined individual before the court for a determination whether the imprisonment is legally warranted. But a court's review in either a damage suit or a habeas corpus action is restricted. The court may not decide whether the individual actually was guilty of the acts charged—that is the prerogative of the legislature. The court may, however, examine whether the House involved had the *jurisdiction* to hold the offender in contempt—e.g., whether the information a witness failed to produce was sought pursuant to an investigation supported by a valid legislative purpose or whether the offending conduct actually obstructed some legislative function.† The court may also pass judgment on whether the rudiments of due process were preserved in the contempt proceeding. The Supreme Court has recently ruled that these rudiments at least require that the alleged contemptor be afforded notice and the opportunity to be heard respecting the legislative proceeding where he is "tried" for past contempt.

This last-mentioned principle emerged in a case involving civil rights activist Father James Groppi. Groppi, whose passion for leftist causes appears to rival that of Rabbi Korff for his more conservative concerns, was held in contempt by the Assembly of the Wisconsin Legislature for leading a demonstration onto its floor which, the Assembly found, constituted "disorderly conduct in the immediate view of the house and directly tend[ed] to interrupt its proceedings." The contempt resolution was voted two days after the demonstration without giving Groppi notice of its imminent presentation or the chance to be heard. That, the Supreme Court said, was improper.

---

* Compare *Kilbourn* v. *Thompson* 103 U.S. 168 (1881) with *Jurney* v. *MacCracken* 294 U.S. 125 (1935).

† See generally *Jurney* v. *MacCracken* 294 U.S., 125 (1935) and *Marshall* v. *Gordon*, 243 U.S. 521 (1917).

While a legislature in a contempt proceeding is not bound to adhere to all the strictures that govern a criminal trial, the Court stated, it must, at a minimum, give notice and a limited right to respond to the subject of the legislature's disfavor.*

STATUTORY CONTEMPT

In the mid-1850's, J.W. Simonton, the Washington correspondent for *The New York Times*, shocked the capital by claiming that certain unnamed congressmen were soliciting bribes to influence their actions regarding the disposal of public lands. Simonton was hauled before the House and commanded to divulge the members' names. When he refused, the House cited him for contempt and imprisoned him for over two weeks until, suitably chastened, he decided to testify. After he testified, several congressmen resigned.

Despite its success regarding Simonton, this episode left Congress disgruntled over the scope of its self-help contempt powers. As the law then stood, Congress could only use "the least possible power adequate to the end proposed" to punish contempts—the power of imprisonment during the current session of Congress. Harsher remedies, it was argued, were needed to deal with obdurate witnesses who refused to answer questions or produce materials. Consequently, in 1857, Congress passed a statute making it a criminal offense to refuse to give testimony or disgorge physical evidence demanded by Congress. This statute, an accompaniment to the ill-fated immunity statute of 1857 described above, remains, with

---

* *Groppi* v. *Leslie*, 404 U.S. 496 (1972). While a state legislature was involved in this case, the same result should apply regarding the national legislature, since the Court's holding rested on basic due process principles. The Court in the Groppi case indicated that a different conclusion might have been reached if Groppi, upon commission of his acts in full view of the entire house, had immediately been found in contempt without a two-day lag. See further, *Marshall* v. *Gordon*, 243 U.S. 521, 545 (1917).

minor amendment, in the current federal code.* The statute, which prescribed a fine between $100 and $1,000
and imprisonment "in the common jail" for one to twelve
months, was specifically passed "to inflict a greater punishment than . . . the House possesses the power to inflict.†

The language of the current contempt provision reads
in part: "Every person who having been summoned as a
witness to give testimony or to produce papers . . . willfully makes default, or who having appeared, refuses to
answer any questions pertinent to the question under
inquiry, shall be deemed guilty of a misdemeanor." The
current penalties are the same as meted out by the 1857
statute. The statute covers various kinds of "willful" (i.e.,
not inadvertent or accidental) failures to respond to congressional demands, including failure to appear, failure
to produce pertinent items subpoenaed, refusal to take the
oath, refusal to answer pertinent questions, and leaving a
hearing before being excused.‡

Although the contempt provisions of the federal code
delineate the procedures to be followed in initiating contempt proceedings, the exact responsibilities of various
officials who play a part in those proceedings are not certain. This lack of certainty is occasioned both by lacunae
in the statutory language and by judicial incrustations onto
the provisions of the code.

The statute declares that when a witness fails to comply with a committee's order

> . . . and the fact of such failure or failures is reported
> to either House while Congress is in session, or when

---

* 2 U.S.C. 192, 194 (1970).

† Cong. Globe, 34th Cong., 3d Sess. 405.

‡ See generally *Hutcheson* v. *United States*, 369 U.S. 599 (1962);
McPhaul v. *United States*, 364 U.S. 372 (1960); *United States* v.
Bryan, 339 U.S. 323 (1950); *Eisler* v. *United States*, 170 F. 2d 273
(D.C. Cir. 1948) *cert. dismissed* 338 U.S. 883 (1949); *Townsend* v.
United States, 95 F. 2d 352 (D.C. Cir. 1937), *cert. denied* 303 U.S.
664 (1937). There are, of course, numerous defenses that may be
available in a prosecution under this statute in appropriate cir-
cumstances. These are discussed in Chapters IV through IX.

Congress is not in session, a statement of fact constituting such failure is reported to and filed with the President of the Senate or the Speaker of the House, it shall be the duty of the said President of the Senate or Speaker of the House, as the case may be, to certify, and he shall so certify, the statement of facts aforesaid under the seal of the Senate or House, as the case may be, to the appropriate United States Attorney, whose duty it shall be to bring the matter before the grand jury for its action.

This turgid language—certainly not a model of artful drafting—appears to make *mandatory* certification of the alleged contempt to the United States Attorney once the committee involved has sent the relevant facts to its parent body. But not so, said the United States Court of Appeals for the District of Columbia in a case growing out of a contempt citation recommended by the House Un-American Activities Committee.* Relying on the statute's legislative history, the past practices of Congress and fragments from other cases, the court held that when Congress is in session, the house in question must vote on whether certification is in order. If Congress is not in session, the court said, the Speaker of the House or the President of the Senate must independently determine that certification is warranted before forwarding the matter to the United States Attorney. This case was decided by a 2–1 vote over a strong dissent, but the decision has received apparent approval in later cases by the same court.† The Supreme Court has not yet ruled on the matter.

On occasion, but infrequently, in the last thirty years, a house has gone against committee recommendations on

* *Wilson* v. *United States* 369 F. 2d 198 (D.C. Cir. 1966).

† *Sanders* v. *McClellan*, 463 F. 2d 894, 899 (D.C. Cir. 1972); *Ansara* v. *Eastland*, 442 F. 2d 751, 754 (D.C. Cir. 1971). The revised House Rules provide that a committee subpoena may be enforced "only as authorized or directed by the House." See Rule XI 2. (m) (2) (B).

contempt. A recent illustration involved the 1971 attempt by the House Interstate and Foreign Commerce Committee to have CBS and its president, Dr. Frank Stanton, cited for contempt. Stanton had refused to comply with a subcommittee subpoena calling for film and sound recordings edited from the award-winning, controversial documentary *The Selling of the Pentagon*. Stanton claimed a First Amendment free press right to protect these "outtakes," but the Committee—25 members voting aye, 13 nay—recommended contempt. After spirited floor debate, the House, by a 226–181 vote, returned the matter to the committee, thus killing the contempt move.

The statute also requires that the United States Attorney bring the contempt certification before the grand jury for its action. The grand jury, of course, can decline to indict, but even if the grand jury returns an indictment, there is no absolute assurance under the statute that a prosecution will be commenced. Under existing law a United States Attorney cannot be forced to sign an indictment he believes ill-advised or proceed with a prosecution he thinks unwise.* There is also no certitude that a prosecution, if it eventuates, will be vigorously pursued and not handled perfunctorily. Additionally, a conviction under the criminal statute is always susceptible to Presidential pardon; President Franklin Roosevelt in fact used the pardon power to rescue an individual convicted of contempt of Congress.† Thus, several obstacles to successful prosecution and punishment may be erected if the executive branch is less than enthusiastic about the case. There are dangers lurking here, for the executive might happily decline to prosecute or allow punishment of those who resist testifying to Congress about executive branch

---

* See, e.g., *United States* v. *Nixon* 418 U.S. 683, 694 (1974); *United States* v. *Cox*, 342 F. 2d 167 (5th Cir. 1965) *cert. denied* 381 U.S. 935 (1965). But see Rule 48(a), Federal Rules of Criminal Procedure, which apparently gives a federal judge some discretion as to whether to dismiss an indictment.

† See *Townsend* v. *United States*, 95 F. 2d 352 (D.C. Cir. 1938), *cert. denied*, 303 U.S. 664 (1938).

corruption or the offenses of the President's friends. Fortunately, the self-help powers of Congress remain an alternate method to nudge intransigent witnesses into giving evidence to Congressional bodies.*

Throughout its history, Congress has not been reluctant to use its contempt powers. The *Congressional Quarterly* reports that between 1789 and 1969 Congress voted 394 contempt citations;† this figure includes citations under both the federal criminal statute and Congress's implied contempt powers. Three hundred and eighty of these citations involved the recalcitrance of witnesses to answer questions or to produce physical evidence. The other fourteen related to alleged obstructions of legislative functions. Of the total, 283 contempt citations occurred since 1945, the bulk growing out of the proceedings of the House Un-American Activities Committee.

For a time after the passage of the 1857 criminal statute, Congress normally opted to use its self-help powers to punish contempts. Several considerations produced this result. Where evidence from a witness was sought, resort to the courts was time-consuming and removed the witness from Congress's control. A few days in jail at Congress's direction, however, could well have the salutary effect of loosening a witness's tongue. Also, the fear pervaded that the judiciary, if contempt matters were dispatched to it, would soon restrict Congress's investigatory authority. In fact, this gradually happened as contempt cases came before the courts.‡

As time passed, however, more and more contempt matters were handled via the criminal statute, principally because other legislative responsibilities became too pressing to allow full-scale congressional trials. Of late, vir-

---

* See *In re Chapman*, 166 U.S. 661, 671–72 (1897).
† *Congressional Quarterly Guide to the United States Congress,* 1971, p. 248.
‡ See Chapters VII and VIII.

tually all contempt matters have been processed under
the federal statute; Congress has not used its implied
contempt powers since 1945.

The Ervin committee declined to seek contempt citations of either type, although a suitable occasion presented itself more than once. A good example involved
Gordon Liddy, the DNC burglar, who refused even to be
sworn, although the committee would have given him
immunity. While the exact reasons for the committee's failure to hold the tight-lipped Liddy in contempt are not
altogether clear, an important factor probably was that
Liddy—a pitiable figure in his arcane, self-inflicted mar-
tyrdom—already had numerous tribulations heaped upon
him, including a six- to twenty-year sentence for his role
in the DNC burglary. However, the more insouciant
House, by a 334–11 margin, did vote a contempt citation
for Liddy in regard to his refusal to take the oath before
the House Armed Services Special Intelligence Subcommittee, and Liddy was later convicted for criminal
contempt under the federal statute.

Although the Watergate committee did not institute
contempt proceedings against any witness, it did use the
threat of contempt to accomplish compliance with its subpoenas. Bebe Rebozo and certain Howard Hughes employees, for example, were informed that contempt proceedings were distinctly possible if they did not honor
committee subpoenas. But Rebozo in particular never
fully complied with the multiple subpoenas against him
despite the committee's warnings.

Senator Ervin's minatory pronouncements early in the
Watergate investigation that he would use the Senate
sergeant at arms to corral reticent White House witnesses
were apparently more effective. On April 17, 1973, President Nixon, reversing his previous stand, announced he
would allow White House aides to testify before the Ervin
committee.*

* To put his threat into effect, Ervin, of course, would have
needed a majority vote of the full Senate.

Ervin's rough persuasion also brought Alexander Butterfield to the witness table. Butterfield had told the Committee's staff in executive session on Friday, July 16, 1973, that President Nixon was taping his own conversations. On Monday, I was instructed to inform Butterfield that we wished his *public* testimony that very afternoon. Butterfield, preparing for a trip to Russia on FAA business, was, with some justification, infuriated by the short notice. In fact, he said, the pique evident in his voice, he would not appear.

I reported Butterfield's retort to Senator Ervin, who was seated at the committee table listening to the testimony of Special Counsel to the President Richard Moore. Now, Ervin is not a man to be thwarted. As I conveyed Butterfield's response, the senator—his eyebrows cavorting and his jaws churning in anticipation of his next remark—grew visibly agitated. "Tell Mr. Butterfield," he said emphatically, "that if he is not here this afternoon I will send the sergeant at arms to fetch him." I faithfully relayed this declaration to Mr. Butterfield, whom I located in a barber's chair. Upon hearing Ervin's ultimatum, his defiance subsided. He would come, he said, as soon as he finished his haircut. Shortly after 1:30 P.M. he arrived—diffident, contrite, and nicely coifed—to meet with Senators Ervin and Baker and staff. Later that afternoon he gave his electrifying testimony to the world.

The Power to Bring Suit

In 1927 another election was under investigation. William S. Vare had been elected senator from Pennsylvania, but his vanquished opponent, William B. Wilson, claimed fraudulent and unlawful practies in connection with both Vare's nomination and election. The Senate, reacting to this charge, authorized a special committee to investigate the circumstances of the campaign. Pursuing its mission, the committee ordered the production of ballots, ballot boxes, and other items used in the election, but was rebuffed by their custodians. The committee then instituted suit against the custodians to obtain the materials sought.

The Supreme Court frustrated the committee's efforts.* It ruled that the Senate, in the committee's enabling resolutions, had not delegated the power to sue to the committee "even if it be assumed that the Senate alone may give that authority." Thus the committee had no authority to bring the action and it could not be maintained.

Almost immediately the Senate acted to rectify this oversight. In 1928 it passed a resolution† which declared:

> That . . . any committee of the Senate is hereby authorized to bring suit on behalf of and in the name of the United States in any court of competent jurisdiction if the committee is of the opinion that the suit is necessary to the adequate performance of the powers vested in it or the duties imposed upon it by the Constitution, resolution of the Senate or other law. Such suit may be brought and prosecuted to final determination irrespective of whether or not the Senate is in session at the time the suit is brought or thereafter. The committee may be represented in the suit either by such attorneys as it may designate or by such officers of the Department of Justice as the Attorney General may designate upon the request of the committee . . .

The House, however, has passed no such resolution, and thus a suit by a House committee lacking specific approval by the full House would be amenable to dismissal for lack of delegation.‡

The suggestion in the Supreme Court decision that the Senate alone might not be able to impart power to sue to

---

* *Reed* v. *County Commissioners*, 277 U.S. 376 (1928).

† Senate Resolution 262, 70th Cong., 1st Sess. (1928). This resolution is now part of the Standing Orders of the Senate. See Senate *Manual*, p. 105.

‡ See House Rule 2. (m) (2) (B).

a committee is mystifying. Each house of Congress, as we have seen, has certain implied powers. It can conduct investigations, issue subpoenas, and cite and jail for contempt. Surely a house of Congress has implied power to institute suit to obtain information needed for its legislative responsibilities—a remedy far less drastic than imprisonment.*

President Nixon, in the Ervin committee's suit against him, did not contend that the Senate was powerless to bring suit. Rather, his complaint was that the committee, under its enabling resolution, could only sue the President with the full Senate's concurrence. This argument was exceedingly strange because it overlooked the 1928 resolution and because the provision of the Ervin committee's enabling resolution which the President relied on stated only that the committee was empowered "to make to the Senate any recommendations it deems appropriate . . . in respect to the willful failure of any officer . . . of the executive branch of the United States Government . . . to produce before the Committee any . . . tapes . . . or materials in obedience to any subpoena."† Although this provision appeared to give complete discretion to the committee regarding recommendations to the full Senate, the President, quoting Yale Law School Professor Charles Black, argued:

Does not this language (at the very least when applied to such an utterly unique and politically charged question as a "willful failure or refusal" *of the President himself*) designate the *exclusive* procedure to be followed by the Committee? Is it not reasonable to infer from it a *direction* by the Senate that the matter of pos-

* In *Minnesota State Senate* v. *Beens,* 406 U.S. 187, 194 (1972), the Supreme Court held that a state Senate might participate in litigation without securing the concurrence of the other house.

† This provision, for example, would have allowed the Committee to recommend initiation of criminal contempt proceedings or the use of self-help powers.

sible contempt be brought back to the whole Senate, for resolution upon action? Is the expressed power to "make recommendations" not an implied exclusion of independent action by the Committee?*

With all deference to the distinguished Professor Black, a more convoluted reading of clear language would be difficult to conceive. However, before a court determination on this issue could be reached, the Senate put the matter to rest. In Senate Resolution 194, passed shortly after the Saturday Night Massacre, the Senate, relying in part on the 1928 resolution, unanimously declared that it was "the sense of the Senate" that the suit against the President was "fully authorized" and did not require the Senate's prior approval. The Senate added that it "approves and ratifies" the committee's actions in instituting and pursuing the litigation

None of the judges ruling on the committee's claims in its suit against the President ever questioned that the Senate had the power—which it could delegate—to initiate suit in a court of competent jurisdiction† to obtain information to make legislative judgments. Whether the Senate or the House can sue to enforce its subpoenas may seem a minor technical matter to some, but it could become of vital importance to the proper harmony between the branches of government. If a house of Congress does not have resort to the courts to resolve conflicts with the executive branch, it may have to rely on other, cruder tests of strength to obtain the evidence it needs which may put severe strain on the constitutional fabric. We shall have more to say later about this issue.

* See *Congressional Record*, E 5321 (daily ed., August 1, 1973).
† The matter of jurisdiction is discussed in Chapters VI and X.

·IV·
Investigating Criminal Conduct: The Doctrine of Legislative Purpose

"Richard M. Nixon," his lawyers said, in answering the Ervin committee's suit, ". . . denies that [the committee and its members] are entitled to investigate criminal conduct." The committee's enabling resolution, his counsel complained, "purports to authorize an investigation of alleged criminal conduct, and . . . the investigation by [the committee] has been, in fact, a criminal investigation and trial conducted for the purpose of determining whether or not criminal acts have been committed and the guilt or innocence of individuals . . . . [The] Resolution and investigation exceed the legislative powers granted to the Congress in Article I of the Constitution." Rabbi Korff, in his litigation to block the committee's public hearings into criminal matters, presented similar contentions.

The President later modified his position. Although

it is proper for the committee to "identify" criminal conduct, his lawyers stated, in attempting to root out the
details of wrongdoing the committee was pursuing an
"inquiry . . . not germane to the Committee's *legislative*
purpose, [which] constitutes a usurpation of those duties
exclusively vested in the executive and the judiciary."
Bebe Rebozo, in his lawsuit to proscribe further committee inquiries into his affairs, presented yet another
variation on this theme. When he brought his suit, Rebozo
was under investigation by the special prosecutor concerning his stewardship of the $100,000 Hughes contribution
to Mr. Nixon's 1972 campaign. Thus he argued: "Now
that the criminal processes have been invoked and investigations of Plaintiff Rebozo begun, it is imperative that the
committee's investigation be terminated. Any possible
criminal violations must be handled by the proper law
enforcement officials and the courts."*

The claims of the President and Rebozo were self-
serving, but they do raise serious issues that have troubled
courts and investigators for generations. Criminal conduct
is, after all, chiefly the province of prosecutors and courts.
What, then, is the legitimate scope of Congress's powers to
probe criminality? What protections are available to impede misuse of that power?

It is useful to begin this discussion by observing that,
as a historical matter, Congress has investigated criminal
conduct since its nascence. In the late eighteenth and early
nineteenth centuries, the House conducted several inquiries in connection with contempt proceedings into alleged attempts to bribe its members by such men as Robert
Randall, Charles Whitney, and John Anderson. Beginning
in 1859, the Senate investigated the treasonous raid by
John Brown on the federal arsenal at Harpers Ferry. And

* The special prosecutor's office eventually decided not to prosecute
Rebozo.

in the 1870's both houses of Congress examined the Credit Mobilier scandal, including efforts to bribe congressmen to abstain from investigating the affairs of the Union Pacific Railroad.

In this century numerous congressional committees have delved into criminal wrongdoing. The Senate Teapot Dome investigating committees fully explored the different aspects of that variegated affair, including the cover-up of the scandal by the Department of Justice. Senator Estes Kefauver's Special Committee to Investigate Organized Crime in Interstate Commerce did just that, and was successful in exposing widespread wrongdoing, particularly corruption in state and local governments. The Senate Select Committee on Improper Activities in the Labor or Management Field, under the direction of Senator John McClellan, scrutinized the illegal activities of numerous union and management officials. At midcentury the House Ways and Means Subcommittee on Administration of the Internal Revenue Laws engaged in a well-publicized investigation of nation-wide corruption in the Internal Revenue Service. More recently, in the 1960's, the Senate Government Operations Permanent Subcommittee on Investigations conducted an inquiry into riots and violent disorders, including the activities of the Ku Klux Klan. And the House Un-American Activities Committee, of which Richard Nixon was an active member, invested considerable time into examinations of alleged espionage.*

The freight of history, therefore, demonstrates conclusively that Congress at least has viewed its investigation of criminal conduct as fully within the parameters of pro-

---

* There also have been various investigations of criminal conduct in connection with impeachment proceedings, but these are a unique breed because the Constitution specifically provides for impeachment for treason, bribery, or other high crimes and misdemeanors. See Art. II, Sec. 3. President Nixon, in the Ervin committee's suit, argued that the House Judiciary Committee, with its impeachment responsibilities, was "the only appropriate committee of Congress for inquiring into specific allegations of crime against individuals within the executive branch of government."

priety. Indeed, the immunity statutes enacted by Congress in 1857, 1954, and 1970 show that the legislators who promulgated them—and the various Presidents who allowed them to become law—had few compunctions about Congress's investigating criminal conduct. Laws giving immunity to witnesses forced to testify before Congress about criminal wrongdoing would not have been written unless it was believed that examination of criminal activities by Congress was permissible. The National Commission for Reform of Federal Criminal Laws that drafted the 1970 immunity statute withheld power to block a congressional request for an immunity order from the Attorney General because it realized that future criminal scandals of the Teapot Dome ilk involving the Attorney General could come under Congress's scrutiny.

The courts have also recognized that Congress, in appropriate circumstances, can probe criminal conduct. Perhaps the most significant Supreme Court decision to that effect is *McGrain* v. *Daugherty*, a case growing out of the Teapot Dome scandal.*

In 1923–24, the Senate became concerned that the Department of Justice—under the supervision of Attorney General Harry M. Daugherty, a political adviser and friend to President Warren Harding—was mired in corruption. After increasing demands for an investigation, the Senate adopted a resolution directing a select committee of five senators

> to investigate circumstances and facts, and report the same to the Senate, concerning the alleged failure of Harry M. Daugherty, Attorney General of the United States, to prosecute properly violators of the Sherman Anti-trust Act and the Clayton Act against monopolies and unlawful restraint of trade; the alleged neglect and failure of the said Harry M. Daugherty, Attorney General of the United States, to arrest and prosecute Albert

* 273 U.S. 135 (1927).

B. Fall, Harry F. Sinclair, E.L. Doheny, C.R. Forbes, and their co-conspirators in defrauding the Government, as well as the alleged neglect and failure of the said Attorney General to arrest and prosecute many others for violations of Federal statutes, and his alleged failure to prosecute properly, efficiently, and promptly, and to defend, all manner of civil and criminal actions wherein the Government of the United States is interested as a party plaintiff or defendant. And said committee is further directed to inquire into, investigate and report to the Senate the activities of the said Harry M. Daugherty, Attorney General, and any of his assistants in the Department of Justice which would in any manner tend to impair their efficiency or influence as representatives of the Government of the United States.

Pursuing this responsibility, the select committee subpoenaed the Attorney General's banker brother, Mally S. Daugherty, to appear and testify, but he ignored the subpoenas. Reacting to this snub, the full Senate—finding that Daugherty's testimony was "material," would aid the committee in executing its functions, and would serve as a basis for "legislative and other action" the Senate might undertake—sent its sergeant at arms to arrest Daugherty and bring him before the bar of the Senate.

Daugherty was taken into custody but was promptly released on a writ of habeas corpus by an Ohio federal district judge. Noting "the extreme personal cast of the original resolutions [and] the spirit of hostility towards the then Attorney General," the District Court (in language resembling Mr. Nixon's claims) declared: "What [the Senate] is proposing to do is to determine the guilt of the Attorney General of the shortcomings and wrongdoings set forth in the resolution. It is 'to hear, adjudge and condemn.' In so doing it is exercising the judicial function . . . This it has no power to do."*

* *Ex parte Daugherty,* 229 F. 620, 639–40 (S.D. Ohio 1924).

The case was immediately appealed to the Supreme Court, which was thus squarely presented with a case directly challenging the prerogatives of Congress to explore criminal conduct. It was, as the Court later noted, a matter "of unusual importance and delicacy."

The Supreme Court—taking *over two years* to decide the case—reversed. Rejecting the contention that the Senate was attempting to prosecute and try the former Attorney General, the Court stated that "plainly" the administration of the Department of Justice was a subject "on which legislation could be had and would be materially aided by the information which the investigation was calculated to elicit. . . . The only legitimate object the Senate could have in ordering the investigation was to aid in legislating; and we think the subject matter was such that the presumption should be indulged that this was the real object."* While the Senate could not try the Attorney General for crimes, the Court said, it was not "a valid objection to the investigation that it might possibly disclose crime or wrongdoing on his part."

Two years later the Supreme Court, in another Teapot Dome case—*Sinclair* v. *United States*†—reaffirmed the principle that Congress may rightfully investigate criminal conduct where there is a legitimate legislative need. The Senate had ordered its Committee on Public Lands to examine government leases of oil reserves and oil magnate Harry F. Sinclair was asked by the committee to testify concerning leases his company had obtained from the Interior Department. Sinclair declined. He argued that the investigation related to his "private affairs," and, pointing to a joint resolution by Congress that had directed the

---

* It should be observed that other cases have indicated that Congress may have other legitimate reasons to investigate besides aiding its lawmaking functions. See Chapters V and VI. But, the Supreme Court has said, "The subject of any inquiry always must be one 'on which legislation could be had.'" *Eastland* v. *United States Servicemen's Fund*, 421 U.S. 491, 504, and n. 15 (1975).

† 279 U.S. 263 (1929).

President to institute appropriate court proceedings regarding these leases, claimed that this resolution "had made the whole matter a judicial question which was determinable only by the court."* For his intransigence, Sinclair was convicted of contempt of Congress. The Supreme Court affirmed, finding that the inquiry did not pertain solely to his private affairs, and that the investigation was not foreclosed because the joint resolution had put the subject before the courts. Said the Supreme Court: "It is plain that investigation of the matters involved in suits . . . under [the] Joint Resolution . . . might directly aid in respect of legislative action."†

In truth, the *McGrain* and *Sinclair* cases were important for reasons that went far beyond their holding that Congress could investigate criminal conduct, for they denoted a new judicial perspective regarding the general nature of the legislature's investigatory powers. Fifty years earlier, in the famous damage action brought by Hallet Kilbourn against the House sergeant at arms for false imprisonment, the Supreme Court had enunciated a much narrower conception of Congress's investigatory authority.‡ There the subject under investigation by the House had been a private real estate pool managed by Kilbourn and participated in by Jay Cooke & Co., a depository of federal funds whose affairs were involved in a bankruptcy proceeding before a federal district court. Kilbourn, it will be recalled, had been imprisoned by the House sergeant

* A civil suit against Sinclair's company had already been brought at the time he declined to testify.

† For a case forcefully holding that an investigation of subversive propaganda did not involve purely private affairs but related to matters on which legislation could be had, see *United States* v. *Josephson*, 165 F. 2d 82, 88–9 (2d Cir. 1947) *cert. denied* 333 U.S. 838 (1948).

‡ *Kilbourn* v. *Thompson*, 103 U.S. 168 (1881). Justice Harlan has stated that this case has been "severely discredited" because of its "loose language," and the decision has received other savage criticism for its lack of accurate scholarship. See, e.g., *Hutcheson* v. *United States* 369 U.S. 599, 613–14 (1962); *United States* v. *Rumely*, 345 U.S. 41, 46 (1953).

at arms for refusing to answer questions concerning the
real estate pool. The Court, in holding that Kilbourn had
been unlawfully confined, ruled that the House had
exceeded its legitimate legislative authority in conducting
an impermissible "investigation into the personal affairs of
individuals . . . that could result in no valid legislation on
the subject to which the inquiry referred." Additiona-
ally, the Court—observing that the matter was before a
bankruptcy court—held that the House had improperly
"assumed a power which could only be properly exercised
by another branch of the government, because it was in its
nature clearly judicial."

The differences in approach between the *Kilbourn* decision and the rulings in *McCain* and *Sinclair* are not difficult to perceive. In the *Kilbourn* case the Court, noting
that a bankruptcy court has assumed jurisdiction over the
matter, found that the House was improperly assuming a
"judicial" function, but in *Sinclair* the investigation was
approved even though a joint resolution had instructed
the President to put the subject under inquiry before the
courts. In *Kilbourn* the Court was quick to find no valid
legislative purpose, although arguably a proper legislative
interest in investigating a bankrupt debtor of the United
States could have been found. The *McGrain* court, on the
other hand, was prepared to indulge the *presumption* that
a legitimate legislative purpose existed. Since *McGrain* the
Supreme Court has indicated on other occasions that it will
presume a legislative body acts with valid legislative reasons. The Court has also announced that it will not inquire
into the actual motives of legislators to establish that an
investigation was not supported by proper legislative
goals. In fact, the Court has said, if a valid legislative purpose otherwise appears, the judiciary "lacks authority to
intervene on the basis of the motives which spurred the
exercise of the investigatory power."* The determination

---

* See also *Eastland* v. *United States Servicemen's Fund*, 421 U.S.
491, 508–9 (1975); *Barenblatt* v. *United States*, 360 U.S. 109, 132–
33 (1959); *Watkins* v. *United States*, 354 U.S. 178, 200 (1957).

respecting validity of legislative purpose must be made by an objective evaluation of the nature of the inquiry and the possible legislative functions it may serve.

It would be misleading, however, to suggest that the *Kilbourn* case has been sapped of all vitality. It remains a credible precedent for the proposition that Congress, without legitimate legislative interest, cannot pry into the purely private affairs of citizens. Indeed, the *McGrain* and *Sinclair* decisions vigorously reexpressed this rule. *Kilbourn* is also an early affirmation of the basic, salutary principle that the federal courts may review Congress's exercise of its investigatory functions. But *Kilbourn* today no longer deserves the unstinting panegyric once bestowed upon it by Justice Stephen Field: "This case will stand for all time as a bulwark against the invasion of the right of the citizen to protection in his private affairs against the unlimited scrutiny of investigation by a Congressional committee."*

The efficacy of Congress's criminal investigatory function is nowhere more apparent than when Congress trains its sights on corruption in the executive branch. Unless prodded by a congressional investigation, the executive may be hesitant to prosecute miscreants in its own ranks, and a forceful congressional probe may provide just the push needed to unstick the clogged wheels of criminal justice. The Watergate and Teapot Dome experiences in particular demonstrate the laudable effect of congressional investigations in ensuring that the corrective processes of prosecution and punishment are allowed to function. Mr. Nixon was not moved to appoint a special prosecutor to handle Watergate matters until it became clear that the Ervin committee's investigation would be rigorous.

The courts have recognized the validity—indeed, the

* *Re Pacific Railway Commission*, 32 Fed. 241, 250 (Cir. Ct., N.D. Cal 1887).

critical necessity—of congressional probes into criminal wrongdoing in the executive branch. Referring to the circumstance where illegal activities of an unindicted public official are under congressional scrutiny, the Court of Appeals for the First Circuit said: "In such a situation the investigative function of Congress has its greatest utility: Congress is informing itself so that it may take appropriate legislative action; it is informing the executive so that existing laws may be enforced; and it is informing the public so that democratic processes may be brought to bear to correct any disclosed executive laxity."*

The Supreme Court has made similar pronouncements. Congress's investigatory power, it has said, "comprehends probes into departments of the federal government to expose corruption." And on several occasions the Court has recognized "the dangers to effective and honest conduct of the Government if the legislature's power to probe corruption in the executive branch [is] unduly hampered."†

What, however, if the executive is or becomes engaged in prosecuting those under examination by Congress? Should a congressional investigation into the same conduct be allowed to proceed? Mr. Rebozo, in his suit against the committee, argued that once prosecutorial authorities had taken up the cause, Congress should fold its tents and gracefully retire. But the few decisions that speak to this issue do not support Rebozo's contentions.

In October 1951 the House Subcommittee on Administration of the Internal Revenue Laws (generally called the King Committee after its chairman) began an investigation of criminal conduct in the IRS office for the District of Massachusetts. The inquiry focused on Denis W. Delaney, who had been collector of internal revenue for that state. The investigation covered, among other things, allegations that Delaney had taken bribes to influence his actions as collector and caused the discharge of tax liens

---

* *Delaney* v. *United States*, 199 F. 2d 107, 115 (1st Cir. 1952).
† See *Watkins* v. *United States*, 354 U.S. 178, 187, 194–95 (1957).

by falsely certifying that the liens had been paid. Delaney, however, had been indicted by a federal grand jury for this perfidy in September 1951, and his trial was scheduled for January 1952. Both Delaney and the federal prosecutors had vigorously appealed to the King committee to postpone its hearings until after trial, but their pleas had fallen on deaf ears. Delaney also asked the trial judge to delay the trial until prejudicial publicity from the King hearings subsided, but this entreaty was also refused. The hearings were held in October and in January Delaney was convicted for his derelictions.

The appellate court reversed on the grounds that Delaney's trial should have been continued to a later date,* but it stated that the King committee, in declining to postpone its hearings, had acted lawfully:

> . . . We mean to imply no criticism of the action of the King Committee. We have no doubt that the committee acted lawfully, within the constitutional powers of Congress duly delegated to it. It was for the committee to decide whether considerations of public interest demanded at that time a full-dress public investigation of the affairs of the Internal Revenue Bureau, including particularly the conduct of Delaney's office in Boston. . . .
> . . . If . . . the legislative committee deemed that an open hearing at that time was required by over-riding considerations of public interest, then the committee was of course free to go ahead with its hearing . . .

An even more significant case, decided by the Supreme Court in 1962, involved Maurice Hutcheson, president of the United Brotherhood of Carpenters and Joiners of America.† In 1958 Hutcheson was called before Senator

---

* *Delaney* v. *United States*, 199 F. 2d 107 (1st Cir. 1952). We shall return to this case in the next chapter when we consider the potential conflict between Congress's informing function and fair trials.

† *Hutcheson* v. *United States*, 369 U.S. 599 (1962).

McClellan's select committee investigating labor corruption. At the time of the hearing Hutcheson was under indictment by an Indiana state grand jury for selling land to the state at a huge profit after promising a kickback to an Indiana official involved in arranging the deal. When Hutcheson was queried by the McClellan committee about the use of union money to bribe a state prosecutor to drop charges against the individuals involved in this fraud, he declined to answer, but not on Fifth Amendment grounds. (As the law then stood—it has since been changed by Supreme Court decision—a claim of the privilege against self-incrimination in a *federal* proceeding could be used against a defendant in a *state* trial either as evidence of guilt or to impeach his testimony if he took the stand.) Hutcheson instead contended he was not required to answer because it would violate his due process rights to force him to testify about matters involved in the upcoming criminal trial and thus aid the prosecution. Additionally, he asserted, his refusal to testify was justified because "the committee invaded domains constitutionally reserved to the executive and the judiciary, in that its inquiry was simply aimed at petitioner's 'exposure' and served no legislative purpose." Hutcheson was convicted on an eighteen-count contempt indictment for his failures to respond.

The Supreme Court affirmed by a 4–2 vote. Justice Harlan wrote the principal opinion, which was concurred in by Justices Clark and Stewart; Justice Brennan concurred in a separate opinion, and Chief Justice Warren and Justice Douglas dissented. Harlan found that the McClellan committee, commissioned by the Senate to investigate "criminal or other improper practices . . . in the field of labor-management relations," was acting with valid legislative purpose, a finding not difficult to arrive at since the Labor-Management Reporting and Disclosure Act of 1959 (the Landrum-Griffin Act) resulted from the committee's inquiries. Speaking to Hutcheson's contentions that he should not have to testify about matters relating to his state indictment, Justice Harlan said "[I]t [cannot] be argued that the mere pendency of the state indictment *ipso facto* constitutionally closed this avenue of interrogation to the Committee." Establishing that Hutcheson had used union money to bribe a prosecutor, Harlan observed, "would have supported remedial federal legislation, even though [it] might at the same time have warranted a separate state prosecution for obstruction of justice, or have been usable at [Hutcheson's] trial . . . as evidence of consciousness of guilt . . . But surely a Congressional committee which is engaged in a legitimate legislative investigation need not grind to a halt whenever responses to its inquiries might potentially be harmful to a witness in some distinct proceeding . . . or when crime or wrongdoing is disclosed." Harlan concluded with this reminder: "[I]t is appropriate to observe that just as the Constitution forbids the Congress to enter fields reserved to the Executive and Judiciary, it imposes on the Judiciary the reciprocal duty of not lightly interfering with Congress' exercise of its legitimate powers."

The opinion in the *Hutcheson* case also speaks to the President's claim in the Ervin committee's suit that, while it was appropriate for the committee to "identify" criminal conduct, it had no authority to explore the details of wrongdoing. After noting that the information sought was pertinent to the legislative inquiry, Justice Harlan stated, "it does not lie with this Court to say when a Congressional committee should be deemed to have acquired sufficient information for its legislative purposes." This position brought a stinging retort from the dissenters, Warren and Douglas: "Conceding that . . . the Committee here had the power to ask general questions along this line, it does not follow that it could make detailed inquiries about the conduct of a witness that related specifically to a crime with which he was already charged and for which he was soon to be tried . . . [I]t is incomprehensible . . . how it can be urged that Congress needed the details of how petitioner committed this alleged crime in order to pass general legislation about union funds . . ." This latter view, however, remains a dissent.*

Despite the rulings in the cases of Messrs. Daugherty, Sinclair, Delaney, and Hutcheson, there is no question that the legislature cannot assume the functions of the executive and the courts and conduct a prosecution and trial. Clear expression of this fundamental principle is found in a 1957 Supreme Court opinion, *Watkins* v. *United States*:

> . . . There is no general authority to expose the private affairs of individuals without justification in terms of the functions of Congress . . . Nor is the Congress a law enforcement or trial agency. These are the functions of the executive and judicial departments of government. No inquiry is an end in itself; it must be related to, and in furtherance of, a legitimate task of the Congress. Investigations conducted solely for the personal aggrandizement of the investigators or to "punish" those investigated are indefensible.†

* Warren's and Douglas' dissents were in part predicated on their view that Hutcheson was confronted with a fundamentally unfair dilemma. Had he claimed his Fifth Amendment privilege, this response—under the law as it then stood—could have been used against him in the state trial. Thus Hutcheson was forced to refuse to testify on other grounds or risk injury in his state trial. The Supreme Court has now ruled that an assertion of the Fifth Amendment privilege in a federal proceeding can no longer be used against the witness in a state proceeding. *Griffin* v. *California*, 380 U.S. 609 (1965).

† 354 U.S. 178, 187 (1957); see also *Quinn* v. *United States*, 349 U.S. 155, 161 (1955). The Congress is also "without authority to compel disclosures for the purpose of aiding the prosecution in pending suits; but . . . its . . . constitutional power is not abridged because the information sought to be elicited may also be of use in such suits." *Sinclair* v. *United States*, 279 U.S. 263, 295 (1929). Compare *Silverthorne* v. *United States*, 400 F. 2d 627, 633–34 (9th Cir. 1968), *cert. denied*, 400 U.S. 1022 (1971) where the court observed that "the Senate Committee [involved in this case] and the federal grand jury are associates in exposing criminal activity and moving toward its curtailment."

This trenchant statement by the high court was an obvious comment on the "legislative trials" of the loyalty-investigations era. According to numerous observers, the legislative trial had become the mechanism for punishing witnesses—usually those suspected of Communist affiliations or sympathies—without bothering with the safeguards inherent in a criminal trial. The congressional zealots who conducted these trials perceived the processes of the courts as frustratingly time-consuming and unreliable. And, in any event, the courts could only punish for crimes, not for "disloyalty" or being a "fellow traveler."

The legislative trial often wreaked onerous penalties on its victims: their affairs and views for decades back were disclosed; they were publicly subjected to stigma, scorn and ridicule; their livelihoods were put in jeopardy. As the Supreme Court observed, "when . . . forced revelations concern matters that are unorthodox, unpopular or even hateful to the general public, the reaction in the life of the witness may be disastrous. This effect is even more harsh when it is past beliefs, expressions or associations that are disclosed and judged by current standards rather than those contemporary with the matters exposed."[*] Individuals appearing before the committees at such proceedings also ran the risk of charges for collateral crimes such as contempt or perjury—witness the case of Owen Lattimore who, after twelve days of grueling testimony before Senator McCarran's Internal Security Subcommittee where his past actions and writings were copiously examined, was forced into many months of litigation to defend himself against spurious perjury charges that were eventually abandoned by the government. It was this type of congressional abuse the Supreme Court sought to reprove.

While investigations conducted to punish those under

[*] *Watkins* v. *United States*, 354 U.S. 178, 197 (1957). For discussions of legislative trials, see Alan Barth, *Government by Investigation* (The Viking Press, 1955), pp. 81–111, and Telford Taylor, *Grand Inquest* (Simon and Schuster, 1955), p. xiv.

scrutiny are rightly condemned, it must be realized that worthwhile, well-intentioned inquiries often bring griev-ous injury to numerous persons. Watergate could not have been investigated without bringing down rebuke upon Nixon, Dean, Mitchell, Haldeman, Ehrlichman, and many, many more. To use Telford Taylor's words, "It is impos-sible to probe deep in the vital tissues of society without drawing blood and leaving scars."*

Moreover, it must be wondered how much actual pro-tection resides in the Supreme Court's remonstration in the *Watkins* case. The Congress, of course, cannot pass an act pronouncing an individual guilty of a crime and inflict-ing punishment upon him. Such action would be a "bill of attainder," and an express constitutional provision pre-vents this kind of legislative transgression.† Beyond that, however, it is difficult to draw lines. Today the federal government reaches into diverse and multitudinous aspects of American life. Some federal interest abides in many matters once considered essentially private—the internal workings of labor unions, the wages paid employees, the makeup of the clientele at the corner diner, the racial composition of local neighborhoods. While the mere sem-blance of some furtive federal interest will not justify a congressional investigation—especially where a protection granted by the Bill of Rights is imperiled—the predilection of most courts is to find a legitimate federal concern that vindicates the legislative inquiry. The Supreme Court, after all, has recognized a "presumption" that a congres-sional inquiry proceeds with valid legislative purpose. And, the Court has said, the motives of legislators cannot be examined to discover if vindicating legislative purpose is missing. This interdiction against prying into legislative motives puts an evident crimp on any attempt to demon-strate that an inquiry is intended to punish a witness or was

* *Grand Inquest*, p. 84.
† United States Constitution, Art. I, Sec. 9; see also *Kilbourn* v. *Thompson*, 103 U.S. 168, 182 (1881).

concocted for the self-aggrandizement of some ambitious politician or staff member.

Indicative of the way many courts would react is the Supreme Court's 1961 decision in *Wilkinson* v. *United States.** Wilkinson was convicted of contempt for refusing to tell a HUAC subcommittee whether he was a member of the Communist Party. One of his defenses—with which four dissenting Justices† basically agreed—was that the subcommittee had acted without valid legislative purpose, that its goal had been to "harass and expose him" because of his public opposition to the committee's very existence. The Court's majority, rejecting this contention, said:

The petitioner's contention that, while the hearing generally may have been pursuant to a valid legislative purpose, the sole reason for interrogating him was to expose him to public censure because of his activities against the Committee is not persuasive. It is true that the Staff Director's statement reveals the subcommittee's awareness of the petitioner's opposition to the hearings and indicates that the petitioner was not summoned to appear until after he had arrived in Atlanta as the representative of a group carrying on a public campaign to abolish the House Committee. These circumstances, however, do not necessarily lead to the conclusion that the subcommittee's intent was personal persecution of the petitioner. As we have noted, a prime purpose of the hearings was to investigate Communist propaganda activities in the South. It therefore was entirely logical for the subcommittee to subpoena the petitioner after he had arrived at the site of the hearings, had registered as a member of a group which the subcommittee believed to be Communist dominated, and had conducted a public campaign against the subcommittee. The fact that the petitioner might not have been sum-

* 363 U.S. 399 (1961).
† Black, Douglas, Warren, Brennan.

moned to appear had he not come to Atlanta illustrates the very point, for in that event he might not have been thought to have been connected with a subject under inquiry—Communist Party propaganda activities in that area of the country.

Moreover, it is not for us to speculate as to the motivations that may have prompted the decision of individual members of the subcommittee to summon the petitioner. . . . "[A] solution to our problem is not to be found in testing the motives of committee members for this purpose. Such is not our function. Their motives alone would not vitiate an investigation which had been instituted by a House of Congress if that assembly's legislative purpose is being served."

In a 1956 perjury case, however, a federal court found that a House subcommittee was conducting a legislative trial and consequently acting without proper legislative purpose.* The case involved an investigation by a subcommittee of the House Committee on Armed Services into the 1944 death of Major William Hallahan while on assignment to the Office of Strategic Services in Italy. The Court held that the subcommittee, as its reports and the testimony before it indicated, was primarily interested in fixing guilt for the major's death. Because the subcommittee was not engaged in a legitimate legislative function, the Court stated, the testimony of the defendant had not been given to a "competent tribunal" as required before a perjury conviction can stand.†

In the course of its opinion, the Court said:

The Chairman of the Armed Services Committee . . . had authority to appoint a special subcommittee to investigate a particular alleged offense, a segment of the whole picture, as an initial step toward reaching a valid

---

* *United States* v. *Icardi,* 140 F. Supp. 383 (D.D.C. 1956).
† See Chapter III.

legislative judgment. * * * While a committee or sub-committee of the Congress has the right to inquire whether there is a likelihood that a crime has been committed touching upon a field within its general jurisdiction and also to ascertain whether an executive department charged with the prosecution of such crime has acted properly, this authority cannot be extended to sanction a legislative trial and conviction of the individual toward whom the evidence points the finger of suspicion.

None of the judges ruling on any of the litigation matters involving the Ervin committee held that the committee had strayed beyond the boundaries of proper legislative conduct in investigating criminal activities. On the contrary, the courts generally registered approval of the committee's role in this regard—albeit in somewhat muted fashion.

Judge Sirica, in his opinion respecting immunity orders for Dean and Magruder, came the closest to outright affirmation of the validity of the committee's criminal investigatory activities. He indicated that nothing had been disclosed suggesting that the investigation fell outside the "constitutional scope of the Congressional investigatory power." Sirica was fully aware that the committee was intending to dig further into the details of criminal conduct, since it was seeking immunity orders allowing it to take the testimony of two men deeply entangled in the crimes under examination. In fact, Sirica, at the conclusion of the first Watergate trial in January 1973, publicly expressed his "hope" that a "Senate committee is granted the power by Congress by a broad enough resolution to try to get to the bottom of what happened in this case."

Noting that the committee was empowered by the Senate "to investigate 'illegal, improper or unethical activities' occurring in connection with the Presidential campaign and election of 1972," the Court of Appeals in the suit against the President remarked that "we have no doubt that the Committee has performed and will continue to perform its duties fully in the service of the nation." Earlier in the same lawsuit, Judge Gesell had observed that the committee's work, including its "criminal investigative aspects," had "ably served" the "Congress's legislative function." Gesell stated that it was left to the committee to judge whether to continue the criminal investigative aspects of its inquiry. But he was concerned that, if he allowed the committee to obtain the tape recordings it sought, the committee, in the exercise of its informing function, would endanger the fair trials of later Watergate defendants by playing those recordings before the microphones and cameras of the broadcast media. His concern leads us to an examination of Congress's informing function and its potential conflict with fair criminal trials.

·V·
The Informing
Function:
The Potential Conflict
with Fair Trials

In 1969 the House of Representatives commissioned its Committee on the District of Columbia to conduct "a full and complete" investigation of the various departments and agencies of the District of Columbia government. The committee was given subpoena power and directed to report the results of its investigation to the House as soon as practicable. The committee promptly launched an inquiry into the District of Columbia's public school system, and on December 8, 1970, submitted a 450-page report on its findings, which the full House immediately ordered printed and distributed.

The report created a furor. The document featured some forty-five pages comprised of copies of absentee records, test papers, and documents relating to the disciplinary problems of certain students who were specifically named. It declared that these materials were included to "give a realistic view of a troubled school" and "the lack of administrative efforts to rectify the multitudinous problems there."*

The Court of Appeals for the District of Columbia Circuit later declared that these materials were "somewhat derogatory" to the students involved. This portrayal was a masterpiece of judicial understatement. Twenty-nine test papers were printed in the report, twenty-one of which bore failing grades. Disciplinary letters were included that accused named children of disrespect, profanity, vandalism, assault, and theft. One letter alleged that a named child, "involved in the loss of fifty cents," had "invited a male substitute [teacher] to have sexual relations with her, gapping her legs open for enticement."

Not surprisingly, the report precipitated a lawsuit. Parents of pupils involved, outraged by the inclusion of their children's names, brought a class action for themselves, their children, and others similarly situated to enjoin further distribution of the report to the public at large and to recall the copies already distributed. Their basic claim was that their children's lawful right to privacy was being violated. This invasion of privacy, they asserted, had caused and would cause grave damage to the children's mental and physical health, reputations, and future careers. Instituted under pseudonyms to avoid revealing the identity of the plaintiffs, the suit was styled *"Doe v. McMillan"*—the first-named defendant being Congressman John McMillan of South Carolina, then the chairman of the House District Committee. Other defendants included the members of the committee, various congressional staff members, the Public Printer, the Superintendent of Documents, several officials of the District of Columbia educational system, and the United States. The suit also sought damages for past distribution from the defendants.

When the case reached the Supreme Court, two princi-

* H.R. Rep. No. 91–1681, 91st Cong., 2d Sess. (Dec. 8, 1970).

pal, closely related issues required resolution. First, was public dissemination of the report a proper legislative function—in other words, could it be validly claimed that distributing the report served "the important legislative function of informing the public concerning matters pending before Congress"? Second, was the suit to stop further distribution of the report and to exact damages for the dissemination already effected barred by various doctrines —most particularly, the principles emanating from the speech or debate clause of the Constitution—that give legislators and other public officials immunity from suit for their official actions? The questions were related because, as discussed elsewhere,* legislators and their functionaries are shielded from suit only where the acts challenged are within the "sphere of legitimate legislative activity."

These two issues provoked a raft of opinions from the Court that revealed discord and fundamental disagreement among the nine Justices.† Justice White wrote the opinion of the Court, which was joined by Justices Douglas, Brennan, Marshall, and Powell. But Douglas also filed a concurring opinion in which Brennan and Marshall joined. Chief Justice Burger concurred in part and dissented in part in a separate opinion. Justice Blackmun did the same in a different opinion that Burger also adopted. Finally, Justice Rehnquist concurred in part and dissented in part in an opinion joined in full by Burger and Blackmun and adopted in part by Justice Stewart. This hodgepodge of views does little to foster clarity and understanding regarding the legitimate scope of Congress's informing function.

Justice White, writing for the Court, emphasized that he did "not doubt the importance of informing the public about the business of Congress." But White refused to agree that the "informing function" automatically justi-

---

* See Chapter X.
† These opinions are found at 412 U.S. 306 (1973).

fied the distribution beyond the halls of Congress of materials "actionable under local law." There might be, the opinion suggested, no valid legislative purpose in the public dissemination of a report that could form the basis for a lawsuit for libel or unwarranted invasion of rights or privacy. But, the Court said, it was unable to judge from the sparse record before it whether "the legitimate legislative needs of Congress . . . have been exceeded." In other words, the Court was saying that it was unable to determine whether distribution of the report to the public at large served some valid legislative function which justified the harm done the children sullied by its contents. The matter was thus remanded to the lower courts for an appropriate finding on this issue.*

In 1974 District Judge John Pratt found that publication and distribution of the report did not exceed Congress's legitimate legislative needs and entered judgment for defendants.† The matter was appealed but subsequently remanded to the District Court when it was discovered that further proceedings were necessary because Judge Pratt's decision had been based on inaccurate facts regarding the extent of distribution of the report. Pratt again dismissed; plaintiffs have appealed.

Judge Pratt's several holdings were not calculated to warm the hearts of Justices Douglas, Brennan, and Marshall, for they had been prepared, when the matter was before the Supreme Court, to go beyond the Court's ruling and hold that the record was sufficient to demonstrate that distribution of the report exceeded justifiable legislative needs. These Justices agreed that "a legislator's function in informing the public concerning matters before Congress or concerning the administration of Government is essential to maintaining our representative

---

* Because of speech or debate clause reasons, the Court only allowed the suit to proceed against the Public Printer and the Superintendent of Documents, as discussed in Chapter X.

† *Doe* v. *McMillan*, 374 F. Supp. 1313 (D.D.C. 1974).

democracy." Nonetheless, noting that "We all should be painfully aware of the potentially devastating effects of congressional accusations," they expressed the view that "Congress, in naming the students without justification exceeded the 'sphere of legitimate legislative activity' . . . The names of specific students were totally irrelevant to the purposes of the study. The functions of the Committee would have been served equally well if the students had remained anonymous."

The other four Justices—Burger, Blackmun, Rehnquist, Stewart—were as adamant in their views regarding the proper scope of the informing function in this case as were Douglas, Brennan, and Marshall, but their conclusions were diametrically opposed to those of their three brethren. Chief Justice Burger wrote that the "acts here complained of were not outside the traditional legislative function of Congress." Justice Blackmun, for himself and the Chief Justice, observed that "the 'informing function' is an essential attribute of an effective Legislative Branch," and stated that "each step in the legislative process, from the gathering of information in the course of an officially authorized investigation to and including the official printing and official distribution of that information in the formal report, is legitimate legislative activity . . ."

Justice Rehnquist, writing also for Justices Burger, Blackmun and Stewart, was likewise of the opinion that distribution of the report served a legitimate legislative need. He declared: "The subject matter of the Committee Report here in question was . . . concededly within the legislative authority of Congress. . . . To the extent that public participation in a relatively open legislative process is desirable, the Court's holding makes the materials bearing on that process less available than they might be."

This congeries of opinions has been reviewed at some length because the various decisions demonstrate that the Supreme Court is troubled and divided about the extent of Congress's informing function.* Five of the Justices seem to be saying that even if an *investigation* is within the scope of Congress's investigatory power, the publicizing and dissemination of the results of that investigation may not fill a legitimate legislative need. Whether or not such "informing" is warranted, the five Justices indicated, must be determined on a case-by-case basis. The other four Justices appear to believe that, when Congress properly investigates, it may lawfully report its full findings to the public as it sees fit. While the matter is, for now, left in some uncertainty, a review of other commentaries on, and uses of, the informing function may help illuminate its proper scope.

Congressional investigations essentially serve four often interrelated purposes. The most apparent is the accumulation of information to allow Congress to determine whether or not to legislate. Legislative investigations also aid Congress in performing its mission of riding herd on the administration of the executive branch—a duty it has under both the Constitution and statutory law.† Congress also investigates to resolve issues concerning its membership—for example, questions as to the right to be seated or the bribery of a member. Finally, certain investigations are conducted in whole or in part to fulfill the informing function.‡

* For further dissension on this subject, see the various opinions in *Gravel* v. *United States*, 408 U.S. 606 (1972). In this case the majority held that Senator Gravel's arrangement with a private firm to publish the Pentagon Papers (which he had introduced at a subcommittee hearing) was "not part and parcel of the legislative process" and thus not protected from grand jury scrutiny by the speech or debate clause. Gravel had argued that private reproduction was an exercise of the informing function and consequently was protected legislative activity.

† See Chapter VI.

‡ See generally W. J. Keefe and M. S. Ogul, *The American Legislative Process* (Prentice-Hall, Inc., 1973), pp. 223–24.

Noting the importance of "the right of an elected representative to inform, and the public to be informed about matters relating directly to the workings of our government," Justice Brennan has written, "The dialogue between Congress and the people has been recognized, from the days of our founding, as one of the necessary elements of a representative system."* The works of Thomas Jefferson, James Madison, and James Wilson do reflect their recognition of the importance of the informing function. Jefferson, for example, wrote that representatives' "communications with their constituents should of right, as of duty also, be free, full, and unawed by any."†

The informing function received significant support from Woodrow Wilson, who, in 1885 long before he became President, wrote a widely read, highly acclaimed, and lastingly influential book entitled *Congressional Government*. In this work Wilson declared:

> It is the proper duty of a representative body to look diligently into every affair of government and to talk much about what it sees. It is meant to be the eyes and the voice, and to embody the wisdom and will of its constituents. Unless Congress have and use every means of acquainting itself with the acts and the disposition of the administrative agents of the government, the country must be helpless to learn how it is being served; and unless Congress both scrutinize these things and sift them by every form of discussion, the country must remain in embarrassing, crippling ignorance of the very affairs which it is most important that it should understand and direct. The informing function of Congress should be preferred even to its legislative function. The argument is not only that discussed

* *Gravel* v. *United States*, 408 U.S. 606, 661 (1972) (Brennan, J., dissenting).

† See generally Ford, ed., *The Works of Thomas Jefferson* (G. P. Putnam's Sons, 1904), Vol. VIII, pp. 322–27.

and interrogated administration is the only pure and
efficient administration, but, more than that, that the
only really self-governing people is that people which
discusses and interrogates its administration.*

The informing function, and Wilson's views of it,
received little judicial recognition until the middle of this
century. In 1953 the Supreme Court, in an opinion by
Justice Felix Frankfurter, called the informing function
"indispensable" and quoted the bulk of the above passage
with apparent general approval.† Several years later, in
Watkins v. *United States*,‡ the Court again dealt with the
informing function. Remarking that "The public is, of
course, entitled to be informed concerning the workings
of its government," Chief Justice Earl Warren wrote:

> [There is a] power of the Congress to inquire into
> and publicize corruption, maladministration or ineffi-
> ciency in agencies of the Government. That was the
> only kind of activity described by Woodrow Wilson in
> Congressional Government when he wrote: "The in-
> forming function of Congress should be preferred even
> to its legislative function." From the earliest times in its
> history, the Congress has assiduously performed an
> "informing function" of this nature.

In the *Watkins* case, however, the Court was quick to
observe that there are limitations to the lawful reach of
the informing function. "We have no doubt," stated the
Court, "that there is no congressional power to expose for
the sake of exposure." This comment appears specifically
directed at legislative committees such as HUAC (which
was involved in this case) bent on conducting legislative
trials where past beliefs and activities bearing scant rela-

* Wilson, *Congressional Government* (Houghton, Mifflin & Co.,
1900), 14th impression, p. 303.
† *United States* v. *Rumely*, 345 U.S. 41, 43-4 (1953).
‡ 345 U.S. 178, 200 and n. 33 (1957). See also *Tenney* v. *Brandhove*,
341 U.S. 367, 377 n. 6 (1951).

tion to legitimate legislative activity were trotted out for public view in an effort to punish witnesses by public scorn and retribution. The prescription against such "exposure" was relied on by Douglas in his concurring opinion in *Doe* v. *McMillan*; including the names of students in the committee report, Douglas contended, was exactly the type of exposure "for the sake of exposure" that the Court had previously condemned.

The *Watkins* case itself gives some clues as to the meaning of its interdiction against "exposure for the sake of exposure." This language, the Court indicated, applies only to exposure of *private* affairs; it has no applicability to the situation where *governmental* corruption, inefficiency, and waste are aired for public consumption. To the contrary, the informing function is perhaps most efficacious when it turns the legislative spotlight on derelictions in government. Furthermore, even exposing matters normally considered private is not improper if there is some "justification in terms of the function of Congress." Thus, to illustrate, in determining whether to legislate in the field of race relations, it should be proper for Congress to investigate and publicize conditions concerning segregation in privately operated dining establishments or other private retail concerns.

To the Ervin committee, meeting its informing responsibilities was one of its most important tasks. Extant from the committee's beginnings was the troublesome suspicion —engendered in part by Judge Sirica's probing questions at the first Watergate trial—that the stench of Watergate permeated, indeed emanated from, the White House itself. If so, it was the committee's job to tell the public the facts. This conception of its responsibilities was perhaps best reflected in Senator Howard Baker's persistent inquiry to committee witnesses: "What did the President know and when did he know it?" Senator Ervin believed that exposing the true nature of the scandal to the country was even more crucial than convicting a few high administration officials for their crimes.

In retrospect, it may be said that the committee's greatest contribution was to heighten public awareness of the corruption that pervaded the 1972 election and the Nixon administration generally. Its hearings presented the broad outlines of the Watergate cover-up, if not all its myriad details, many of which appeared only after the tapes were publicly played. Its work on the Hughes-Rebozo and Milk Fund affairs suggested that campaign contributions had been spent for the President's personal benefit and that campaign contributions from milk cooperatives had been slipped to administration officials as a bribe for hiking milk price supports and other government favors. The committee's labors also bared an outrageous White House plan to transmogrify the federal bureaucracy into an instrument for the President's reelection. The facts surrounding these transgressions were facts the public had a right to know and needed to know. If the actions of the President and his men had gone undetected, if these officials had fully succeeded in their nefarious ventures, our present system of government might have been imperiled. The President's claim in the tapes litigation that the committee was unlawfully seeking to "expose for the sake of exposure" was fatuous and diversionary.

While Congress's part in revealing such scandals may justify its role as "informer," there are other reasons why the legitimacy of the informing function should be recognized. The knowledge that the Congress exercises a vigorous bloodhound role may serve as a powerful deterrent to official wrongdoing. As Louis D. Brandeis once observed in a different context: "Sunshine is said to be the best of disinfectants; electric light the most efficient policeman."* Public realization that Congress will keep watch on the executive branch also helps

* Brandeis, *Other People's Money* (Harper Torchbooks, 1967), p. 62.

to promote confidence in the processes of government as a whole.

In addition, the informing function is often a vital aid to the lawmaking function. Legislation that is controversial, drastic, or far-reaching frequently cannot be enacted —or escape a Presidential veto—unless it has public support. Informing the public of the evils to be corrected can evoke the constituent approbation necessary to enact critical laws. Enlightening the public also creates the possibility that the feedback to Congress will produce ideas that strengthen future legislation.

The Ervin committee realized that the legislation it would recommend might be controversial. Indeed, some of it is—for example, the committee's call for a permanent special prosecutor. Thus, on several occasions in its various litigations, the committee broached the needs of lawmaking as another justification for carrying out the committee's informing responsibilities.

Predictably, the committee's opponents in its various lawsuits denigrated its informing role. Rabbi Korff attempted to portray the committee's performance of the informing function as a public blight rather than a public boon. Through its broadcast hearing, his suit said, the committee has "deliberately and inequitably disrupted the domestic tranquility of the United States . . . by undermining the confidence of citizens" in the Justice Department and the judiciary to the detriment of the nation. The committee met this contention with the assertion that, far from injuring the country, the committee's hearings had been beneficial and therapeutic to the citizenry, that they had helped expose shameful corruption to public view, reinvigorate the system of criminal justice, and reinstill the notion that integrity in government is vital.

But a more fundamental objection should be raised to the rabbi's claim. His notion appeared to be that some form of censorship should be imposed on the revelation of governmental corruption because the nation is harmed by unexpurgated portrayals of administration shortcomings. This concept is invidious to free man. It ignores two of the inveterate tenets of our democracy: (1) that ours is a government of and by the people; and (2) that the people govern best when fully informed. As James Madison wrote years ago: "A popular government without popular information or the means of acquiring it, is but a prologue to a farce or a tragedy or perhaps both. Knowledge will forever govern ignorance: And a people who mean to be their own Governors, must arm themselves with the power knowledge gives."* These bedrock principles are as relevant and vital today as when the nation was founded.

President Nixon offered an argument in the committee's suit against him that was comparably specious. Reacting to the committee's claims that the informing function can legitimately be used to gain public support for legislation, the President—through his counsel, James St. Clair, Charles Alan Wright, and others—declared that the committee's intention "to arouse public support for future legislation . . . is the antithesis of the legislative process intended by the Framers and found in our Constitution." "It should be noted," the President's lawyers continued, "that [the committee's] argument does a great disservice to the Congress and to the American people. It implies that Congress will not act unless it is emotionally stirred up by disclosures of alleged wrongdoing. The Framers thought that the merits of a proposal were what should gain it support. . . . The whole suggestion of using information relating to public wrongdoing as a legislative catalyst . . . militates against the very essence of constitutional government and due process of law . . ."

The President's argument may have come bedecked in nicely honed lawyer phrases, but, pared to its essentials, it raps at the fundamentals of democracy. The denizens

---

* Hunt, ed., *The Writings of James Madison* (Belknap Press, 1910), Vol. IX, p. 103.

of Congress are not anchoritic philosopher-kings, aloof
from their constituents, who, in legislating, should seek
no other counsel but their own. Rather, they are *representatives* of the people and answerable to them. In a
democracy the people govern through their representatives and, if the people are to participate in government,
if they are to advise their representatives whether or not
to legislate, they must know the facts about conditions to
be remedied. Stripped of its rhetoric the President's argument threatens the people's right to govern.

There is another flaw in Nixon's position—the suggestion that it is improper for congressmen to persuade their
constituents to support needed legislation by revealing
conditions that cry for rectification. To hold this view is to
overlook that congressmen are not mere pawns of those they
represent but also leaders who have the duty to build
support for crucial reforms. While demagoguery is to be
deplored, leadership is not. The New Deal era was characterized by congressional leaders who, by exposing the
causes and effects of the Great Depression, evoked the
public support necessary for the wrenching changes
wrought by the corrective legislation of that age.

The Supreme Court recognizes that a valid purpose of
the informing function is to allow the people to participate in government. The majority opinion in *Doe* v.
McMillan declared, "We do not doubt the importance of
informing the public about the business of Congress."
Observing that the informing function was "essential to
maintaining our representative democracy," Justice Douglas—for Justices Brennan and Marshall also—stated in
the *Doe* case that "unless we are to put blinders on our
Congressmen and isolate them from their constituents,
the informing function must be [protected]." Justice
Blackmun, writing also for Chief Justice Burger, offered
the most expansive comments:

. . . More often than not, when a congressional committee prepares a report, it does so not only with the

object of advising fellow Members of Congress as to the subject matter, but with the further objects (1) of advising the public of proposed legislative action, (2) of informing the public of the presence of problems and issues, (3) of receiving from the public, in return, constructive comments and suggestions, and (4) of enabling the public to evaluate the performance of their elected representatives in the Congress.

This statement—which effectively refutes the President's claims set forth above—drew no challenge from the other members of the Court and is not likely to do so.

Where they offered comments on the matter, the reactions of the courts to the Ervin committee's advocacy of the informing function were mixed. Judge Sirica, in ruling that the committee was free to allow broadcast coverage of the immunized testimony of Dean and Magruder, observed, "It is apparent . . . that a committee's legislative purpose may legitimately include the publication of information."* The Court of Appeals' declarations on the informing function in the tapes suit were more niggardly. "In the circumstances of this case," that court said, "we need neither deny that the Congress may have, quite apart from its legislative responsibilities, a general oversight [and informing] power, nor explore what the lawful reach of that power might be . . ." Because the Congress through the House Judiciary Committee had obtained the tapes the Ervin committee sought, the court stated, "we think the need for the tapes premised solely on an asserted power to investigate and inform cannot justify enforcement of the Committee's subpoena."† Judge Gesell, in his opinion in this case, did not deny Congress's general right to inform, but voiced his worry that allowing the committee to air the tapes would prejudice

* Application of United States Senate Select Committee on Presidential Campaign Activities, 361, F. Supp. 1270, 1281 (D.D.C. 1973).

† *Senate Select Committee on Presidential Campaign Activities* v. *Nixon*, 498 F. 2d 725, 732 (D.C. Cir. 1974).

incipient Watergate trials.* His views necessitate an examination of the potential conflict between the informing function and the fair criminal trial by an impartial jury guaranteed by the Sixth Amendment and the due process clause of the Fifth Amendment.

Gerhard Gesell is one of the strengths of the federal bench. He is the son of Dr. Arnold Gesell, whose books on child rearing were gospel before the advent of Dr. Benjamin Spock. Gesell came to the court from the establishment Washington law firm of Covington and Burling, which has nurtured other legal giants and men of affairs, such as Dean Acheson, John Lord O'Brien, Edward Burling, Judge Harry Covington, Hugh B. Cox, Charles Horsky, Daniel Gribbon, and Graham Clayton, now the president of the Southern Railway Company. When Gesell left private practice for the bench, he was among the leading corporate antitrust counsel in the country, but his kaleidoscopic practice had ranged into many diverse fields.

Gesell possesses formidable legal abilities. His mind is like a vice—he clamps onto an important fact at first telling and holds it in store for future use. Moreover, he has an uncanny knack for cutting to the core of a complicated problem to identify the crux issues in a case. This ability to go to the jugular made him a feared opponent during his days as an advocate.†

The sturdily built, ruddy-faced judge has long displayed a concern for individual rights. During his days in private practice, for example, he served Presidents Kennedy and Johnson as chairman of the President's Committee on Equal Opportunity in the Armed Forces and was active in the President's Lawyers Committee for Equal Rights under Law. As momentarily appears, his judicial opinions manifest this concern.

* *Senate Select Committee on Presidential Campaign Activities* v. *Nixon,* 370 F. Supp. 521 (D.D.C. 1974).

† I make these observations in part from firsthand experience. During my initial year in law practice, Gesell was my principal mentor.

Gesell's performance on the bench has been gritty. He has not shied from innovative ruling that rankled traditionalists and officials of the Nixon administration. Thus he held that the firing of Archibald Cox as special prosecutor was illegal, struck down the District of Columbia anti-abortion law as unconstitutionally vague, and in the Ellsberg break-in case, issued barely veiled threats that he might dismiss the case against John Ehrlichman if Ehrlichman was not given fuller access to White House files. (A compromise between the judge and the White House which defused the issue was later reached.) In the Cox firing case, Gesell went beyond the issues before him and pointedly expressed his view that because the judiciary should not engage in prosecutorial functions, Congress ought not to pass a law entrusting to the courts the task of appointing a new special prosecutor—a position, incidentally, at odds with that taken by the Ervin committee, which recommended a permanent special prosecutor selected by a panel of three retired federal judges.

At times Gesell's bold rulings have brought him trouble from higher courts. His decision that members of Congress could not hold reserve military commissions and his ruling that the Hatch Act—which prohibits a broad range of political activities by government employees—was unconstitutional were both rejected by the Supreme Court.

Before the Ervin committee's suit reached his court, Gesell, who once was a counsel to the joint committee that investigated the Pearl Harbor disaster, had demonstrated his distaste for congressional investigatory extravagance. In 1970 he was faced with a case that was a precursor to *Doe* v. *McMillan*.* The House Internal Securities Committee—the successor to HUAC—had prepared a report entitled "Limited Survey of Honoraria Given Guest Speakers for Engagements at Colleges and Universities." The report included the names of sixty-five individuals who

---

* *Hentoff* v. *Ichord*, 318 F. Supp. 1175 (D.D.C. 1970).

had recently spoken on the campuses whom it branded as "Pied Pipers of pernicious propaganda." It also listed the affiliations of these individuals with one or more of twelve organizations or groups which the committee viewed as suspect, including the Communist Party, the National Mobilization Committee to End the War in Vietnam and, interestingly, the National Committee to Abolish HUAC. The report recommended no legislation.

This document was deeply disturbing to Gesell, for the danger it presented to free speech and assembly was apparent. Gesell found that the report was prepared "with the hope and expectation that college officials, alumni and parents would bring social and economic pressures upon the institutions that had permitted these speeches in order to ostracize the speakers and stultify further campus discussion." In fact, the report, noting the amounts of honoraria paid the sixty-five speakers, stated that "the committee believes that the limited sampling made is sufficient to alert college and university administrators, alumni, students, and parents to the extent of campus speaking in promoting the radical revolutionary movement."

Gesell could find no legitimate legislative purpose in this document, which he considered a "blacklist." "The conclusion is inescapable," he stated, "that the Report neither serves nor was intended to serve any purpose but the one explicitly indicated in the Report: to inhibit further speech on college campuses by those listed individuals and others whose political persuasion is not in accord with that of the members of the committee. If a report has no relationship to any existing or future proper legislative purpose and is issued solely for the sake of exposure or intimidation, then it exceeds the legislative function of Congress; and when publication will inhibit free speech and assembly, publication and distribution in official form at government expense may be enjoined. This is such a report."

Gesell closed his novel opinion in this case with a

short homily of the type that occasionally creeps into his decisions: "The Court notes the increasing tendency of the legislative branch to investigate for exposure's sake, and expresses the hope that members of Congress will by rule and attitude limit congressional inquiry to those matters amenable to constitutional legislative action."*

Because of the Constitution's speech or debate clause, the injunction Gesell issued was not directed at the committee or its members, but instead at the Public Printer. No appellate review of Gesell's ruling was had because the matter was mooted when the committee modified its report. Thus a nasty collision was avoided with the House which, with the judge's opinion in mind, had passed a resolution stating, "All persons, whether or not acting under color of office, are hereby . . . ordered . . . to refrain from doing any act . . . which . . . obstructs, or prevents the performance of the [House's] work . . ."

The judge's decision in the Ervin committee's suit against Nixon reflected his interest in individual rights and his propensity to extend the traditional reaches of the law. It also contained more of his individualistic views on the foibles, limitations, and proper role of Congress.

As previously discussed, Gesell concluded that he should assign "priority to the integrity of criminal justice" and ruled that he would not order production of the tapes to the committee because the resultant publicity "would bolster contentions that unbiased juries cannot be impaneled for trial." The President could raise this consideration, the judge said, because of his "constitutional mandate to see that the laws are faithfully executed," which made him "quite properly . . . concerned with the dangers inherent in excessive pretrial publicity."†

---

* Compare Gesell's recent ruling in *Anonymous* v. *McCormick*, C.A. 75–1918 (D.D.C., Nov. 17, 1975).

† In *Nader* v. *Butz*, 372 F. Supp. 175, 177–78 (D.D.C. 1974), Judge William Jones, relying in part on Gesell's ruling, held that the Ervin committee could not have access to certain documents relating

In beginning an analysis of Gesell's opinion, it is important to recognize that beyond doubt congressional hearings are capable of producing damaging publicity that can prejudice criminal trials. This happened in the case of Denis Delaney, which was discussed in the preceding chapter.* Delaney, it will be remembered, was tried and convicted in January 1952 for his misdeeds as collector of internal revenue for Massachusetts. His conviction came less than three months after the King committee's explosive hearings into this activity and other putative wrongdoing by Delaney, including larceny and embezzlement, irregularities in respect to his own tax returns, and influence peddling. Comments made near the close of the hearings by Chairman King displayed his belief that Delaney was a felon and had "seriously betrayed" his trust.

The Court of Appeals for the First Circuit described the publicity stemming from the King committee hearings as follows:

The newspaper publicity was characterized by flamboyant, front-page headlines in large, heavy type, covering colorful feature stories emphasizing the more striking aspects of the testimony. This was supplemented by radio and television exploitation of the same material. Naturally, due to local interest, the publicity was intensified in the Boston area, but it was also carried by the big press associations far and wide throughout the nation, for the generalized charges of corruption in the Internal Revenue Bureau had elicited public

---

to milk fund matters which the court had placed under a protective order. Judge Jones stated that "it . . . is the obligation of this Court to consider the integrity of the criminal process both before the grand jury [handling that affair] and with respect to any resulting indictments involving the issuance of milk price orders in 1971."

* *Delaney* v. *United States*, 199 F. 2d 107 (1st Cir. 1952). Compare *Sheppard* v. *Maxwell*, 384 U.S. 333 (1966).

interest and concern throughout the nation. One of the exhibits in the record is an issue of "Life" for November 19, 1951 (a weekly with an advertised circulation of over 5,000,000), containing an article entitled "The Hands in the Taxpayer's Pockets," with the subtitle: "The Truman Administration's Worst Scandal is in the Making as Corruption is Found Throughout Internal Revenue Bureau." The article displayed pictures of ten Internal Revenue employees, including Delaney, who allegedly had committed wrongs in connection with their respective offices. After a general treatment of the "tax scandal," the article summarized, purportedly on the basis of testimony before the King Committee, the particular situations existing in various cities, including that of Delaney's office in Boston. Also the article reproduced a drawing depicting four vultures (labeled, respectively, San Francisco, Boston, St. Louis, Brooklyn) roosting on the roof of the Internal Revenue Bureau, with the explanation below: "Shame of the Cities is dramatized in this drawing of gathering vultures by Daniel Fitzpatrick, famed cartoonist of the St. Louis Post-Dispatch."

The court was equally explicit in describing the effect of that publicity: "It is fair to say that, so far as the modern mass media of communication could accomplish it, the character of Delaney was pretty thoroughly blackened and discredited as the day approached for his judicial trial on narrowly specified charges. In large part, at least, this result must be attributed to the publicity which the King Committee invited and stimulated when it decided that it was its duty to hold open hearings on the Delaney case after he had been removed from office by the Executive and his indictment had been procured by the Department of Justice."

Because the trial court had not granted Delaney a postponement of his trial until the pejorative publicity dissipated, the Court of Appeals reversed his conviction and sent the case back for a new trial.* But it refused to dismiss the indictment as irrevocably tainted, as Delaney had asked. It could not be said "in this case," the court declared, "if indeed it could be said in any case, as a matter of law, that the prejudicial effect of this publicity was so permanent, and ineradicable by mere lapse of time, that the court should have recognized the impossibility of a fair trial being held at any time within the foreseeable future."

Given the fact that congressionally inspired publicity can prejudice criminal trials—at least for a time—two significant questions remain about the rightness of Gesell's decision: Was the court correct in deciding that the danger to fair trials produced by surrendering the tapes to the committee was substantial enough to deny it access to this material? And, should a court in any case rule that a congressional committee had no right to evidence because its revelation might endanger some future criminal proceeding? Both these issues bear implications that extend well past the immediate concerns of the litigants in the tapes case.

Several considerations, the committee felt, necessitated a negative answer to the first question. The President's assertion that fair trials must be protected, the committee contended, "is both belated and unconvincing now that the President and his present and former aides, with his permission, have spread voluminous evidence regarding the conversations at issue on the public record." The duplicity in the President's position was further revealed a few weeks later when he voluntarily released partial, edited transcripts of the five conversations involved to the public

---

* Compare, e.g., *Beck* v. *United States*, 298 F. 2d 622, 628–29 (1962) where the court held that a further continuance to dispel the effect of pretrial publicity, some of it caused by congressional hearings, had not been necessary. See also *United States* v. *Mitchell*, 372 F. Supp. 1239, 1259–62 (S.D.N.Y. 1973) *appeals dismissed, petitions for mandamus denied sub nom. Stans* v. *Gagliardi*, 485 F. 2d 1290 (2d Cir. 1973); *Calley* v. *Callaway*, 44 U.S.L.W. 2127 (5th Cir., Sept. 10, 1975) (*en banc*).

at large, a move which either bespoke his conviction that fair criminal proceedings actually would not be harmed by their publication or in effect said, "Fair trials be damned where my own skin is concerned."

The committee also argued that releasing the tapes would not create any significant *additional* prejudice to potential criminal trials because there had already been massive public testimony and comment concerning the contents of the conversations at issue. In this same vein, Special Prosecutor Jaworski had suggested to the court that "any publicity stemming from compliance with the subpoenas would add only marginally to previous publicity."

Furthermore, the committee said and Mr. Jaworski agreed, the courts have a variety of devices to ensure fair trials which would sufficiently counteract any detrimental publicity caused by release of the tapes. As Judge Sirica observed in the committee's litigation with Special Prosecutor Cox, federal judges "can draw on a well-stocked arsenal of measures designed to preserve the integrity of proceedings and the rights of individuals." This "arsenal" includes the authority to continue (postpone) a trial until the effect of injurious publicity is dispelled. A judge can also grant a change of venue—that is, shift the location of trial. Or he can increase the number of preemptory challenges allowed a defendant which permit him to remove a juror from the panel without convincing the presiding judge that there is some specific cause mandating dismissal.

During the trial the judge may order the jury sequestered. He can take stringent steps to preserve decorum in the courtroom and prohibit out-of-court statements by lawyers, defendants, and witnesses. At the end of trial before jury deliberations begin, the court can and should instruct the jurors not to consider news accounts regarding the defendants to which they have been exposed.

Some of the remedies so far mentioned have limitations. While a continuance may be an effective and legal exercise of judicial power to ensure fair proceedings, postponement of trial for many months does in fact prevent the speedy trial guaranteed by the Sixth Amendment.* A change of venue is of reduced utility where—as in the *Delaney* and Watergate cases—the adverse publicity has been nation-wide. And the actual remedial effect of a charge ordering the jury not to consider negative publicity has long been viewed askance by jurists. As Justice Robert Jackson once wrote, "the naive assumption that prejudicial effects can be overcome by instructions to the jury . . . all practicing lawyers know to be unmitigated fiction."†

Perhaps the most useful judicial device to safeguard fair trials is an assiduously thorough voir dire—that is, the questioning of prospective jurors to ensure that they can render judgment free of prejudice. Judge Gesell exercised particular care in picking the jury for the Ellsberg break-in trial, conducting the voir dire himself on a person-by-person basis. His questioning took place in a locked court-room to avoid distraction and potentially harmful media coverage. In choosing the jury for the Watergate cover-up trial Judge Sirica adopted comparable procedures.

To date, there has been no ruling by any court that any jury sitting on Watergate cases was prejudiced by the Ervin committee hearings, the proceedings of the House Judiciary Committee, or the publicity resulting from those inquiries, despite the fact that charges to that effect by defendants have been plentiful. There is irrefutable evidence that the New York jury which tried John Mitchell and former Secretary of Commerce Maurice Stans for their alleged involvement in a purported attempt by financier Robert Vesco to secure government favors by healthy campaign contributions was not harmfully prejudiced against them by the Ervin committee hearings or otherwise

---

* The new federal statute generally requiring that trial commence within sixty days after a defendant is arraigned permits continuances where "the ends of justice served by taking such action outweigh the best interest of the public and the defendant in a speedy trial." See 18 U.S.C. 3161 (1975).

† *Krulewitch* v. *United States*, 336 U.S. 440, 453 (1949) (Jackson, J., concurring).

because that jury *acquitted* those former officials. Similarly, Kenneth Parkinson, attorney for the Committee to Re-elect the President, whose name had been mentioned prominently by John Dean and others before the Ervin committee, was found not guilty by the Watergate cover-up jury. And former Secretary of the Treasury John Connally, whose exploits are always heavily covered by the media, was acquitted by an unsequestered jury of charges that he received money from milk cooperatives in payment for his support of their causes.

Sirica and Gesell, who tried the major Watergate-related cases, were able to assemble juries they believed fair. Gesell's juries were quickly picked. The Ellsberg panel was chosen in a day and a half, despite the extraordinary publicity regarding the break-in of Ellsberg's psychiatrist's office engendered by the Ervin committee and other investigatory bodies. The jury for the perjury trial of Dwight Chapin, Nixon's former appointments secretary, was selected in only four hours, although the alleged perjury related to Chapin's connection with the "dirty tricks" activities of Donald Segretti on Nixon's behalf during the 1972 campaign and that noxious chicanery had been the subject of a month of televised Ervin committee hearings. Though Chapin's name had been prominently mentioned during those hearings, few prospective jurors were even aware of his identity.

It has been suggested that the Supreme Court will eventually rule that the trials of some or all Watergate defendants have been *irredeemably* tainted by the mammoth publicity that accompanied the various crimes falling under the Watergate rubric from first discovery. Perhaps, but it is doubtful. We live in the media age. Massive publicity stalks all events of national import, and any significant congressional hearing will be widely covered by the media. Often public interest—as with the Watergate hearings—demands live television and radio coverage. Reams of printed matter are devoted to congressional hearings on sensational issues. For the high court to hold that fair trials of Watergate defendants are impossible would be an admission of defeat. It would be to say that the courts, when faced with rampant publicity, are incapable of picking juries that will be fair, that the courts in such circumstances cannot protect the integrity of criminal proceedings. It would mean that some of the worst offenders in our society—the Charles Mansons, the Lee Harvey Oswalds, the Sirhan Sirhans—would go free. The rule would become "the more heinous, scandalous or notorious the crime, the better the chances for freedom." Surely this is not and should not be the law.

Special Prosecutor Jaworski's statement to both Gesell and the Court of Appeals in the tapes case is pertinent in this regard. "[T]he existence of pre-trial publicity, even wide-spread publicity," he said, "does not support, *ipso facto*, a claim of prejudicial publicity . . . . The courts 'are not concerned with the fact of publicity but with the assessment of its nature'. * * * It must be remembered [that] the issue presented to the courts is not whether a prospective juror is ignorant of the allegations surrounding a prosecution, or even whether he may have some impression about them, but whether 'the juror can lay aside his impression or opinion and render a verdict based on the evidence presented in court.' " *

---

* Jaworski quoted from *Silverthorne* v. *United States*, 400 F. 2d 627, 631 (9th Cir. 1968) *cert. denied*, 400 U.S. 1022 (1971), and *Irvin* v. *Dowd*, 366 U.S. 717, 723 (1961). The Supreme Court recently reaffirmed these principles in upholding, over a pretrial publicity defense, the Florida state court conviction of flamboyant Miami hoodlum Jack Roland Murphy—sometimes known as "Murph the Surf"—whose notoriety rests partially on the fact that he once stole the Star of India sapphire. See *Murphy* v. *Florida* 421 U.S. 794 (1975). But the Court did suggest that adverse publicity going beyond mere factual reporting might create an atmosphere in a given community at a given time that was so "inflammatory" that prejudice would be presumed. The Court also noted its right under its supervisory powers to reverse a *federal* court conviction for insufficient steps to minimize the effect of pretrial publicity even if the circumstances do not warrant a finding that a defendant's constitutional rights have been violated.

Jaworski told both courts that even if the five tapes were released to the Ervin committee he was "confident that notwithstanding prior publicity, if jurors are selected with the care required by the decisions in this Circuit, all defendants will receive a fair and prompt trial." Furthermore, despite prolonged and vehement objections by indicted Watergate defendants who claimed their trials would be harmed, Jaworski strongly urged Judge Sirica and later the Court of Appeals to allow transmittal of the grand jury's report concerning Nixon's involvement in Watergate—which contained a number of tape recordings of presidential conversations—to the House Judiciary Committee, which was considering the President's impeachment. Jaworski argued that the potential danger to fair trials was not great enough to counsel against making the report available to the House committee. Sirica and the Court of Appeals, downplaying the injury to future trials, indicated their agreement, and the report was forwarded to the House.* It is interesting to note that even Judge Gesell in the Ervin committee's suit would go no further than to say that release of the tapes would "bolster contentions" that impartial juries could not be empaneled; he did not find that release of the tapes to the Ervin committee would actually prejudice future trials.

These rulings presage eventual holdings that the Watergate trials were not prejudiced beyond all redemption by congressional action, release of the tapes, or media coverage of such events. It is a reasonable wager that the Supreme Court will in essence rule that jurors could be found who "can lay aside [their] impression[s] or opinion[s] [on Watergate] and render . . . verdict[s] based on the evidence presented in court."

---

* See *Haldeman* v. *Sirica*, 501 F. 2d 714 (D.C. Cir. 1974). In the Ervin committee's suit for the tapes, Gesell, without offering further explanation, stated: "Congressional demands, if they be forthcoming, for tapes in furtherance of the more juridical constitutional process of impeachment would present wholly different considerations."

The second question brought to the fore by Gesell's opinion in the tapes suit is whether a court should, in any event, conclude that a congressional committee should be denied relevant evidence because its revelation might harm upcoming criminal proceedings.

There is surface appeal to Gesell's notion that the President—who is sworn to see that the laws are faithfully executed—should be able to withhold executive branch materials whose release would unduly endanger the integrity of criminal trials. Why is this not, in proper circumstances, as valid a reason to deny production of evidence as the need to preserve military secrets, protect the conduct of foreign affairs, or safeguard the confidentiality of presidential conversations—all grounds which at times the chief executive has asserted in refusing evidence to the Congress and others?* Relevant in this respect is a 1974 amendment to the Freedom of Information Act stating that the executive can deny governmental investigative files to citizens making demands under the act if revelation of the files would "deprive a person of a right to a fair trial or an impartial adjudication."†

But other factors suggest that Gesell's views are askew. No decision—the judge cited none—directly supports his conception that legislative requirements can be subjugated to a judge's view of the need for fair trials. In fact, the *Hutcheson* case‡ discussed above—while not a square precedent—would appear to run counter to Gesell's holding. Hutcheson claimed he was justified in refusing to respond to the McClellan committee's interrogations because the inquiry was simply aimed at his "exposure," and to require him to answer in the face of his pending indictment would deny him due process of law in his future criminal trial in an Indiana state court. Justice Harlan, employing broad language, held that "a Congressional committee which is engaged in legitimate legislative

* See Chapter VI.
† 5 U.S.C. 552 (b) (7) (1974).
‡ *Hutcheson* v. *United States*, 369 U.S. 599 (1962).

investigation need not grind to a halt whenever responses to its inquiries might potentially be harmful to a witness in some distinct proceeding . . . or when crime or wrong-doing is disclosed." And, he observed, "to deny the Com-mittee the right to ask the [questions at issue] would be . . . to limit congressional inquiry to those areas in which there is not the slightest possibility of . . . prosecution . . . . Such a restriction upon congressional investigatory powers should not be countenanced."

The *Hutcheson* case, therefore, strongly suggests that it is improper to refuse evidence to a congressional commit-tee because adverse publicity might be generated. In addi-tion, the *Delaney* case—which involved executive branch corruption—indicates that Congress, to accomplish its important missions, may lawfully demand evidence regard-ing criminal conduct despite the probability that injurious publicity will occur.* The Court of Appeals in the com-mittee's suit against the President, perhaps made wary by the committee's citations of *Hutcheson* and *Delaney*, ducked the issues Gesell had raised and instead decided the appeal on presidential confidentiality grounds.†

Moreover, the Gesell rule that in some circumstances the President may withhold materials that might inspire derogatory publicity regarding the defendants in some future proceeding is susceptible to obvious abuse. As noted above, the courts have remarked that congressional investi-gations have their greatest efficacy when they focus on cor-ruption in the executive branch. But a President may be loath for many reasons to hand over information relating to the transgressions of his closest friends and associates. The claim that pending or possible criminal trials might be prejudiced could offer an easy out; certainly the pro-

---

* Recently the Supreme Court, in foreclosing a suit because of the speech or debate clause, stated, "Collateral harm which may occur in the course of a legitimate legislative inquiry does not allow us to force the inquiry to 'grind to a halt.' " *Eastland* v. *United Service-men's Fund*, 421 U.S. 491, 510, and n. 16 (1975). See Chapter X.

† See Chapters II and VI.

clivity of most courts would be *not* to second-guess the President as to possible adverse effects on future trials. And, because the President normally controls prosecutions, there is usually no assurance that such criminal trials will ever be begun or, if held, conducted with vigor. Competent prosecutions, in fact, may not be realized in certain circumstances unless Congress actually has obtained information allowing it to spotlight malfeasance in the executive branch. In the Teapot Dome situation, to give one illustration, prosecutions came long after Congress began to probe the various aspects of that multifaceted scandal.

Another factor is also arresting. The new "privilege" to protect fair trials recognized by Gesell apparently would not be available only to the President. It would seem that the "privilege" could also be claimed by actual or potential criminal defendants who might present with substantial force their fears that giving testimony or other evidence to Congress would impede their chances of a fair hearing in some future proceeding. In particular, this "privilege" would give defendants in congressional contempt cases another defense against prosecutions for failing to respond to committee inquiries. But is such a "privilege" necessary? Under the Fifth Amendment a defendant has the absolute right to refrain from giving incriminating evidence to a congressional committee. To condone reliance on a right to restrain adverse publicity as a proper reason to refuse production of evidence would in some circumstances render meaningless the protection afforded by that amendment. As Justice Harlan said in *Hutcheson*, it "would be to turn an 'option of refusal' into a 'prohibition of inquiry' " and thus "would in effect . . . obliterate the need" for the Fifth Amendment guarantee. Additionally, because the courts have a "well-stocked arsenal" of protective devices that can be employed to mitigate the effect of harmful publicity, because they can deal with the fall-out of adverse publicity by regulating their own proceedings, it is dubious that basic principles of fairness require the erection of a pretrial publicity "privilege" which allows a witness to withhold evidence relevant to committee undertakings.

Gesell's ruling also seems to cut against the grain of Congress's investigatory history and the various court rulings relating to it in addition to *Hutcheson* and *Delaney*. As described, Congress has investigated criminal conduct since its beginnings, and the courts have generally sanctioned these endeavors notwithstanding the fact that the possibility of precipitating publicity that might endanger future trials has been ever-present. Wholesale utilization of Gesell's theory could seriously debilitate Congress's vital role in investigating criminal conduct in the executive branch and elsewhere where there is a legitimate federal interest. This result, history has shown and the courts have recognized, would be unfortunate, perhaps catastrophic.

If the Gesell rule receives wider judicial acceptance, the courts will perhaps be able to strike appropriate balances between legislative requirements and fair trial needs which will not unduly frustrate congressional investigations. Some courts undoubtedly would "assume that . . . legislators are sensitive to, and will endeavor to act conformably to, the principle that the Bill of Rights applies to the legislature's investigations"* and that Congress will use the evidence it seeks so as to minimize that injury to criminal proceedings. But the peril remains that other courts would incline to rulings overly protective of their own processes and thus hamper critical legislative inquiry.

In this regard, Gesell's opinion should be compared with Judge Sirica's approach in Special Prosecutor Cox's case with the Ervin committee. Here also was an attempt on pretrial publicity grounds to keep the committee from giving key evidence—the testimony of Dean and Magruder —to the public. But Sirica refused to use the court's "inherent powers in the interest of preserving the rights

---

* *Ansara v. Eastland,* 442 F. 2d 751, 754 (D.C. Cir. 1971).

of potential defendants." He refused to "go beyond administering of [the court's] own affairs and attempt to regulate
proceedings before a coordinate branch of government,"
commenting that appellate court decisions (including
Hutcheson and *Delaney*) "mandate[d] a hands-off policy
on the court's part." Sirica also aided the committee's performance of its informing function by entering orders
allowing Watergate burglars Howard Hunt and Bernard
Barker to leave prison to testify publicly before the committee.

It would be remiss to leave Gesell's opinion without a
few additional comments on his views. In the course of his
opinion the judge wrote: "The public interest does not
require that the President should be forced to provide
evidence, already in the hands of an active and independent prosecution force, to a Senate committee in order to
furnish fuel for further hearings which cannot, by their
very nature, provide the procedural safeguards and adversary format essential to fact finding in the criminal justice
system. . . . To suggest that at this juncture the public
interest requires pretrial disclosure of these tapes either to
the Committee or to the public is to imply that the judicial
process has not been or will not be effective in this matter."
Continuing further in this vein, Gesell said:

> The Court recognizes that any effort to balance con-
> flicting claims as to what is in the public interest can
> provide only an uncertain result, for ours is a country
> that thrives and benefits from factional disagreements
> as to what is best for everyone. In assigning priority to
> the integrity of criminal justice, the Court believes that
> it has given proper weight to what is a dominant and
> pervasive theme in our culture. To be sure, the truth can
> only emerge from full disclosure. A country's quality is
> best measured by the integrity of its judicial processes.
> Experience and tradition teach that facts surrounding

allegations of criminal conduct should be developed in an orderly fashion during adversary proceedings before neutral fact finders, so that not only the truth but the whole truth emerges and the rights of those involved are fully protected.

As Gesell anticipated, his remarks are open to disagreement. To begin with, many people—especially nonlawyers—might quarrel with the judge's assessment that "a country's quality is best measured by the integrity of its judicial processes." Men of the cloth, for example, might believe that the "quality" of a nation is better signified by its citizens' concern for spiritual values. Others might hold that national "quality" is better judged by how the government—particularly its legislature through the passage of laws—feeds its hungry, attends its sick and aging, shelters its homeless, educates its children, and ensures that the willing can earn a livelihood. Still others might contend that the measure of "quality" is the extent to which the ideal of participatory democracy is realized and the conduct of government charted and scrutinized by the people's representatives. To be considered in this regard is the remark of Senator Edmund Muskie of Maine that "Legislative bodies since the time of King John have been recorded as frontline fighters for the protection of the rights of the free people to influence and control their government."* Also pertinent is the observation of Justice Oliver Wendell Holmes that "it must be remembered that legislatures are ultimate guardians of the liberties and welfare of the people in quite as great a degree as the courts."†

* See *Hearings before the Subcommittee on Intergovernmental Relations, et al.*, April 10, 1973, Vol. I, p. 49.

† Missouri, *Kansas & Texas Ry. Co.* v. *May*, 194 U.S. 267, 270 (1904). See also *United States* v. *Lovett*, 328 U.S. 303, 319 (1946) (Frankfurter, J., concurring). Justice Brandeis once noted the English and American conviction that "the people must look to representative assemblies for protection of their liberties." *Myers* v. *United States*, 272 U.S. 52, 294–95 (1926) (Brandeis, J., dissenting).

Beyond this, there is room for disagreement respecting Gesell's exaltation of the criminal over the legislative process as a vehicle to inform the public. While the criminal process may result in a final determination that an individual is guilty or not guilty of a crime, it sometimes falls woefully short of exposing facts relating to wrongdoing which the public has a need and a right to know. A grand jury may fail to return an indictment, leaving undisclosed the results of its explorations, which by law are secret. Criminal cases may be dropped by the prosecution or resolved by guilty pleas, thereby prohibiting full revelation of the facts. The strictures of the rules of evidence may prevent the introduction of facts of interest to the public which could be brought forward in a legislative format.

It may be argued that the protections granted by the rules of evidence and the other safeguards that surround criminal trials form a principal basis for the contention that the criminal process is the desirable means to present publicly the facts regarding criminal conduct. But this argument would seem to overlook the consideration that there are many facts surrounding criminal activities not strictly relevant to a criminal proceeding or admissible at a trial which the public should know in order to make judgments about the qualities and capabilities of its leaders, the administration of its government, or the needs for legislative reform. Congress, through its independent informing function, may be able to present this information better than the courts. To recognize Congress's informing role is not to denigrate that of the courts in the criminal process; it is simply to affirm that both Congress and the courts have unique functions to fulfill in exposing wrongdoing to public scrutiny.

If Congress is to play the informing role, it must recognize the problems its activities pose for the criminal process and its concomitant obligation for self-regulation. Justice

Brennan, concurring in the *Hutcheson* case, put it this way: "When a congressional inquiry and a criminal prosecution cross paths, Congress must accommodate the public interest in legitimate legislative inquiry with the public interest in securing the witness a fair trial. . . . Surely it cannot be said that a fair criminal trial and a full power of inquiry are interests that defy accommodation. . . . Even within the realm of relevant inquiry, there may be situations in which fundamental fairness would demand postponement of inquiry until after an immediately pending trial, or the taking of testimony in executive session. . . ." Perhaps, for example, the King committee, knowing that Denis Delaney's trial was less than three months hence, should have delayed its hearings into the shortcomings of that hapless official.

The Watergate committee—led by Senator Ervin, a former judge whose concern for individual rights and liberties has shown itself in many ways—made significant attempts to accommodate the interests of Congress and the courts. Mitchell and Stans, testifying in televised session after the return of their indictments in the Vesco matter, were asked no questions concerning that situation by the committee. The committee in early 1974 postponed its public hearings so as not to interfere with the Mitchell/ Stans trial and later canceled those hearings altogether to avoid impairing the upcoming Watergate trials and the impeachment inquiry. The committee also delayed the release of its final report for several weeks in part to wait until the jury in the Ellsberg case was chosen and sequestered.*

Despite Cox's ardent pleas the committee did not forgo its hearings in the summer of 1973. As remarked, Senator Ervin felt that informing the public about Watergate was more important than a few convictions, which, in any

---

* The committee also took the extraordinary step of informing the Court of Appeals that it would accede to a protective order prohibiting it from using the tapes in a fashion that would endanger fair trials.

event, he did not believe would be imperiled by public hearings at that stage, for there were then no indictments in the main Watergate case and that case obviously would not be tried for many months. The final word is not yet written, but so far Senator Ervin's prognostication remains untarnished.

·VI·
Investigating
the Executive Branch

In early April 1973 the national environment was vastly different from the present. The country was burdened with an ignoble President, his administration not yet cut to tatters by revelations of its various scandals. Indeed, the Nixon administration, fresh from its landslide victory in the November elections, appeared impregnable in its power and impervious to the growing importunings of those seeking full exploration of the Watergate affair.

Richard Kleindienst, in April 1973, was Attorney General of the United States. He was called before a joint session of three subcommittees of the Senate Government Operations and Judiciary committees to give the Nixon administration's views on executive privilege. His testimony, which reflected the imperiousness that the Nixon administration still displayed, was characterized more by audacity than sagacity.

The Constitution contains no express provision granting the President an executive privilege. Nonetheless, in his formal statement Kleindienst declared that "the separation of powers doctrine" gives the President "the constitutional authority . . . in his discretion to withhold certain documents or information in his possession or in possession of the executive branch from compulsory process of the legislative or judicial branch of the Government, if he believes disclosure would impair the proper exercise of his constitutional functions." And when Kleindienst was interrogated by Senators Muskie and Ervin, the full extent of the Nixon administration's views regarding the absolute authority of the President to secrete executive branch materials from Congress became apparent.

Senator MUSKIE. Now, I would like to ask this question. I understand your definition. Congress has no power at all to command information or receive information from the executive branch; is that your definition?

Mr. KLEINDIENST. Only if the President of the United States directs a member of the executive branch not to appear or provide it.

Senator MUSKIE. So my statement is correct that the Congress in your view, has no power to command the production of testimony or information by anyone in the executive branch under any circumstances?

Mr. KLEINDIENST. If the President of the United States so directs.

Senator MUSKIE. If the President of the United States, as he rarely does, can veto, the Congress has no power to command; is that not true?

Mr. KLEINDIENST. You command my presence up here all the time and I am up here all the time, Mr. Muskie. If the President called me up at 8 o'clock and said, "Kleindienst, you are to go up there and testify before that committee but I am telling you not to do it," I will not come here. We will stipulate to that.

Senator MUSKIE. But you come here because you have

decided you will do so, not because you concede our right to command you to do so. I have heard words all morning about [how] we work this out with . . . cooperative discussion, with some kind of amicable arrangement. I am talking now about what the rights of Congress are. Do we have the right to command you to testify against your will and better judgment?

Mr. KLEINDIENST. Well, my will or better judgment would have nothing to d   h it.

Senator MUSKIE. But against the will of the President of the United States?

Mr. KLEINDIENST. If the President directs me not to appear I would not appear, no more than I would appear in your office and give you information you ask for.

Senator MUSKIE. So it is your opinion that the Congress has no power to command anyone in the executive branch or command the production of information in the executive branch; is that your definiton?

Mr. KLEINDIENST. Or conversely, we will provide it unless the President directs us to the contrary.

Senator MUSKIE. So our power to command is in the President's hands?

Mr. KLEINDIENST. Well, your power to get what the President knows is in the President's hands. Your power to get information from citizens is in your hands.

Senator MUSKIE. I am talking about 2½ million employees of the executive branch; do we or do we not have the power to command him to testify and—

Mr. KLEINDIENST. You do not have the power to command President Nixon to come up here.

Senator MUSKIE. That is not my question.

Mr. KLEINDIENST. That was an extension of your question which I have been trying to answer on three or four occasions, Senator Muskie.

Senator MUSKIE. You have fudged every answer.

Mr. KLEINDIENST. You do not have the power to compel me to come up here if the President directs me not to and even if you would attempt to compel me, I would not come here.

Senator MUSKIE. Does that apply to every one of the employees of the [executive] branch of the United States?

Mr. KLEINDIENST. I think if the President directs it, logically, I would have to say that is correct.

*   *   *

Senator ERVIN. Maybe I can sum up your testimony on executive privilege. You concede, I take it, that Congress does have the power to gather information for the purpose of enabling it to legislate wisely?

Mr. KLEINDIENST. Yes, sir.

Senator ERVIN. But you take the position that notwithstanding the fact that the Constitution impliedly gives this power to the Congress, that Congress cannot obtain any information whatsoever from anybody in the executive branch of the Government, or any document in the possession of the Government, unless the President specifically directs that it have it?

Mr. KLEINDIENST. Or conversely, if the President directs anybody who has a document or information or directs anyone not to appear, that person would have the power not to comply with the congressional request.

Senator ERVIN. Is that not what I said?

Mr. KLEINDIENST. I like the way I put it better in emphasis, for one, this President, all Presidents, 99.9 percent of the time cooperate with the Congress.

Senator ERVIN. Your position is the President has implied power under the Constitution to deny to the Congress the testimony of any person working for the executive branch of the Government or any document in the possession of anybody working for the Government?

Mr. KLEINDIENST. Yes, sir, and you have a remedy, all kinds of remedies, cut off appropriations, impeach the President.*

Kleindienst's testimony has been recounted at length because it reveals both the absurdity and the danger of the Nixon position. Perhaps realizing the implausibility of this stand, Kleindienst drew back from presenting it in starkest terms until forced to do so by Senators Ervin and Muskie.

Viewed historically, Kleindienst's testimony was an opening salvo in the battle between Nixon, on the one hand, and the special prosecutors and Congress, on the other, over the executive privilege issue. The tapes had not yet been discovered, but in early April Nixon was determined to prohibit his top aides—principally Haldeman, Ehrlichman, and Dean—from testifying before the Ervin committee. These were the men who could link him to the Watergate cover-up. Later he allowed those aides to testify after Senator Ervin threatened to dispatch the Senate sergeant at arms to transport them to the Senate, and by July 1973 the tapes had become the focus of the executive privilege controversy.

But it is important to look beyond the Watergate milieu and recognize the general threat to Congress's oversight function posed by Nixon's views, a threat heightened by the burgeoning of the executive branch and its increasing control over national affairs. Indisputably, the Constitution gives Congress the implied power to examine the activities of the executive. The Supreme Court has affirmed that " 'It is the proper duty of a representative body to look diligently into every affair of government' " and remarked that "The power of Congress to conduct investi-

* United States Senate, *Hearings before the Subcommittee on Intergovernmental Relations et al.*, "Executive Privilege, Secrecy in Government, Freedom of Information," 93rd Cong., 1st Sess. (April 10, 1973), Vol. I, pp. 20, 45–46, 51.

gations . . . comprehends probes into departments of the Federal Government to expose corruption, inefficiency or waste."* And in *McGrain* v. *Daugherty*† the Court specifically approved a Senate investigation of the Justice Department. Without authority to probe the executive, Congress frequently could not obtain the information necessary to pass or repeal laws, to appropriate funds, to determine whether to confirm presidential appointments, to decide whether to consent to treaty obligations. If Congress could not investigate the executive branch, it could not keep the public informed about the state of its government. In short, without its powers of oversight, Congress would be emasculated. As Justice Stewart once said, "with the people and their representatives reduced to a state of ignorance, the democratic process is paralyzed."‡

Not only does the Constitution imply oversight responsibilities, but provisions of federal law specifically affirm Congress's role as overseer of the executive branch. A 1971 amendment to the Legislative Reorganization Act of 1946 states:

In order to assist the Congress in—

(1) its analysis, appraisal, and evaluation of the application, administration, and execution of the laws enacted by the Congress, and

(2) its formulation, consideration, and enactment of such modifications of or changes in those laws, and of such additional legislation, as may be necessary or appropriate,

each standing committee of the Senate and the House of Representatives shall review and study, on a continu-

---

* See *United States* v. *Rumely*, 345 U.S. 41, 43 (1953) and *Watkins* v. *United States*, 354 U.S. 178, 187 (1957).

† 273 U.S. 135 (1927).

‡ *EPA* v. *Mink*, 410 U.S. 73, 95 (1973) (Stewart, J., concurring).

ing basis, the application, administration, and execution of those laws, or parts of laws, the subject matter of which is within the jurisdiction of that committee.*

A statute putting a more direct responsibility on the executive branch to provide information to Congress is a law, originally passed in 1789, providing that "The Secretary of the Treasury . . . shall make report and give information to either branch of the legislature in person or in writing, as may be required, respecting all matters referred to him by the Senate or House of Representatives, or which shall appertain to his office."† Another provision states that "An Executive agency, on request of the Committee on Government Operations of the House . . . or . . . the Committee on Government Operations of the Senate . . . shall submit any information requested of it relating to any matter within the jurisdiction of the committee."‡ And there are statutes allowing certain committees to obtain tax returns and related materials from the Internal Revenue Service;§ the Ervin committee made use of these provisions.

Also relevant is the Freedom of Information Act,‖ enacted in 1966, which gives citizens—including congressmen—the right to obtain vast amounts of executive branch material. In essence this statute provides that, with specifically enumerated exceptions, executive records must be made available to citizens upon request. The law establishes court procedures by which obdurate officials can be forced to produce materials covered by the statute. A citizen's right to records designated by the act is absolute; there is no requirement that he demonstrate need for the items demanded.

* 2 U.S.C. 190d (a) (1971).
† 31 U.S.C. 1002 (1970).
‡ 5 U.S.C. 2954 (1970). See further, 7 U.S.C. 2207 (1970) and 31 U.S.C. 54 (1970).
§ 26 U.S.C. 6103(d), 6104(a) (2) (1970).
‖ 5 U.S.C. 553 (1970).

But the Nixon administration's view, parroted by Kleindienst, was that under the doctrine of separation of powers the President, by executive fiat, could plug the entire fount of executive branch information. Whether this position was produced by fear, megalomania, or both, it was not an accurate accounting of the law. As the Court of Appeals for the District of Columbia Circuit said in its opinion regarding Cox's effort to obtain Nixon tapes: "If the claim of absolute privilege was recognized, its mere invocation by the President or his surrogates could deny access to all documents in all the Executive departments to all citizens and their representatives, including Congress. . . . The Freedom of Information Act could become nothing more than a legislative statement of unenforceable rights. Support for this kind of mischief simply cannot be spun from incantation of the doctrine of separation of powers."*

This rather hostile critique of Kleindienst's exaggerated contentions should not obscure the fact that the President, particularly in regard to demands from private parties, has legitimate needs to protect confidential information. For example, in certain circumstances the President, in the interest of national security, may properly protect sensitive matters pertaining to foreign relations or military affairs. Although no decisions have directly dealt with Congress's right to such evidence, the courts have generally held that the executive has the prerogative to withhold materials of this nature from other supplicants. The courts, however, have asserted authority to review claims of privilege on national security grounds.† Also instructive is the Freedom of Information Act, which recognizes that the executive can deny national security information to private parties.‡

* *Nixon* v. *Sirica*, 487 F. 2d 700, 715 (D.C. Cir. 1973).
† E.g., *United States* v. *Reynolds*, 345 U.S. 1 (1952).
‡ However, the act states that it "is not authority to withhold information from Congress." 5 U.S.C. 552(c) (1970).

The executive also may be justified in safeguarding certain government investigative files where their release, for instance, might interfere with the progress of an investigation, disclose the identity of an informer, reveal investigative techniques, or endanger the safety of law enforcement personnel. Again, no court decisions have directly ruled on Congress's right to such files. In cases involving demands for such materials by private litigants the courts have generally recognized that investigative files are privileged, but have held that the privilege must give way if the fair administration of justice so requires. A defendant in a criminal case, for example, may be allowed to ascertain the identity of an informer against him in order to prepare his defense. Where the government is a party to the litigation, it must drop its prosecution or concede the matter at issue if it declines to produce materials which a court has ordered revealed.* As with national security secrets, the executive's right to protect certain investigatory files from disclosure to private parties is affirmed by the Freedom of Information Act.

The species of privilege involved in the Ervin committee suit against Nixon was that which protects the confidentiality of presidential communications. The concept was abused by Nixon, who claimed he had absolute authority to determine what communications the courts and Congress could secure, but strong policy reasons support a limited privilege of this nature. If the President is to receive frank advice—written or oral—his aides must know that their communications to him are protected. If a President's advisers were constantly beset by trepidations that their comments, opinions, and recommendations might filter into the public domain, their views would become highly moderated, qualified, or bowdlerized. Reduced to

---

* See, e.g., *Roviaro v. United States,* 353 U.S. 53 (1957); *Jencks v. United States,* 353 U.S. 657 (1957); *Center on Corporate Responsibility, Inc. v. Shultz,* 368 F. Supp. 863 (D.D.C. 1973); and Raoul Berger, *Executive Privilege: A Constitutional Myth* (Harvard University Press, 1974), pp. 209–33.

a tepid state, their advice and opinions would be unreliable and largely useless. Similarly, a President might not express himself freely if he had no power to ensure that his comments are not broadcast to a world waiting to be informed of sensitive government policies or titillated by revelations of presidential peccadilloes.

There is nothing unusual about the requirement of government officials to protect the confidentiality of their official communications. The law recognizes the needs of congressmen to converse freely with their aides. The confidentiality of discussions among judges, and among judges and their law clerks, is normally protected. Similarly, heads of executive departments and other high government officials generally have a right to preserve the confidentiality of their deliberations.* The President has similar—indeed heightened—needs.

The requirement of presidential confidentiality has been expressed by numerous writers of diverse persuasions. With special reference to congressional requests for evidence, Justice William O. Douglas wrote in his book *Anatomy of Liberty*:

> Each President—from Washington to Kennedy—has deemed it to be in his prerogative not to disclose certain information to the legislative branch. . . . Certainly much information must be kept secret; at least, the President might so believe. Defense items, the operations of diplomatic missions, the communications with our embassies or legations—these are sensitive matters. Moreover, employees of the executive branch are in a chain of command leading up to the President. If any of them can be summoned and interrogated as

* See, e.g., *NLRB* v. *Sears, Roebuck & Co.,* 421 U.S. 132 (1975); *EPA* v. *Mink,* 410 U.S. 73 (1973); *Gravel* v. *United States,* 408 U.S. 606 (1972); *Soucie* v. *David,* 448 F. 2d 1067 (D.C. Cir. 1971) (note particularly Judge Wilkey's concurring opinion); *Carl Zeiss Stiftung* v. *V.E.B.* Carl Zeiss, Jena, 40 F.R.D. 318 (D.D.C. 1966) *affirmed* 384 F. 2d 979 (D.C. Cir. 1967) *cert. denied* 389 U.S. 952 (1967); Statement of the Judges, 14 F.R.D. 335 (1953).

to how he advised his superior, what memoranda he wrote, what conversation he has had, a disruptive influence would be injected into the executive branch. Then the employee would look to Congress and not have undivided loyalty to his superior in the executive branch.*

A more personal statement of similar principles came from Margaret Truman Daniel, who, commenting on her father's presidency, said:

Lately some historians have criticized Dad because he has refused to open his confidential files. But Dad is not acting out of selfish motives. From the day he left office he was conscious that he still had heavy responsibilities as an ex-President. During his White House years a President gets advice from hundreds of people. He wants it to be good advice. He wants men to say exactly what they think, to tell exactly what they know about a situation or a subject. A President can only get this kind of honesty if the man who is giving the advice knows what he says is absolutely confidential, and will not be published for a reasonable number of years after the President leaves the White House.†

Others have stressed the more human requirements of a President. "The President needs to discuss with a sympathetic person ideas and plans that are still in an amorphous state and to gain some respite from the cares of office by talking over trivial matters that interest him or by chatting about men of affairs, with the confidence that his remarks will not go beyond the room."‡

---

* Douglas, *Anatomy of Liberty* (Trident Press, 1963), pp. 74–5.

† Truman, *Harry S. Truman* (William Morrow & Co., Inc., 1973, p. 562.

‡ See Carr, Bernstein, Morrison, Snyder, and McLean, *American Democracy in Theory and Practice* (Holt, Rinehart & Winston 1956), pp. 609–10.

President Nixon succinctly stated the general requirement of confidentiality for presidential communications in a July 6, 1973, letter to Senator Ervin where he declined the Ervin committee's request for access to certain presidential papers. "No President," wrote Nixon, "could function if the private papers of his office, prepared by his personal staff, were open to public scrutiny." And, he continued, "Formulation of sound public policy requires that the President and his personal staff be able to communicate among themselves in complete candor, and that their tentative judgments, their exploration of alternatives, and their frank comments on issues and personalities at home and abroad remain confidential." Nixon later adopted this rationale in rejecting the committee's requests for tapes of his conversations. The baseness of Nixon's motives notwithstanding, these contentions are cogent.

History is replete with requests from the Congress to Presidents, ex-Presidents, and officials of executive departments for confidential materials.* On numerous occasions the executive has declined to honor such requests. Of particular historical interest are the Eisenhower administration's responses to demands for information by Senator Joseph McCarthy.

In 1953–54, Senator McCarthy held lengthy hearings where he repeatedly and savagely attacked the loyalty

* On historical matters generally, see, e.g., Berger, *Executive Privilege: A Constitutional Myth* (Harvard University Press, 1974), "Executive Privilege v. Congressional Inquiry," 12 UCLA *Law Review* 1044, 1056–60 (1965), and "Congressional Subpoenas to Executive Officials," 75 *Columbia Law Review* 866 (1975); Rotunda, "Presidents and Ex-Presidents as Witnesses: A Brief Historical Footnote," *The University of Illinois Law Forum* No. 1 (1975), p. 1; *Hearings before the Subcommittee on Intergovernmental Relations, et al., United States Senate,* "Executive Privilege, Secrecy in Government, Freedom of Information," 93rd Cong., 1st Sess. (1973); and *Hearings before the Subcommittee on Separation of Powers,* "Executive Privilege: The Withholding of Information by the Executive," 92d Cong., 1st Sess. (1971). Professor Berger is the leading authority on executive privilege.

and competence of various senior military officials. For a while his broadsides were met with appeasement by the Eisenhower administration—particularly Secretary of the Army Robert T. Stevens. The executive branch appeared determined at all costs to avoid a major confrontation with the senator even if Army morale suffered greatly, as it did. McCarthy, emboldened by his successes and the lack of meaningful opposition, openly called for disgruntled administration employees to bring him confidential material relating to subversion in government, and he was in fact leaked a summary of a confidential document prepared by FBI chief J. Edgar Hoover respecting thirty-four suspect employees of the Army Signal Corps. Eventually the administration stiffened. The Army counterattacked with charges that McCarthy and his chief counsel, Roy Cohn, had sought preferential treatment from the Army for Private David Schine, a former McCarthy staff member. These allegations became part of the sensational Army-McCarthy hearings. When McCarthy attempted to inquire into consultations among high administration officials leading to a release of the Army's charges, Eisenhower issued a broad directive prohibiting disclosure of any conversations, communications, and documents reflecting Defense Department decision-making processes.

This directive, which bore the seeds of Nixon's later claims of absolute executive privilege, declared:

> Because it is essential to efficient and effective administration that employees of the Executive Branch be in a position to be completely candid in advising each other on official matters, and because it is not in the public interest that any of their conversations or communications or any documents or reproductions concerning such advice be disclosed, you will instruct employees of your Department that in all their appearances before the subcommittee of the Senate Committee on Government Operations regarding the inquiry

now before it, they are not to testify to any such conversations or communications or to produce any such
documents or reproductions.*

This directive was hailed by many observers who believed
that McCarthy, through his attacks on the Army and the
International Information Administration (Voice of America), was actually attempting to achieve operative control
of executive departments in violation of separation-of-
powers principles. Among those delivering plaudits to the
administration were *The New York Times* and *The Washington Post*, newspapers which, during the Nixon years,
became staunch foes of exaggerated executive privilege
claims.

Another prominent example of reliance on presidential
confidentiality from the loyalty investigations era concerned the 1953 refusal of former President Truman to
comply with a HUAC subpoena to appear and testify
regarding charges that he had knowingly supported an
alleged Russian spy (former Assistant Secretary of the
Treasury Harry Dexter White) for a position with the
International Monetary Fund. Observing that many
Presidents had declined congressional requests for evidence, Truman delcared: "The doctrine [of presidential
confidentiality] would be shattered, and the President,
contrary to our fundamental theory of constitutional government, would become a mere arm of the Legislative
Branch of the government if he would feel during his
term of office that his every act might be subject to official
inquiry and possible distortion for political purposes."

---

* The Eisenhower administration's full views concerning the executive's inviolate prerogative to withhold information from Congress were later embodied in a much criticized memorandum
delivered to the Senate Subcommittee on Constitutional Rights in
1958 by Attorney General William P. Rogers. Earlier the Eisenhower
administration had also resisted McCarthy's attempts to subpoena
members of the appeals board that reviewed security cases involving
Army employees.

Numerous other illustrations of presidential reluctance
to honor congressional demands could be adduced. These
include Washington's refusal in 1796 to release to the
House his instructions to Chief Justice John Jay concerning Jay's negotiations leading to the controversial treaty
with Great Britain that eventually bore his name;* Lincoln's refusal in 1861 to surrender dispatches to the War
Department on the fall of Fort Sumter; Franklin Roosevelt's and Harry Truman's various denials of congressional
requests for FBI reports; and John Kennedy's refusal to
allow the Secretaries of Defense and State to reveal the
names of officials who reviewed certain speeches.

As President Nixon's lawyers happily remarked in the
Ervin committee suit, influential members of Congress
have at times conceded that executive officials may
decline to testify on grounds of presidential confidentiality. In 1951 General Omar Bradley, called before the
Senate Armed Services and Foreign Relations committees
concerning President Truman's dismissal of General
Douglas MacArthur, refused to answer questions about a
meeting with the President, George Marshall, and Dean
Acheson. Senator Richard Russell, then chairman of the
Armed Services Committee, agreed that silence was justified, stating:

> I know that in my opinion any conversation with
> respect to any of my actions that I might have, any
> conference I might have with my administrative assist-
> ant in my office I think should be protected, and it is
> my own view, and I so rule, that any matter that tran-
> spired in the private conversation between the President
> and the Chief of Staff as to detail can be protected by
> the witness if he so desires, and if General Bradley

---

* Washington, however, did supply this information to the Senate,
observing that it, and not the House, has the constitutional duty to
ratify treaties.

relies upon that relationship, so far as the Chair is concerned, though I regret very much that the issue was raised and I am compelled to pass on it, I would rule that he be protected.*

A similar colloquy occurred during the Senate Judiciary Committee confirmation hearings of Abe Fortas for Chief Justice of the United States. In response to a query from Senator Ervin about a conversation between Justice Fortas and President Johnson, Justice Fortas replied:

Senator, I will not go into my conversations, either to affirm them or deny them, that I have had with the President. I ask you please to understand that, and please to excuse me. I know how easy it is to say no, the President did not say something to me. But the question "What did he say?" would follow, and so on. I have endeavored Senator, and Mr. Chairman, to err, if I erred, on the side of frankness and candor with this committee. But I think that it is my duty to observe certain limits, and one of those limits is any conversation, either affirmance or denial, that I may have had with the President of the United States.

Senator Ervin agreed that Justice Fortas should not be compelled to answer such questions, remarking that nondisclosure in these circumstances was a "prerogative" of the executive branch.† Throughout the controversy with Nixon, Senator Ervin's position was never that the President has no executive privilege. Rather, in regard to the

* See United States Senate, *Hearings before the Committee on Armed Services and the Committee on Foreign Relations,* "Military Situation in the Far East," 82nd Cong., 1st Sess. (1951), pp. 763–765.

† See United States Senate, *Hearings before the Committee on the Judiciary,* "Nominations of Abe Fortas and Homer Thornberry," 90th Cong., 2nd Sess. (1968), p. 124 et seq.

secrecy of executive communications, the senator contended that the President may keep confidential only those communications between him and his advisers, or among the advisers themselves, which enable the President to exercise his constitutional or legal obligations. Communications in furtherance of crimes or relating solely to political matters, Senator Ervin asserted, are not covered by the doctrine.

The historical record, however, is mixed and certainly does not support the claim that the President has an absolute executive privilege. An examination of pre-constitutional history reveals that both the English Parliament and the colonial legislatures engaged in examinations of executive conduct and asserted the right to executive information. As William Pitt the elder stated in 1742 regarding the powers of Parliament, "We are called the Grand Inquest of the Nation, and as such it is our Duty to inquire into every step of public Management, either Abroad or at Home, in order to see that nothing has been done amiss." There was no pre-constitutional recognition of a right in the executive to withhold information from the legislature at will.

On many occasions Congress has investigated the conduct of the executive branch. In fact, most of its investigations during its first hundred years concerned executive conduct. And, as Kleindienst's testimony suggests, in numerous significant instances Presidents and ex-Presidents have acceded to congressional demands for evidence. A few illustrations will suffice.

During the 1792 House investigation of the calamitous defeat of General St. Clair, President Washington allowed the Secretaries of the Treasury and War departments to appear before the House and give testimony. Washington also submitted the available documentary evidence on the matter to the House, although he first unsuccessfully asked the House to withdraw its request for this material. In the words of Washington's biographer, "not even the ugliest line on the flight of the beaten troops was eliminated".* In 1846 Daniel Webster was accused of making improper disbursements from a "Presidential Secret Service Fund"—a fund established by Congress for use in clandestine foreign operations. During the House inquiry that followed, President Polk provided a schedule of amounts in the fund during the relevant time period (although he refused to produce documentation on the uses of the money expended), ex-President Tyler testified under subpoena before two House select committees, and ex-President John Quincy Adams filed a sworn deposition with one of those committees. President Lincoln, according to several contemporaneous newspaper accounts, gave evidence in early 1862 to the House Judiciary Committee concerning the purported involvement of his wife in the leak of an undelivered message to Congress which had been published in the New York *Herald*. Theodore Roosevelt testified before Congress on two occasions after he left the White House. In 1911 he appeared before a special House committee regarding the 1907 acquisition of the Tennessee Coal and Iron Company by United States Steel, and the next year testified before a Senate subcommittee investigating corporate contributions to his 1904 presidential campaign.

During the Teapot Dome investigations, a beleaguered President Harding sent the Senate a report on the leasing of Naval oil reserves prepared for him by Secretary of the Interior Albert Fall, later convicted for his role in that scandal. Earlier Fall had forwarded voluminous Interior Department documents to the Senate. President Eisenhower provided the Senate Kefauver committee with controversial documentation relating to the well-publicized Dixon-Yates affair, which involved conflicts of interest

---

* Douglas S. Freeman, *Biography of Washington* (Charles Scribner's Sons, 1954), Vol. VI, p. 339. However, Washington and his Cabinet apparently held the view that the President could refuse to disclose such information if the public interest demanded it. Raoul Berger, *Executive Privilege: A Constitutional Myth* (Harvard University Press, 1974), p. 167.

regarding an Atomic Energy Commission contract to build a power plant. Nixon, of course, was pressured to allow his closest aides to testify before both the Ervin committee and the House Judiciary Committee, and also released tape recordings and edited transcripts of his conversations to the House committee. Most recently, President Gerald Ford, confronted with public outcry over his pardon of Nixon, voluntarily appeared before the House Judiciary Committee to testify about that action, a move that created warmer executive-congressional relations but did little to assuage the views of those who saw the pardon as a blunder of major proportions.

On occasion Presidents have acknowledged Congress's right to executive information. President Andrew Jackson (who later found occasion to reject congressional demands for information concerning frauds in the sale of public lands) declared in 1834 that "cases may occur in the course of [Congress's] legislative . . . proceedings in which it may be indispensable to the proper exercise of its powers that it should inquire or decide upon the conduct of the President, or other public officers, and in every case its constitutional right to do so is cheerfully conceded." Similarly, President Polk stated in 1846, "If the House of Representatives, as the grand inquest of the nation, should at any time have reason to believe that there has been malversation in office . . . and should think proper to institute an inquiry into the matter, all the archives and papers of the Executive Department, public or private, would be subject to the inspection and control of a committee of their body and every facility in the power of the Executive be afforded to enable them to prosecute the investigation."

Also instructive is the pre-presidential conduct of Richard Nixon. While a member of the House Un-American Activities Committee in 1948, Nixon challenged President Truman's assertion, accompanying his refusal to produce FBI records on a governmental scientist, that the President had absolute power to deny executive branch information to Congress. To make this claim, Nixon argued on the floor of the House, was erroneously to contend "that the President could have arbitrarily issued an Executive order in . . . the Teapot Dome case . . . denying the Congress . . . information it needed to conduct an investigation of the executive department and the Congress would have no right to question his decision"

History, therefore, presents a contradictory, ambiguous picture. But this brief, selective historical review is an important prelude to an examination of the law that has recently evolved concerning executive privilege because this issue must be kept in proper perspective. While the heroes and the villains change, the basic systemic questions relating to the prerogatives of the two branches remain.

In the early 1970's for example, the national bugbear was a President who asserted claims of executive privilege bordering on the fanatical, one who attempted to use the doctrine to hide his crimes and those of his coterie. In Nixon's last days Congress was—to many—the knight on a white stallion come to rescue the country from creeping despotism, or at least from perversion of basic principles. But in the 1950's Senator McCarthy was considered America's affliction by a large segment of the population. Then the claim was that Congress was overreaching, that the Eisenhower administration too long stood silent while Congress attempted to usurp executive functions. Although the personalities and politics in these struggles were different, they both revolved around the central issue of congressional right to information from the executive branch.

The various judges who ruled on Nixon's claim of privilege were all aware of the not-so-distant history of the McCarthy period. They undoubtedly realized that their decisions would have consequences far beyond the immediate facts before them, and that they must produce solutions workable in the future when the major threat to constitutional government might be not a Nixon but a McCarthy. Whether they succeeded is next examined.

The Supreme Court's decision on executive privilege in July 1974 was President Nixon's eviction notice.* This decision allowed Special Prosecutor Jaworski access to numerous tapes of presidential conversations, including a tape of a June 23, 1973, conversation which showed beyond cavil Nixon's early knowledge of and complicity in the Watergate cover-up. This tape, soon revealed to the House Judiciary Committee and the nation, put the lie once and for all to that less than elevating presidential proclamation, "I am not a crook."

The case began on April 18, 1974, when Judge Sirica, at the request of Special Prosecutor Jaworski, issued a subpoena to the White House for sixty-four recordings of presidential conversations and certain documents for use in the Watergate cover-up trial. Claiming executive privilege, the President quickly moved to quash the subpoena, but Sirica denied the motion and ordered the President to produce the subpoenaed items for examination in chambers. While finding that the items were "presumptively privileged"—as the Court of Appeals had ruled in October 1973 in Cox's clash with Nixon—Judge Sirica held that the special prosecutor had made a "sufficiently compelling" showing of need to warrant production of the materials to the court for final determination whether they should be delivered to Jaworski. Sirica's ruling was taken directly to the Supreme Court; the Court of Appeals was by-passed through an unusual procedure allowing immediate high court review of matters of extraordinary importance.

The Supreme Court's 8–0 opinion is a forceful confirmation that the President does have an executive privilege rooted in the doctrine of separation of powers and the supremacy of the executive branch in the exercise of its

* *United States v. Nixon*, 418 U.S. 683 (1974).

constitutional duties. The privilege, however, is not absolute, and it lies with the courts to define its scope. Quoting Chief Justice John Marshall's opinion in the venerated case of *Marbury* v. *Madison,** the Court observed that " 'it is emphatically the province and duty of the judicial department to say what the law is.' " This Court, it said, is the " 'ultimate interpreter of the Constitution.' "† The Court's decision thus echoed that handed down in the infancy of the nation in the famous Aaron Burr case by Chief Justice Marshall, who ruled that a federal court had "the right to issue a subpoena against the President," and declared that claims of executive privilege are for the courts to judge.‡

A President's assertion of privilege is entitled to the "utmost deference" when he claims a need to protect military, diplomatic, or sensitive national security secrets, the Court said, citing earlier Supreme Court decisions.§ Indeed, when a court is convinced that confidential materials of this nature would be disclosed, it should uphold a claim of privilege *without* in-chambers inspection no matter what interests demand disclosure. But, the Court stated, "No case of the Court has extended this high degree of deference to a President's generalized interest in confidentiality."

Nonetheless, the Court recognized "the valid need for protection of communications between high government officials and those who advise and assist them in the performance of their manifold duties." "[T]he importance of this confidentiality," it said, "is too plain to require further discussion. Human experience teaches that those who expect public dissemination of their remarks may well temper candor with a concern for appearances and for their own interests to the detriment of the decisionmaking

---

* 1 Cranch (5 U.S.) 137, 177 (1803).
† This quote is from *Baker* v. *Carr*, 369 U.S. 186, 211 (1962).
‡ *United States* v. *Burr*, 25 Fed. Cas. 187 (No. 14, 694) (1807).
§ *C. & S. Air Lines* v. *Waterman Corp.*, 333 U.S. 103, 111 (1948); *United States* v. *Reynolds*, 345 U.S. 1, 10 (1953).

process." Thus the Court, agreeing with the lower courts which had handled Nixon's various claims, ruled that presidential communications are "presumptively privileged."

This presumption, however, is outweighed by the needs of criminal justice for evidence that will permit a fair trial. The Court said: "We conclude that when the ground for asserting privilege as to subpoenaed materials sought for use in a criminal trial is based only on the generalized interest in confidentiality, it cannot prevail over the fundamental demands of due process of law in the fair administration of criminal justice. The generalized assertion of privilege must yield to the demonstrated, specific need for evidence in a pending criminal trial." The Court was not fearful that this inroad into presidential privilege would harshly affect the quality of presidential advice. "[W]e cannot conclude that advisers will be moved to temper the candor of their remarks by the infrequent occasions of disclosure because of the possibility that such conversations will be called for in the context of a criminal prosecution." The Court ordered the items subpoenaed transmitted to Sirica so he could ascertain what should be protected and what released to the special prosecutor.

In considering the ramifications of this opinion, it is important to understand the precise scope of its holding. The Court dealt only with the claim of executive confidentiality *vis-à-vis* the requirements of criminal justice. The Court was not, in its words, "concerned with the balance between the President's generalized interest in confidentiality and the need for relevant evidence in civil litigation, nor with that between the confidentiality interest and congressional demands for information, nor with the President's interest in preserving state secrets."* Thus the

---

* Since Nixon's forced retirement, several lower courts, on reasoning similar to that in the Supreme Court's opinion, have overruled his claims of executive privilege in *civil* litigation and required the production of documents and his submission to deposition. *Sun Oil*

opinion left the Court of Appeals decision in the Ervin committee case as the most authoritative final ruling on executive privilege assertions against the Congress. That case must be looked at again to understand its full implications.

That the Ervin committee case was decided at all is significant. Nixon had claimed it was not the type of dispute the courts should resolve, that it was not—to use a misty legal term—"justiciable." To be justiciable a dispute must have several attributes. For example, there must be, in constitutional language, a legitimate "case or controversy," that is, the parties must have adversary interests affected by the outcome of the case and not merely seek an advisory opinion. Most important for the present discussion, the issue before the court must not involve a "political question" whose resolution is solely the province of the executive or the legislature.*

To simplify the matter, a dispute involves a "political question" if the Constitution specifically commits its resolution to the executive or the Congress, or if the judiciary has no discernible standards for resolving the dispute, or if it otherwise appears that the issue should be decided by the exercise of executive or legislative discretion. President Nixon claimed that the tapes suit presented a political question primarily because the Constitution vested him with absolute discretion to protect his conversations by invocation of executive privilege.

Because no express provision in the Constitution affords the President an executive privilege, Nixon's lawyers had to comb its provisions to shore up his absolutist claim.

Co. v. *United States,* 514 F. 2d 1020 (Ct. Cl. 1975); *Halperin* v. *Kissinger,* Civ. No. 1187–73 (D.D.C. Sept. 24, 1975); *Nixon* v. *Administrator of General Services Administration,* Civ. No. 74–1852 (D.D.C., July 16, 1975).

* See, e.g., *Powell* v. *McCormack,* 395 U.S. 486 (1969); *Flast* v. *Cohen,* 392 U.S. 83 (1968); *Baker* v. *Carr,* 369 U.S. 186 (1962).

Their conclusions were imaginative, if not convincing. Their principal assertion was the historically unsupported contention that the constitutional grant of "executive powers" to the President gives him absolute power to deny executive information to Congress. (As already discussed, when the Constitution was drafted the prevailing view endorsed the legislature's right to executive information; there was no accepted theory that the executive could with impunity ignore legislative demands for relevant facts.) To bolster their contentions, his lawyers argued further that "The President . . . is charged 'from time to time [to] give to the Congress Information of the State of the Union . . .' This [provision] vests in the President, not in the subpoena power of a Senate Committee, the power to determine when and what information he will provide to Congress." The committee's answer to this "last-ditch grasping at verbal straws" was that a provision instructing the President to give information to Congress is hardly authority for withholding it.

The President's lawyers also pointed to his constitutional "duty to 'take Care that the Laws be faithfully executed'" and asserted, "As the President has clearly and forcefully maintained, the meetings and the conversations that the Senate Committee seeks to make public were participated in by the President pursuant to this Constitutional mandate." The committee mordantly responded that there was substantial evidence of the President's own involvement in crimes and that "the President's duty faithfully to execute the laws [does not] empowe[r] him to suppress evidence of Executive lawbreaking." The committee also observed that courts are accustomed to ruling on claims of privilege by the executive branch, so the case presented no novel judicial task.

In any event, the Court found the matter proper for judicial resolution, a result that has far-reaching ramifications for the future regulation of executive-legislative relationships. Judge Gesell had stated that "application of [the] tests [for determining the existence of a 'political question'] leaves no doubt that the issues presented in the instant controversy are justiciable." The Court of Appeals did not disturb this ruling, although Judge Malcom Wilkey expressed his view that under separation-of-powers principles, full discretion regarding executive privilege rested with the President and thus the matter involved a "political question" and was nonjusticiable.

The Court's position had been foreshadowed by the conclusions of Judge Sirica and the Court of Appeals in the Cox-Nixon dispute that the judiciary could rule on presidential claims of privilege. This principle, which was affirmed in July 1974 by the Supreme Court in Special Prosecutor Jaworski's suit for additional tapes, had found expression in other opinions before the tapes issues arose. Twenty years earlier, in a case brought by private litigants involving military secrets, the Supreme Court resolutely stated that "judicial control" over evidence "cannot be abdicated to the caprice of executive officers."* Additionally, in a 1971 suit brought by private parties concerning claims of executive privilege by five agency heads to protect documents relating to the proposed underground nuclear test on Amchitka Island, the District of Columbia Court of Appeals declared in language worthy of repetition:

> In our view, this claim of absolute immunity for documents in possession of an executive department or agency, upon the bald assertion of its head, is not sound law.

> * * *

> . . . An essential ingredient of our rule of law is the authority of the courts to determine whether an executive official or agency has complied with the Constitution and with the mandates of Congress which define

---

* *Reynolds* v. *United States*, 345 U.S. 1, 9–10 (1953).

and limit the authority of the executive. Any claim to executive absolutism cannot override the duty of the court to assure that an official has not exceeded his charter or flouted the legislative will.

. . . Otherwise the head of an executive department would have the power on his own say so to cover up all evidence of fraud and corruption when a federal court or grand jury was investigating malfeasance in office, and this is not the law.*

In the Ervin committee suit, the Court of Appeals' attention "was directed solely to one species of executive privilege—that premised on 'the great public interest in maintaining the confidentiality of conversations that take place in the President's performance of his official duties.'" Such presidential conversations, it declared, "are 'presumptively privileged,' even from the limited intrusion represented by [an in-chambers] examination of the conversations by a court." This presumption can be overcome, according to the court, only by a "strong showing" of need by the institution of government seeking the materials at issue—"a showing that the responsibilities of that institution cannot responsibly be fulfilled without access to records of the President's deliberations."

But the committee, the court stated, could not meet this threshold requirement: "Particularly in light of events that have occurred since this litigation was begun and, indeed, since the District Court issued its decision, we find that the Select Committee has failed to make the requisite showing." The principal "events" the court referred to were the release of the five tapes at issue to the House Judiciary Committee and the edited transcripts of those tapes to the public at large. Because the House Judiciary Committee had the tapes, Congress's informing

* *Committee for Nuclear Responsibility, Inc.* v. *Seaborg,* 463 F. 2d 788, 792–94 (D.C. Cir. 1971).

function would be met whether or not the Ervin committee received them. Similarly, the committee could not make a strong showing of need regarding the lawmaking function. Edited transcripts of the five recordings were available to the committee, and indications were that the House's findings on impeachment would not be long in coming.

During its discourse on the lawmaking function the court offered the following comments:

> There is a clear difference between Congress's legislative tasks and the responsibility of a grand jury, or any institution engaged in like functions. While fact-finding by a legislative committee is undeniably a part of its task, legislative judgments normally depend more on the predicted consequences of proposed legislative actions and their political acceptability, than on precise reconstruction of past events; Congress frequently legislates on the basis of conflicting information provided in its hearings. In contrast, the responsibility of the grand jury turns entirely on its ability to determine whether there is probable cause to believe that certain named individuals did or did not commit specific crimes. . . . We see no comparable need in the legislative process, at least not in the circumstances of this case. Indeed, whatever force there might once have been in the Committee's argument that the subpoenaed materials are necessary to its legislative judgments has been substantially undermined by subsequent events.

Fuel for the court's finding that the committee did not need the tapes to meet its legislative functions was supplied by committee members Edward Gurney and Daniel Inouye, who had publicly stated that the committee's final report and recommendations could be prepared without the tapes. In a CBS interview Senator Gurney had said: "In answer to the . . . question [whether] we need the tapes in order to write our report I said no, we didn't.

The tapes would shed light on the Watergate affair, that is true but that is really not what our charter is and that is to write our report and make recommendations to the Senate." Earlier, Gurney had remarked, "Now, getting the presidential tapes really has nothing to do with that charter at all."

Had the committee surmounted the threshold requirement of demonstrating substantial need for the actual tapes, the court would have had to balance the committee's needs against the President's requirements of confidentiality. In such circumstances, the court said, "application of Executive privilege depends on a weighing of the public interest protected by the privilege against the public interests that would be served by disclosure in a particular case." In a balancing test of this nature several factors presumably would have been relevant. One such factor was that the conversations in question were no longer confidential, the President having breached their confidentiality in many ways, not the least of which was the release of edited transcripts. Also pertinent in a balancing situation would have been the court's observation that "the Executive cannot, any more than the other branches of government, invoke a general confidentiality privilege to shield its officials and employees from investigations by the proper governmental institutions into possible criminal wrongdoing."

Whatever its merits, the Court of Appeals opinion has a surrealistic ring. The court invoked the doctrine of presidential privacy to protect conversations which, especially after release of the tapes and edited transcripts, had lost their confidentiality. Indeed, in the Cox-Nixon dispute the same court, as to four of the five conversations at issue in the committee's litigation, had declared in October 1973, "The simple fact is that the conversations are no longer confidential."

In fairness, it should be recognized that the court was attempting to propound and apply a general rule of law that would have significant implications beyond the immediate facts, to promulgate a standard which would squelch future efforts by the next wave of marauding McCarthys to rummage through presidential files and papers. Arguably, the establishment of suitable protection was worth an odd result in the Ervin committee's case, because, in truth, release of the tapes to the committee was in no respects as crucial as it had been in August 1973 (the month the suit was instigated), when neither the special prosecutor nor the House Judiciary Committee had secured any tapes.

That said, the question remains whether the test the court established is too severe, whether it unduly restricts congressional powers of inquiry. And, it should be noted, the opinion leaves open a number of issues perhaps of more importance than that directly before the court.

The threshold demonstration required in a test with the President—"a showing that [Congress's] responsibilities . . . cannot responsibly be fulfilled without access to records of the President's deliberations"—may be extremely difficult to make. The Supreme Court apparently believes that when presidential conversations contain evidence relevant to criminal prosecutions, the processes of criminal justice cannot function "responsibly" without access to records and testimony concerning those conversations. Thus the Supreme Court, repeatedly stressing the need for "all relevant and admissible evidence," ruled flatly that a President's claims of privilege "cannot prevail over the fundamental demands of due process of law in the fair administration of criminal justice" where a "specific need for evidence in a pending criminal trial" is demonstrated. (Earlier the Court of Appeals in Cox's case with Nixon held that the grand jury's "uniquely powerful showing" of need surmounted the President's presumption of privilege; this ruling—as does the Supreme Court's—undoubtedly reflects the pronounced judicial propensity to protect the integrity of court processes, a propensity also evinced in Judge Gesell's opinion in the committee's suit.) But even if Congress can show a "specific need" for presidential communications, it has not won the battle under the Court of Appeals' standard because, given the nature of its tasks, Congress may be able to fulfill its missions "responsibly" without the items sought.

The Court of Appeals was not charitable in its remarks regarding Congress's oversight and informing functions, stating that it "need neither deny that the Congress may have, quite apart from its legislative responsibilities, a general oversight [and informing] power, nor explore what the lawful reach of that power might be" because the House Judiciary Committee was fulfilling such functions for the Congress as a whole. This reticence to take a stand is somewhat surprising in light of the Supreme Court's assertions that Congress should "look diligently into every affair of government" and may probe the "departments of Federal Government to expose corruption, inefficiency or waste." Moreover, in the November 1973 resolution following the Saturday Night Massacre, the full Senate had affirmed that the Ervin committee was validly engaged in "informing . . . the public" of corruption regarding the 1972 presidential election and was seeking materials "vital" to the performance of that function.

The opinion of the Court of Appeals—which did not comment on these affirmations of the informing function by the Supreme Court and the Senate—indicates that this court, an important forum in the regulation of intragovernmental relationships, would be hesitant in the future to adjudge that Congress's oversight and informing responsibilities supply the strong showing of congressional need required to bring a President's assertion of privilege into challenge. Its predilection might be to find that these functions could be "responsibly" met by the discovery and revelation of other evidence without violating presidential confidentiality.

Congress's need for information to meet its lawmaking responsibility is less controversial, but the Court of

Appeals' discourse on that function also raises the question whether lawmaking needs could ever comprise the "strong showing" of necessity which allows a test of the President's privilege. The court observed that, generally speaking, the lawmaking process does not require "precise reconstruction of past events" but depends rather "on the predicted consequences of proposed legislative actions and their political acceptibility," a view similar to that expressed by Justices Warren and Douglas in their dissent in the *Hutcheson* case where they suggested that "Congress [does not] nee[d] the details [of] alleged crime in order to pass general legislation . . ."* Were this view rigidly adhered to, it would be extraordinarily difficult in most situations to demonstrate that Congress cannot fulfill its lawmaking missions "responsibly" without invading the sanctity of presidential conversations

On the other hand, Congress, in its impeachment role, could more easily make a strong showing of need for presidential communications involving the crimes of executive officials. In that capacity, Congress must render judgments of a judicial nature respecting executive lawbreaking, a function it cannot "responsibly" fulfill without all relevant evidence. In this role, Congress's need can be equated with that of the courts in criminal proceedings.

But the impeachment context is the exception, and in the more normal situation there are yet other factors that militate against giving Congress ready access to presidential conversations. The Supreme Court commented that making presidential conversations available to the criminal process would not move the President's advisers "to temper the candor of their remarks" for fear that their statements would be publicized because the chance that the criminal process would reveal such statements was exceedingly remote. But if advisers were fearful that Congress—which has interests ranging far beyond criminal concerns—could

---

* See 369 U.S. at 636 and Chapter IV.

readily intrude on presidential confidentiality, frank advice and opinion might vanish. Also the danger exists that confidential materials may be leaked by congressmen or staff—a consideration, it is reasonable to speculate, which the Court of Appeals had in mind when it formulated its stringent standard protecting presidential confidentiality.

In response to this last consideration it may be observed that executive officials leak too, often with a passion that rivals or exceeds that exhibited on Capitol Hill. Thus a claim by executive officials that information must be withheld because Congress cannot be trusted rings hollow. Furthermore, a great many congressmen exercise their functions responsibly, fully protecting the sensitive information they frequently receive, and the possibility of abuse should not generally deny the legislature the opportunity to fulfill its constitutional functions.

These functions, of course, are of the utmost significance to the nation. Because of their crucial import, the Supreme Court has said that Congress—as well as the courts—has the right to every man's evidence and that all witnesses have an "unremitting obligation" to respond to Congressional subpoenas.* Judge George MacKinnon has written that a congressional subpoena carries "at least as much weight" and serves interests as "vital" as a judicial subpoena.† In the same vein, the District of Columbia Court of Appeals has said, "A legislative inquiry may be as broad, as searching and as exhaustive as is necessary to make effective the constitutional powers of Congress."‡ Should the President, therefore, have greater power to resist congressional subpoenas than those issued by courts to further

---

* *United States* v. *Bryan*, 339 U.S. 323, 331 (1950); *Watkins* v. *United States*, 354 U.S. 178, 187–88 (1957).

† See *Nixon* v. *Sirica*, 487 F. 2d 700, 737 (D.C. Cir. 1973) (MacKinnon, J., dissenting). Judge MacKinnon, who voted against the committee in its suit, did not view his position there as opposed to his statements in *Nixon* v. *Sirica*. See 498 F. 2d at 734.

‡ *Townsend* v. *United States*, 95 F. 2d 352, 361 (D.C. Cir. 1938), *cert. denied* 303 U.S. 664 (1938).

the administration of criminal justice?* Justice Robert Jackson's comment in another context is pertinent here: "When the President takes measures incompatible with the expressed or implied will of Congress, his power is at its lowest ebb. . . ."† Congress's responsibilities and its corollary need for executive branch information should be kept in mind as we consider further questions left unanswered by the opinion in the Ervin committee suit.

———————

The Court of Appeals decision concerned only one brand of executive privilege—that resting on the public interest in preserving the confidentiality of presidential conversations. It did not deal with assertions of privilege to protect military secrets, materials relating to foreign relations, communications among heads of departments and other high government officials, investigative files, or the myriad other records generated and maintained by the executive branch. What are the rules governing congressional requests for such information? Are they also presumptively privileged against a request by Congress?

To some degree no firm answers follow these questions. As a general rule, when a President claims privilege the assertion will be given considerable judicial deference. But to say this does not answer the question "How much deference?" or supply any solid assessment of what showing in various circumstances Congress must make to overcome the

———

* In considering Congress's right to presidential materials it is significant that in several recent civil cases lower courts, employing balancing tests somewhat similar to those used by the Supreme Court in Jaworski's case, have overruled former President Nixon's claims of executive privilege and required that he submit to deposition and that the government produce evidence. E.g., *Sun Oil Co. v. United States*, 514 F. 2d 1020 (CT. Cl. 1975); *Halperin* v. *Kissinger*, Civ. No. 1187–73 (D.D.C. Sept. 24, 1975). These decisions did *not* rest on the still disputed proposition that a former President can no longer invoke executive privilege.

† *Youngstown Sheet & Tube Co.* v. *Sawyer*, 343 U.S. 579, 637 (1952) (Jackson, J., concurring).

assertion. As in many areas of the law, the specific factual contexts in which the claims of privilege arise will be all-important.

As to military secrets and matters of foreign affairs affecting national security, the Supreme Court has stated that the President's assertion of privilege must be afforded "utmost deference," declaring that regardless of the interests calling for production, the claim must be upheld without in-chambers inspection if the facts indicate that materials relating to these subjects are involved.* But these rulings were not made in the context of demands for evidence by Congress. The issue is different where Congress is involved because Congress has constitutional responsibilities respecting both military matters and foreign relations. Congress, for example, is empowered by Article I of the Constitution to regulate commerce with foreign nations, declare war, and raise and support armies. Article II states that the President can enter into treaties with foreign nations only upon the advice and consent of two-thirds of the Senate. Do not these provisions give Congress some type of presumptive right to executive branch information relating to such matters?

An important consideration here is the proclivity of some government officials to use security classifications to excess, to protect materials whose release would in no way endanger national security. Justice Douglas has commented on this phenomenon: "[A]nyone who has ever been in the Executive Branch knows how convenient the 'Top Secret' or 'Secret' stamp is, how easy it is to use, and how it covers perhaps for decades the footprints of a nervous bureaucrat or a wary executive. . . . '[A]s has been revealed by such exposés as the Pentagon Papers, the My Lai massacres, the Gulf of Tonkin incident, and the Bay of Pigs invasion, the Government usually suppresses damaging news but highlights favorable news. In this filtering

---

* *United States* v. *Nixon*, 418 U.S. 683 (1974); *Reynolds* v. *United States*, 345 U.S. 1 (1952).

process the secrecy stamp is the officials' tool of suppression and it has been used to withhold information which in "99½%" of the cases would present no danger to national security.'"* Clearly, overclassification and subsequent resort to a national security privilege would threaten the right of Congress to critical information relating to its functions.†

In December 1969 Secretary of Defense Melvin Laird, responding to a request by Senator J. William Fulbright, chairman of the Foreign Relations Committee, stated that certain documents—which later became known as the Pentagon Papers—could not be released to the Senate because they contained "an accumulation of data of the most delicate sensitivity, including national security papers and other presidential communications which have always been considered privileged." Laird's position prompted a telling retort by Fulbright: "If the Senate is to carry out effectively its Constitutional responsibilities in the making of foreign policy, the Committee on Foreign Relations must be allowed greater access to background information which is available only within the Executive Branch than has been the case over the last few years."

To put the problem in another practical context, two select committees on intelligence operations—one from each house—are at this writing investigating the Central Intelligence Agency and other federal intelligence organizations. The purpose of the investigations is not only to ascertain whether the CIA has violated its current charter, but also to determine if further statutory regulation of the agency is warranted. These investigations undoubtedly

---

* *EPA* v. *Mink*, 410 U.S. 73, 108–9 (1973) (Douglas, J., dissenting).

† An exception to the federal statute making criminal the unauthorized release of certain classified information provides that the statute does not prohibit supplying such information, upon lawful demand, to duly constituted congressional committees. See 18 U.S.C. 798 (c) (1970). The congressional committees investigating intelligence activities engaged in a dispute with the Ford administration which raised the unresolved issue of a committee's right to declassify and release classified information.

touch on matters of extreme sensitivity regarding foreign relations and military affairs. But Congress needs intimate knowledge of the operations of that Byzantine organization to decide what additional legislative strictures are necessary. Congress also requires specific information regarding CIA activities to fix the amount of appropriations the agency will receive. Does the President, in these circumstances, have a presumptive right to seal CIA files to Congress?

The intelligence investigations also raise the issue of Congress's access to investigatory files. It appears necessary, for example, to examine records maintained by the FBI on congressmen to determine if the FBI exceeded the bounds of proper conduct. Nothing will encourage abuses of investigatory power more than freedom from scrutiny. But if the President asserts privilege, are these files presumptively privileged?

As a general rule, the privilege attaching to investigative files against demands by private parties must give way when the fair administration of justice requires production. There appear to be no cases, however, where the government has been *actually compelled* to produce such evidence.* If the government is a party to the litigation— the situation in which most evidentiary demands have arisen—it can continue to resist court-ordered disclosure by dropping its prosecution or conceding the matter at issue. Still, it must be asked whether a rule more stringent than applied to nongovernmental requests—one that includes a presumption of privilege—should pertain where Congress is the supplicant. A simple balancing of the needs of Congress and the executive—unaffected by the application of any presumption—seems the appropriate test. It is interesting, perhaps ironic, that Attorney General Kleindienst, who so strongly advocated the Nixon absolutist theory of executive privilege, allowed the Ervin

* Raoul Berger, *Executive Privilege: A Constitutional Myth*, (Harvard University Press, 1974), p. 209.

committee access to certain FBI files concerning the department's Watergate inquiries.

Other questions concern the protection of nonpresidential communications among government officials. The Supreme Court's opinion in Jaworski's case recognized "the valid need for protection of communications between high government officials and those who advise and assist them in the performance of their manifold duties," and other decisions contain similar statements.* If the President asserts executive privilege to protect the communications of Cabinet officials or his chief White House advisers, would such communications be presumptively privileged? Can such officials and advisers assert the privilege on their own? If they can, are their communications protected by a presumption of privilege?

The position that only the President may claim executive privilege was at least formally adopted by Presidents Kennedy and Johnson. Further, Judge Gesell ruled in the Ervin committee suit that a statement asserting privilege for presidential conversations "must be signed by the President for only he can invoke the privilege at issue."† Other—and higher—courts, however, in respect to privilege claims concerning military secrets and communications of government officials besides the President, have indicated that privilege may be asserted by the head of the department or agency involved,‡ and historically claims of privilege even with respect to presidential communications

---

* E.g., *EPA* v. *Mink*, 410 U.S. 73, 87 (1973); *New York Times Co.* v. *United States*, 403 U.S. 713, 727–28 (1971) (Stewart, J., concurring); *Committee for Nuclear Responsibility* v. *Seaborg*, 463 F. 2d 788, 792 (D.C. Cir. 1971); *Carl Zeiss Stiftung* v. *V.E.B. Carl Zeiss, Jena*, 40 F.R.D. 318, 324–25 (D.D.C. 1966) *affirmed* 384 F. 2d 979 (D.C. Cir. 1967) *cert. Denied* 389 U.S. 952 (1967).

† See also *Center on Corporate Responsibility* v. *Schultz*, 368 F. Supp. 863 (D.D.C. 1973).

‡ E.g., *United States* v. *Reynolds*, 345 U.S. 1 (1953); *Committee for Nuclear Responsibility* v. *Seaborg*, 463 F. 2d 788 (D.C. Cir. 1971); *Carl Zeiss Stiftung* v. *V.E.B. Carl Zeiss, Jena*, 40 F.R.D. 318 (D.D.C. 1966), *affirmed* 384 F. 2d 979 (D.C. Cir. 1967), *cert. denied* 389 U.S. 952 (1967).

have been put forth by lesser officials, e.g., the Laird refusal to supply the Pentagon Papers to the Senate Foreign Relations Committee. While instances of nonpresidential refusals to supply information to Congress were greater in the Nixon administration, they occurred even during the terms of Kennedy and Johnson.*

The private litigant decisions on nonpresidential communications involving matters other than national security secrets indicate that the needs of the government must be balanced against the requirements of the litigant without the intrusion of a presumption to tilt the scales. Thus the District of Columbia Court of Appeals has stated, "When such demand is made in conjunction with discovery sought in the courts, the settled rule is that the court must balance the moving party's need for the documents in the litigation against the reasons which are asserted in defending their confidentiality."† It appears unreasonable to apply a stricter test where the President officially (rather than privately) gives his blessing to a claim of privilege, or where Congress, not a private party, makes the request for information.

Another issue is whether the privilege can be claimed only concerning policy-making communications or whether it has a broader scope. Decisions under the Freedom of Information Act limit its exception to production for "inter-agency or intra-agency memorandums or letters" to records "reflecting deliberative or policy making processes"; materials containing "purely factual, investigative matters" are not exempt.‡ These holdings suggest that purely factual, nonclassified information held by government employees is not privileged. However, during the

---

* See United States Senate, *Hearings before the Subcommittee on Intergovernmental Relations, et al.*, "Executive Privilege, Secrecy in Government, Freedom of Information," 93d Cong, 1st Sess. (1973), Vol. III, Appendix, pp. 222–26.

† *Committee for Nuclear Responsibility* v. *Seaborg*, 463 F. F. 2d 788, 791 (D.C. Cir. 1971).

‡ E.g., *EPA* v. *Mink*, 410 U.S. 73, 89 (1973).

Ervin committee's investigation, members of the Secret Service, asserting executive privilege, declined to testify regarding the operation of Nixon's taping system. This refusal was not tested in court.

There must come a point where a President's claim of privilege over executive branch materials would be, in Ronald Ziegler's famous phrase, "inoperative." Certain statutes give the Congress rights to specific types of executive information. Should the President's claim of privilege be allowed to negate demands under these statutes unless it is compellingly shown that application of a statute would clearly impinge upon his constitutional prerogatives? Moreover, the Freedom of Information Act makes huge amounts of executive information available to ordinary citizens. Amendments to the act passed in 1974 over President Ford's veto facilitate citizen access to executive materials, including information from the executive office of the President. To be sure, there are restrictions in the act regarding the production of certain types of records. To give a partial list, a citizen cannot secure (1) certain classified records concerning national defense or foreign policy, (2) materials exempted from disclosure by statute, (3) records containing confidential trade secrets and commercial or financial information, (4) inter- and intra-agency memoranda reflecting deliberative or policy-making processes, (5) personnel and medical files and other records whose production would constitute an unwarranted invasion of privacy and (6) certain investigative files compiled for law enforcement purposes. These exemptions are exclusive and, the courts have said, must be narrowly construed; the burden is on the government to prove that the exemptions are applicable.* Thus, taken as a whole, the statute is a forceful declaration of the rights of citizens to executive information which is totally contrary to sweeping claims of executive privilege.

* See, e.g., *EPA* v. *Mink*, 410 U.S. 73 (1973); *Soucie* v. *David*, 448 F. 2d 1067 (D.D. Cir. 1971).

The Freedom of Information Act concludes with the admonition that "this section [shall not] be authority to withhold information from Congress," thereby tacitly recognizing that Congress has more rights to executive branch materials than ordinary citizens. The Court of Appeals for the District of Columbia has noted this, commenting that the "right [of] a Congressman [to executive information] is presumably greater" than that of an average citizen.* But the precise nature of congressional rights is yet to be authoritatively determined.

More definitive rulings regarding executive privilege issues may soon be forthcoming. Wending their way through the courts at this writing are complicated litigations which concern Nixon's ownership of the tapes and records accumulated during his term in the White House, his right to assert executive privilege after he has left office, and the validity of the "Presidential Recordings and Materials Preservation Act." This act, which Nixon has vigorously challenged, gives control of his tapes and records to the General Services Administration and regulates access to this material by the special prosecutor, other litigants, executive agencies and departments, and the general public. The determination whether Congress has power to pass this statute may shed further light on Congress's right to presidential and other executive branch information.

This conglomeration of uncertainties presents the further question how best to resolve disputes between the Congress and the executive over access to executive branch information. That the result of the Ervin committee's resort to the courts was less than auspicious suggests that there may be better ways—at least from Congress's standpoint—to deal with such conflicts. Traditionally other methods have predominated; the Ervin committee suit was

* *Soucie* v. *David*, 448 F. 2d 1067, 1070 n. 6 (D.C. Cir. 1971).

the first civil action to enforce a congressional subpoena issued to the executive.*

Congress and its committees have a variety of tactics at their command to force production of executive evidence. An administration bill may be shelved in committee until information is forthcoming or defeated on the floor. Appropriations sought by a President may be denied or reduced. An ambassadorial or Cabinet appointment may be rejected. Additional investigations of the executive branch may be initiated. Prominent Congressmen may use their national forums to castigate a President for guile, lack of cooperation, or worse.

Such approaches may work. If, for example, the President declines to provide information relevant to legislation he seeks, refusal by Congress to pass it may be sufficient impetus to force production. Similarly, a President may not secure congressional confirmation of a Cabinet appointment until information relating to his or her past performance in government is revealed.

But such approaches may prove rough-hewn remedies unsuitable to the task. When executive refusal, as in Nixon's case, does not involve specific legislation, it may not be appropriate to employ a wholesale attack on administration legislative proposals as a lever to pry loose facts. Likewise it may not be propitious to cut off an appropriation to gain information not related to it. Demonstrations of strength of this order often do little to promote workable government and may backfire on Congress by creating a negative public image.

An intransigent President is always subject to impeachment for failure to produce materials, but as the disquieting, enervating struggle to oust Nixon showed, this is a remedy not lightly pursued, one that is hardly practi-

---

* The Ervin committee's subpoena to the President was also the first congressional subpoena issued to a sitting President. The House Judiciary Committee later followed suit. There are a number of examples of congressional subpoenas issued to lesser executive officials, some predating the Watergate investigation.

cal to resolve normal disputes between legislature and executive. Judge Sirica recognized this in the Cox-Nixon struggle for the tapes. "[I]mpeachment," he said, "is not a reasonable solution" to executive obduracy and "is not so designed that it can function as a deterrent in any but the most excessive cases."*

The realization that trials of strength between the two branches may be destructive suggests that a judicial solution, in some circumstances, may be the preferable mode of resolution. The question then becomes, "How is the issue raised in court?" As described previously,† the courts have traditionally tested Congress's subpoena powers and right to information in several ways. They have ruled on habeas corpus petitions or damage actions by those detained by a sergeant at arms for failure to testify or produce records. And they have determined the propriety of demands for evidence in the context of criminal contempt proceedings brought against those who defied congressional orders. But congressional action putting in motion either of these processes may be undesirable. It would be unseemly—and probably futile—to send a sergeant at arms to arrest the President or to instigate criminal contempt proceedings against him, as the Ervin committee realized when it deliberated the proper course to combat Nixon's defiance of its subpoenas. Similarly, using a sergeant at arms or initiating criminal contempt actions against other high executive officials—or even lower-echelon employees who are only following orders— may be inappropriate. Moreover, in a criminal or habeas corpus case—where the liberty of an individual is at stake —the courts tend to construe the powers of Congress strictly. Even if a court ruling eventually favors the congressional claim, the final holding, which may come long after the issue was at a head, may not actually produce the materials sought.

* *In re Subpoena to Nixon,* 360 F. Supp. 1, 5 n. 9 (D.D.C. 1973).
† See Chapter III.

These considerations bring us back to the proposition that a congressionally instigated civil action—with its opportunity for full exploration of constitutional issues and its flexibility for fashioning a just relief—may be the most efficacious method to resolve serious disputes between Congress and the executive branch. This may be the case even though language in the Ervin committee tapes decision suggests that Congress's chances of success in a court battle with the President are less than sanguine. (On the other hand, the precedental value of that case is limited; it involved only presidential communications and the determinative facts—that the evidence at issue had been released in full to another congressional committee and in part to the general public—are so rarefied that anything resembling them will unlikely reappear.)

In deciding how to resolve legislative-executive disputes attention should be given to the Supreme Court's repeated proclamation that "it is the responsibility of [the judiciary] to act as the ultimate interpreter of the Constitution."* A clash between Congress and the executive over information is a constitutional confrontation of the highest magnitude, one that the courts in a civil action may be best suited to handle. As Justice Robert Jackson once said, "Some arbiter is almost indispensable when power . . . is . . . balanced between different branches, as the legislature and the executive. . . . Each unit cannot be left to judge the limits of its own power."†

There is, however, a troublesome hurdle that must be overcome before a federal court can rule on the merits of a congressional request for evidence.

A federal court cannot hear a case unless it determines that some specific provision of the federal code gives it authority or "jurisdiction" to do so. If no such provision

* See, e.g., *Powell* v. *McCormack,* 395 U.S. 486, 549 (1969); *Marbury* v. *Madison,* 1 Cranch (5 U.S.) 137, 177 (1805).

† Jackson, *The Struggle for Judicial Supremacy* (Knopf, 1941), p. 9.

appears, the case must be dismissed. Because of the implications for future judicial resolutions of executive-legislative conflicts, the Ervin committee's efforts to satisfy jurisdictional requirements in the tapes suit warrant a brief review.

The federal code contains a wide variety of jurisdictional provisions covering different types of federally oriented cases. The Ervin committee considered two most applicable to its suit. One provision states in part, "Except as otherwise provided by Act of Congress, the district courts shall have original jurisdiction of all civil actions, suits or proceedings commenced by the United States."* Relying on this statute, the committee brought suit against Nixon in the name of the United States. The committee also acted pursuant to a 1928 Senate resolution delegating it authority to sue in the name of the United States.† This resolution was passed after a 1928 Supreme Court decision dismissed an action, brought by a Senate committee under the predecessor statute to the act invoked by the Ervin committee, on the grounds that the Senate had not delegated power to sue to the committee.‡ The resolution was intended to dovetail with the earlier statute, which also provided jurisdiction for suits brought by the United States.

In the 1950's the statute was successfully relied on by the Senate Banking and Currency Committee before an Illinois District Court, although apparently no ruling on the statute's applicability was obtained. The committee's litigation involved a petition for an order—a *writ of habeas corpus ad testificandum*—allowing a federal prisoner to leave jail to testify before the committee.§ At the Ervin

---

* 28 U.S.C. 1345.

† See Chapter III.

‡ *Reed* v. *County Commissioners*, 277 U.S. 376 (1928).

§ See the discussion in *In re Hearings by the Committee on Banking and Currency*, 245 F. 2d 667 (7th Cir. 1957) (appeal dismissed for mootness and other reasons); see also 19 F.R.D. 410 (N.D. Ill. 1956). Papers filed by this committee establish that it proceeded under 28 U.S.C. 1345.

committee's behest, Judge Sirica issued several such writs prior to his jurisdictional ruling in the tapes suit which allowed federal prisoners such as Howard Hunt and Bernard Barker to testify. At no time had he questioned the committee's jurisdictional right to apply for these writs.

Judge Sirica, however, declared the statute inapposite in the tapes suit.* He found determinative another federal statute which states, "Except as otherwise authorized by law, the conduct of litigation in which the United States, an agency, or officer thereof is a party, or is interested . . . is reserved to officers of the Department of Justice, under the direction of the Attorney General."† The statute, Judge Sirica said, "reserves to the Attorney General and the Department of Justice authority to litigate as United States. . . . While this section does not require a congressional litigant to be represented by the Justice Department, it does deny such a litigant the right to sue as the United States when jurisdiction derives from [this statute]."

Sirica's opinion clearly runs counter to the district court result in the Banking and Currency Committee matter (where the committee used its own attorney) and the intention of the Senate memorialized in its 1928 resolution. And his holding ignores the Ervin committee's observation that the conduct-of-litigation provision is a housekeeping statute designed to resolve conflicts between executive departments and to regulate the relationships between the Attorney General and the various United States Attorneys, and was not intended and had never been applied to deal with representation of the legislative branch or its right to be in court.‡

---

* *Senate Select Committee on Presidential Campaign Activities* v. *Nixon*, 366 F. Supp. 51, 56–7 (D.D.C. 1973).

† 28 U.S.C. 516 (1970); see also 28 U.S.C. 519 (1970).

‡ Congressional litigants frequently employ attorneys of their own choosing. See e.g., *Gravel* v. *United States*, 408 U.S. 606 (1972) (Senate appeared as a friend of the court and was represented by Senators

Sirica's ruling on another jurisdictional provision proffered by the Ervin committee is even more susceptible to criticism. The code provides, "The district courts shall have original jurisdiction of all civil actions wherein the matter in controversy exceeds the sum or value of $10,000 . . . and arises under the Constitution, laws or treaties of the United States."* Mr. Nixon did not dispute that the "matter in controversy"—the President's executive privilege rights against the Congress—arose "under the Constitution." The contested issue was whether this "matter" exceeded "the sum or value of $10,000." The Supreme Court has said that a plaintiff's allegations respecting jurisdictional amount must be accepted unless it appears "to a legal certainty that the claim is less than [the] jurisdictional amount."†

The Ervin committee made several arguments why the case was worth $10,000, two of which are important here. The committee contended that its "constitutional rights and duties to investigate criminality and corruption in high administrative places and to propose legislation to prevent future rot in the presidential elective process" clearly had a value more than $10,000 and, perforce, jurisdiction existed. The committee also argued that the amount was present because the case was worth more than $10,000 to Nixon. As authority for the proposition that the value of the litigation to Nixon was relevant, the committee cited a distinguished work by the President's coun-

---

Ervin, Saxbe, and others); *Williams* v. *Phillips*, 360 F. Supp. 1363 (D.D.C. 1973), *motion for stay denied*, 482 F. 2d 669 (D.C. Cir. 1973) (suit brought by four senators); *Kennedy* v. *Sampson*, 364 F. Supp. 1075 (D.D.C. 1973), *affirmed* 511 F. 2d 1075 (D.C. Cir. 1974) (Senator Kennedy appeared as his own lawyer in this case; the United States Attorney for the District of Columbia represented the executive branch defendants.) In none of these cases, however, was jurisdiction premised on 28 U.S.C. 1345. The 1928 Senate resolution authorizing suit in the name of the United States allows a committee to use attorneys of its own selection.

   * 28 U.S.C. 1331(a) (1970).
   † *St. Paul Mercury Indemnity Co.* v. *Red Cab Co.*, 303 U.S. 283, 288–89 (1938).

sel, Professor Wright, which declared that the "desirable rule" allows consideration of the suit's value to the defendant in the jurisdictional determination because "the purpose of a jurisdictional amount, to keep trivial cases away from the court, is satisfied where the case is worth a large sum to either party."*

In making this latter argument the committee's tone was restrained. It said in part:

> We trust, moreover, that it is not untoward to suggest that the outcome of this litigation means [much] to the defendant President . . . If the accuracy of John Dean's account is substantiated in all particulars, the continuance of his Presidency may be in jeopardy and he may be subjected to criminal penalties. In these circumstances the outcome of this case is clearly worth more than $10,000 to defendant President.

The President's reply bristled with indignation. "The suggestion," his lawyers told Sirica, "that the tapes have a monetary value to the President in excess of $10,000 does not need to be dignified with a response."

Sirica was not moved by either committee argument concerning the $10,000 amount. He rejected the contention that constitutional rights, including the rights of legislators, are susceptible of valuation for jurisdictional amount purposes. "While some decisions have held to the contrary . . . it is the near-universal view that a right or matter in controversy must be capable of valuation in dollars and cents to sustain jurisdiction under [the statute]. . . . The restriction to a dollars and cents evaluation of the matter in controversy . . . logically precludes an assumption that the value of [legislative rights] can satisfy [the statute]. The value of the right or duty must be quantifiable. There must be some financial gain or loss associated directly with sustaining, rejecting or declaring the right. . . . Any direct

* Wright, *Handbook of the Law of Federal Courts*, 2d ed. (West Publishing Co., 1970), pp. 118–19.

financial consequence to rights or duties is not apparent in this case."

Sirica added: "As plaintiffs note, a court in this district has apparently ruled that the inherent value of a constitutional right to vote 'must be equal to any amount set for jurisdictional purposes'* . . . This Court, however, cannot justify a conclusion that [this case] represents the law in this or any Circuit with the possible exception of the Third,† and accordingly, with due respect, cannot regard that precedent. . . . Such value . . . is simply not the type intended to satisfy the monetary restrictions of [the statute]."

Sirica's opinion, however, failed to come to grips with a decision by the Court of Appeals for the District of Columbia Circuit, decided less than two months before he ruled, *which the committee had cited to him on the jurisdictional amount question and which he referred to in his decision.*‡ In that case—which involved an attempt to block a Senate subpoena because it impinged on First Amendment freedoms—the court ruled that constitutional rights could be valued to meet jurisdictional strictures declaring, "the fact that plaintiffs claim that their First Amendment rights were violated in an amount exceeding $10,000 brings this dispute within the purview of [the statute]." The Court of Appeals ruling was thus similar to that of a New York district court which had said: "[The] better and modern view in cases when the complaint alleges abridgment of constitutional rights by federal officials is to give jurisdictional allegations . . . a broad and liberal interpretation . . . Certainly [such

---

* *West End Neighborhood Corp.* v. *Stans*, 312 F. Supp. 1066, 1068 (D.D.C. 1970).

† See *Spock* v. *David*, 469 F. 2d 1047, 1052 3d Cir. 1972) *cert. granted* 95 S. Ct. 1556 (1975).

‡ *United States Servicemen's Fund* v. *Eastland*, 488 F. 2d 1252, 1261 (D.C. Cir. 1973). This case was reversed by the Supreme Court in *Eastland* v. *United States*, 421 U.S. 491 (1975) on the ground that suit was prohibited by the speech or debate clause. (See Chapter X). The Court did not rule on the jurisdictional issue.

rights] may be difficult of evaluation, but 'priceless' does not necessarily mean 'worthless.' "* The Supreme Court has not yet definitively passed on this issue, but in his circuit, Sirica's general premise regarding the impermissibility of valuing constitutional rights is erroneous.†

Sirica also ruled that jurisdiction could not be predicated on the value of the suit to Nixon. "[R]egarding value from defendant's viewpoint, the Court cannot find any basis on which to assign a dollar value to the matter in controversy. Just as the constitutional obligations of legislators, defendant's interest, whatever it may be termed, is incapable of such an appraisal." From the perspective of subsequent events—including Nixon's fall from power because of revelation of tapes covered by the subpoenas involved in this suit—this statement seems singularly myopic.

It is perhaps impolitic to be too critical of Sirica at this stage of history, for the nation is in his debt. His gutsy, dogged probings into the inconsistencies and gaps in the original Watergate story were the catalyst for the more penetrating examinations that followed. He was the first judge to defy the White House and rule that the courts had the last word on Nixon's claims of privilege. Justifiably he has shed his former reputation as "Maximum John"—a sobriquet earned by his stiff sentences—and is now proclaimed an exemplar of judicial probity, an image that in part earned him recognition as *Time* magazine's 1973 Man of the Year.

Nonetheless, it is important to demarcate clearly where Sirica erred in the Ervin committee suit, for his ruling may be significant as precedent when the legislature next takes the executive to court over executive branch information. If, as suggested, resort to the courts may be the

* *Fifth Ave. Peace Parade Committee* v. *Hoover,* 327 F. Supp. 238, 241–42 (S.D.N.Y. 1971).

† For another case in Sirica's circuit allowing valuation of constitutional rights for jurisdictional amount purposes, see *Gomez* v. *Wilson,* 477 F. 2d 411, 419–21 (D.C. Cir. 1973).

best method to resolve serious disputes over evidence between Congress and the executive, stumbling blocks to meaningful litigation based on fallacious perceptions of law should be exposed and removed.

Fortunately, Sirica's jurisdictional ruling did no lasting harm in the Watergate context. Much of the central material at issue was later made available to Congress and the public. The President's perfidy was exposed and he was forced to abdicate. And the committee—through legislation—achieved a favorable jurisdictional ruling from the courts, although the delay occasioned by Sirica's opinion allowed the factual circumstances to change to such degree that an ultimate decision supporting the committee was foreclosed.

The original jurisdictional bill introduced by Senator Ervin would have established permanent federal court jurisdiction for suits to enforce congressional subpoenas issued to executive officials by either house of Congress, any committee or subcommittee of either house, or any joint congressional committee. When Senator Roman Hruska of Nebraska objected that the bill was too broad, Senator Ervin introduced a substitute bill—which eventually became law—limited to suits brought by his committee to enforce its subpoenas.*

---

* The new statute also provided that the committee had "standing" to bring such actions and could prosecute these suits in the name of the United States by attorneys of its choosing, a need palpably evident when Congress litigates against the executive. A person has "standing" to bring an action if he has a "personal stake" in the controversy at issue, e.g., *Sierra Club* v. *Morton*, 405 U.S. 727, 732 (1972). While the President had perfunctorily attacked the committee's standing, it was always clear that the committee's "stake" in obtaining needed evidence and in reaffirming its subpoena authority conferred standing. Courts had previously held that a legislator's interest in discharging his official duties provided the requisite standing to litigate. *Minnesota State Senate* v. *Beens*, 406 U.S. 187 (1972); *Coleman* v. *Miller*, 307 U.S. 433, 438 (1939). The Ervin statute obviated any further discussion on this issue. The initial statute proposed by Senator Ervin had likewise provided that congressional entities had standing and could litigate with their own attorneys.

The Ervin committee's final report recommended a statute ensuring congressional bodies the right to sue in federal court similar to that first introduced by Senator Ervin. The suggested statute has one new feature—that the courts handle congressional claims with expedition. Enactment of such a law would not remove Congress's other remedies—criminal contempt, self-help, power over legislation and appropriations—but would make certain that Congress, where appropriate, could implore the courts to decide disputes with the executive branch. Congress's right to court review on the merits of its claims should not be left to the vagaries of judicial decision. To foreclose court determinations on claims of privilege could force Congress to employ provocative sanctions which would rend the harmonious interworkings of the legislative and executive branches. The United States Congress should have easy access to the United States courts.*

---

* In fact, a bill similar to that recommended by the committee passed the Senate in 1973. It provided that a committee can sue to enforce its subpoenas only on the approval of its parent house, a provision that could interdict errant committees bent on headline hunting or partisan gain. The House Rules in effect require this now; the Senate Standing Orders do not. See House Rule 2. (m) (2) (B); Senate *Manual*, p. 105.

·VII·
Restrictions on Investigatory Powers

The discussion thus far has focused, in the main, on the powers of Congress to investigate and force production of information. Now it is time to shift emphasis, to concentrate on the rights afforded ordinary citizens by the Constitution, statutes, congressional regulations, and court-made rules to resist unjustified legislative incursions into their private lives, their business affairs, their associations, their thoughts.

Chapter III began with quotations from Justices Warren and Harlan—two jurists at different ends of the jurisprudential spectrum—concerning the exceptionally broad powers of Congress to probe matters of federal interest. Perhaps it sets a proper tone for the commentary that follows to quote again from these Justices as to the limitations of investigatory powers.

First from Chief Justice Warren: "[T]he constitutional

rights of witnesses [must] be respected by the Congress as they are in a court of justice. The Bill of Rights is applicable to investigations as to all forms of governmental action. Witnesses cannot be compelled to give evidence against themselves. They cannot be subjected to unreasonable search and seizure. Nor can the First Amendment freedoms of speech, press, religion, or political belief and association be abridged."*

Now Justice Harlan: "Broad as it is, the power [to investigate] is not . . . without limitations. . . . [T]he Congress, in common with all branches of the Government, must exercise its powers subject to the limitations placed by the Constitution on governmental action, [including] the relevant limitations of the Bill of Rights."†

While the threat to basic liberties today may not be as foreboding as during the loyalty investigations era, the need for vigilance remains, for the *potential* for abuse is greater. This condition exists simply because there are increasingly more investigations conducted by larger staffs at greater expense to taxpayers. The burgeoning of investigatory activity can be chiefly explained by several factors. The first is the great growth of the executive branch and the corresponding expansion of areas of federal interest. This phenomenon means additional oversight responsibilities for Congress. Another factor is the increased availability of subpoena power. All Senate standing committees received subpoena power by the 1946 Legislative Reorganization Act. And since January 1975 all House standing committees have this right by virtue of an amendment to the House Rules. Before that date, various House committees had received subpoena authority by statute or House resolution.‡

The growth of investigations can be demonstrated by cost figures. During 1955–56 both houses of Congress authorized around $10,355,000 for investigative activities.

---

* *Watkins v. United States,* 354 U.S. 178, 188 (1957).
† *Barenblatt v. United States,* 360 U.S. 109, 111–12 (1959).
‡ See Chapter III.

In 1961–62 the approximate total was $15,800,000; in 1967–68, $22,000,000. But in 1973–74 the figure rose to around $64,400,000, a staggering sum, even allowing for rampant inflation. The cost for 1975–76 is expected to be much higher.*

The Ervin committee expended $2,000,000 during its eighteen-month probe. Its staff, at peak, numbered around ninety, and much time on Watergate activities was spent by committee members' personal staff not paid from committee appropriations. The price tag for the House Judiciary Committee's impeachment investigation was around $2,120,000.

When the availability of staff and funds is considered along with Congress's ability to compel production of evidence, punish for contempt, and command national attention for its investigations, the tremendous clout inherent in the investigatory process comes into clearer perspective. Because there is increasing potential for abuse, the necessity of delineating the protections afforded those under scrutiny is likewise increased in importance.

We have already touched on certain restraints limiting Congress's investigations of citizens, most particularly the restrictions imposed by the legislative purpose doctrine.† This doctrine proclaims that Congress cannot probe and expose wholly private affairs that have no relevance to legislative tasks. Congress cannot assume the functions of the executive or the judiciary and prosecute and try individuals for criminal conduct. It cannot, in the guise of investigating, assert operational control over executive agencies and departments. The legislative purpose doctrine should be kept in mind as the other limitations on congressional probes are discussed because judges' views on the legitimacy of legislative purpose are often intimately related to their opinions whether or not fundamental freedoms have been transgressed.

---

* These statistics come from the Congressional Research Service.
† See Chapter IV.

The Fifth Amendment

On its face the Fifth Amendment seems *not* to apply to legislative proceedings. It reads in part, "No person . . . shall be compelled in any criminal case to be a witness against himself . . ." A legislative proceeding is not a "criminal case," and the language of the Amendment thus permits the argument that a witness in a congressional inquiry can be forced to incriminate himself.

Members of Congress have taken this position in the past.* In 1879, during an investigation of the State Department, a House investigating committee ordered George F. Steward, recently consul general in Shanghai, to answer questions and produce records relating to that office. Steward refused, relying on his Fifth Amendment privilege. A majority of the investigating committee ruled the claim inappropriate, but the House Judiciary Committee later unanimously concluded that Steward could assert the privilege, a position subsequently adopted by the full House.

That the matter was the subject of such dispute is curious. In 1857 the Congress had passed statutes compelling witnesses to testify fully before Congress but giving immunity to those who incriminated themselves. Had it not been assumed that the privilege against self-incrimination applied to congressional testimony, the immunity provision would not have been necessary.

Moreover, the Steward case was by no means the first instance where a congressional witness declined to testify on grounds of self-incrimination. In 1834 Nicholas Biddle and other directors of the Bank of the United States refused for this reason to appear before a Housing committee investigating the bank. Three years later, while President Jackson's use of the spoils system was under scrutiny, a House committee called on Jackson and his

* Chapter VII of Telford Taylor's *Grand Inquest* provides an illuminating look at the history of the Fifth Amendment and its use during the McCarthy period.

Cabinet to produce the names of all civil servants appointed without consent of the Senate. Jackson hotly refused, stating, "You request myself and the heads of the Departments to become our own accusers, and to furnish the evidence to convict ourselves . . . If you either will not make specific accusations, or if, when made, you attempt to establish them by making free men their own accusers, you will not expect me to countenance your proceedings."

In 1876 President Grant also invoked the privilege against Congress. Grant—although not blessed with retreats at Camp David, San Clemente, or Key Biscayne—frequently vacationed away from Washington. The Democratically controlled House, scenting political benefit, passed a resolution asking Grant to list all executive acts performed away from the "seat of government." Grant rejected the request. If the information was sought in connection with impeachment, Grant declared, ". . . it is asked in derogation of an inherent natural right, recognized in this country by a constitutional guarantee which protects every citizen, the President as well as the humblest in the land, from being made a witness against himself."

The refusals by Jackson and Grant to produce information on self-incrimination grounds provide an interesting contrast to Nixon's tactics during the Watergate investigations. Claiming total innocence, Nixon asserted executive privilege as justification for holding back tapes and documents. In papers filed by the Ervin committee in its suit against the President, the committee, with tongue in cheek, raised the possibility that invocation of his privilege against self-incrimination might be more fitting than reliance on executive privilege. Not unexpectedly, considering the circumstances, Nixon declined to follow this helpful lead.

Today there is no doubt that the privilege applies to legislative investigations. The Fifth Amendment is read to mean that no one shall be required to incriminate himself *in regard to any actual or potential criminal charge.* It protects not only witnesses in legislative proceedings, but also those in civil and criminal litigation who also are not immediately defendants "in any criminal case."

The federal courts were surprisingly late in declaring that the privilege applied in legislative proceedings: the first federal decision flatly stating this was not handed down until 1950.* Fifth Amendment questions in the congressional context reached the Supreme Court in 1955 in three cases involving refusals to testify before the House Un-American Activities Committee. The issue there was not whether the amendment was apposite to legislative inquiries—that was conceded. Rather, the questions before the Court concerned the language necessary to invoke the privilege, the scope of its protection, and the conditions under which the privilege is considered waived.† The details of these three cases are not important for our purposes, but the principles emerging from them (and other related decisions) are.

No talismanic phrase is required to invoke the privilege. The Supreme Court has said: "It is agreed by all that a claim of privilege does not require any special combination of words. Plainly a witness need not have the skill of a lawyer to invoke the protection of the Self-Incrimination clause. If an objection to a question is made in any language that a committee may reasonably be expected to understand as an attempt to invoke the privilege, it must be respected . . . by the committee. * * * When a witness declines to answer a question because of constitutional objections and the language used is not free from doubt, the way is always open for the committee to inquire into the nature of the claim before making a ruling."‡

---

* *United States* v. *Yukio Abe*, 95 F. Supp. 991 (D. Hawaii 1950).

† See *Quinn* v. *United States*, 349 U.S. 155 (1955); *Emspak* v. *United States*, 349 U.S. 190 (1955); *Bart* v. *United States*, 349 U.S. 219 (1955).

‡ *Quinn* v. *United States*, 349 U.S. 155, 162–64 (1955).

The privilege protects an individual not only against incrimination for federal offenses. The Supreme Court has ruled that a witness cannot be forced in a federal forum to give testimony incriminating under state law. Conversely, a witness in a state proceeding cannot be compelled to incriminate himself under federal law*

The privilege against self-incrimination is a personal one: it protects only the individual making the claim and cannot be asserted to shield others† At times during the loyalty investigations this precept was neglected. Playwright Lillian Hellman, prior to her appearance before HUAC, wrote the committee that, while she was willing to talk about her own opinions and actions, she would not answer questions about the activities of others. "I am not willing, now or in the future," she said, "to bring bad trouble to people who, in my past association with them, were completely innocent of any talk or any action that was disloyal or subversive. . . . I am prepared to waive the privilege against self-incrimination and to tell you anything you wish to know about my views or actions, if your committee will agree to refrain from asking me to name other people. If the committee is unwilling to give me this assurance, I will be forced to plead the privilege of the Fifth Amendment at the hearing." The committee declined to accept her conditions and Miss Hellman asserted her privilege. Miss Hellman, who had been identified to HUAC as a former Communist and publicly accused by the committee of membership in Communist "front" organizations, may have had legitimate grounds to assert the privilege, but if the *sole* legal basis for her claim was protection of others, the assertion was improper.

The rule that the privilege is "personal" has another interesting twist. The privilege protects an individual from disclosing personal records that may tend to incrimi-

---

* *Murphy* v. *Waterfront Commission,* 378 U.S. 52 (1964).
† E.g., *Rogers* v. *United States,* 340 U.S. 367, 371 (1951).

nate him. But "books and records 'kept in a representative rather than in a personal capacity cannot be the subject of the personal privilege against self-incrimination, even though production of the papers might tend to incriminate [their keeper] personally.' "* To illustrate, corporate records must be handed over by their custodian even though they show him guilty of a crime.

How can a committee or court judge whether putative answers would or would not incriminate a witness? If a witness were made to prove that his answers would be incriminating, he would have to surrender the protection the privilege affords. Recognizing this, the Supreme Court, in a 1955 HUAC case, declared that "it need only be evident from the implications of the question, in the setting in which it is asked, that a responsive answer to the question or an explanation why it cannot be answered might be dangerous because injurious disclosure could result."† The Court then cited an oft-quoted statement by Chief Justice John Marshall issued a hundred and fifty years before: "Many links frequently compose that chain of testimony which is necessary to convict any individual of a crime. It appears to the court to be the true sense of the rule that no witness is compellable to furnish any one of them against himself."‡

The Fifth Amendment privilege, like other constitutional privileges, can be waived by declining to assert the privilege and testifying, or by revoking a claim of privilege previously made. But once the privilege is asserted, revocation of the claim must be unequivocal because "waiver of constitutional rights . . . is not lightly to be inferred."§

The waiver doctrine has proven troublesome. Much of the problem stems from nagging uncertainties left by the

* *McPhaul v. United States*, 364 U.S. 372, 380 (1960).

† *Emspak v. United States*, 349 U.S. 190, 198 (1955); see also, *Hoffman v. United States*, 341 U.S. 479 (1951).

‡ *United States v. Burr*, 25 Fed. Cas. 38, at 40, No. 14 692e (1807).

§ *Emspak v. United States*, 349 U.S. 190, 196 (1955).

Supreme Court's 1951 decision in *Rogers* v. *United States*.* Before a grand jury, Jane Rogers, treasurer of the Denver Communist Party, testified freely concerning her Communist connections. But when asked to name the person to whom she had turned over the Denver Party's books, she declined. The Court upheld her contempt conviction, finding that she had waived her privilege by incriminating herself, would not suffer further crimination by revealing the recipient's name, and thus was required to answer the question. "[I]f the witness . . . elects to waive [the] privilege . . . and discloses his criminal connections," the Court stated, "he is not permitted to stop, but must go on and make a full disclosure. * * * [W]hen incriminating facts have been voluntarily revealed, the privilege cannot be invoked to avoid disclosure of the details."

Justice Black, joined by Justices Frankfurter and Douglas, dissented.

> Apparently, the Court's holding is that at some uncertain point in petitioner's testimony, regardless of her intention, admission of associations with the Communist Party automatically effected a "waiver" of her constitutional protection as to all related questions. . . . [T]oday's holding creates this dilemma for witnesses: On the one hand, they risk imprisonment for contempt by asserting the privilege prematurely; on the other, they might lose the privilege if they answer a single question. The Court's view makes the protection depend on timing so refined that lawyers, let alone laymen, will have difficulty in knowing when to claim it.

Despite the *Rogers* decision, the government has generally been unsuccessful in its attempts to rely on the waiver doctrine. The courts, for example, have held that testimony before another tribunal or at another time will

* 340 U.S. 367 (1951).

not effect a waiver. Nonetheless, the waiver doctrine has had its influence. After *Rogers,* some Congressional witnesses have given only their names and other such basic information before refusing to testify on privilege grounds. This practice was followed by several witnesses before the Ervin committee. Blanket refusals to testify of this nature have been upheld by the courts.*

To Senator McCarthy, the waiver doctrine was a potent weapon. He would, for instance, ask a witness whether he had engaged in Communist espionage. If the witness answered, McCarthy then asserted that he had waived his privilege concerning "the field of espionage" and proceeded to inquire into possible Communist associations. A witness who then asserted privilege and declined to respond further was threatened with contempt prosecution. If the witness refused to answer the initial espionage question, McCarthy called him a spy.

Despite McCarthy's tactics, the privilege was well used before his Permanent Investigations Subcommittee. The subcommittee's annual report for 1953 proclaimed that 71 persons invoked the Fifth Amendment in that year alone. Senator John McClellan's select committee on labor and management saw even greater reliance on the privilege; during 1957–59, 343 witnesses declined to testify on this ground.

Numerous persons claimed their privilege before the Ervin committee. Some—including Dean, Magruder, Howard Hunt, and Bernard Barker—later gave evidence to the Committee under grants of immunity. Others remained silent after they claimed privilege. G. Gordon Liddy—his bearing military as if under interrogation by a foreign enemy—refused even to be sworn, although the Committee was prepared to grant him immunity. Joseph Johnson, chairman of the 1972 [Wilbur] Mills for President Committee, and Jack Chestnut, campaign manager

* See generally, Emerson, Haber, and Dorsen, *Political and Civil Rights in the United States* (Little, Brown & Co., 1967), pp. 404–6.

for Senator Hubert Humphrey's 1972 presidential campaign, declined to testify about the illegal infusion into
those campaigns of corporate funds from a milk cooperative. Chestnut was later convicted for similar activity during Senator Humphrey's 1970 senatorial campaign.

The most memorable invocation of the Fifth was
Charles Colson's. In August 1973 Colson was almost beat-
ing down the committee's door to testify. To discredit
John Dean was his special mission. But in September,
after being informed he was a target of the grand jury
examining the Ellsberg break-in, his ardor understandably subsided. Colson clearly did not want to assert his
privilege. Perhaps he recalled the opprobrium that dogged
"Fifth Amendment Communists" during the loyalty investigations. His lawyer tried to persuade the committee not
to question him at all. When it did, Colson, near tears,
claimed privilege. To see this man—who had boasted he
would walk over his grandmother to reelect Mr. Nixon—
on the verge of weeping was sobering, even to the more
cynical among us.

For present purposes, the important factor is not who
asserted privilege before the Ervin committee, but how
they were allowed to do so. It would have been great
theater to parade Liddy and Colson before television
cameras and force them publicly to refuse testimony.
But no legislative purpose would have been served by
such display—the Committee already knew these men
would remain silent and offer no information the public
should hear. Thus they were allowed to claim their rights
privately in executive session.

In addition, the various claims of privilege were
accepted as valid assertions of a constitutional right that
historically has served as a refuge to the innocent as well
as the guilty. No one was vilified—publicly or privately—
as a "Fifth Amendment conspirator." Those claiming
privilege were permitted to do so with as much dignity as
the situation allowed.

The atmosphere was often different during the loyalty

investigations. While witnesses who admitted Communist backgrounds were frequently allowed the privacy of executive session, those taking the Fifth were often hauled forth to do so under public gaze. Senator William Jenner's Internal Security Subcommittee was particularly notorious for calling in open session witnesses who it knew would assert privilege. A throwback to this practice occurred in 1975 during an investigation of nursing home frauds when New York Rabbi Bernard Bergman was repeatedly forced to assert his privilege at a public session of the Subcommittee on Long-Term Care of the Special Senate Committee on Aging.

Senator McCarthy was guilty of worse abuses. When a witness pleaded privilege during McCarthy's investigation of the Army Signal Corps, McCarthy exploded: "Julius Rosenberg was convicted as a spy and executed. From your refusal to answer you apparently engaged in the same type of espionage. Do you feel you should be walking the streets free—or have the same fate as the Rosenbergs?" After Dashiell Hammett, author of *The Maltese Falcon* and *The Thin Man*, declined to say whether he was or had been a Communist, McCarthy exclaimed:

> Well, now, you have told us that you will not tell us whether you are a member of the Communist Party today or not, on the ground that if you told us the answer might incriminate you. That is normally taken by this committee and the country as a whole to mean that you are a member of the Party, because if you were not you would simply say, "No," and it would not incriminate you. You see, the only reason that you have the right to refuse to answer is if you feel a truthful answer would incriminate you. An answer that you were not a Communist, if you were not a Communist, could not incriminate you. Therefore, you should know considerable about the Communist movement, I assume.

It is not surprising that the Ervin committee did not engage in diatribes of this sort nor seek by public display to persecute those asserting privilege. Senator Ervin, long a battler for civil liberties, was a leader in the Senate fight to restrain McCarthy, although Ervin was just a freshman senator at the time. That his own hearings would degenerate into a McCarthy spectacle was inconceivable.

But credit also belongs to Chief Counsel Sam Dash. Dash brought many talents to the committee and made significant contributions to its success. He has an extraordinarily retentive mind, second only to the committee's computer in the ability to recall obscure factual details uncovered by the investigations. This trait—considering the enormous scope of the committee's inquiries—was essential. Another Dash characteristic crucial in a pressure-laden, fast-moving investigation, is the capacity to take and weigh criticism and shift course when convinced he is wrong. As important as these two traits was his sense of fairness; he shared Ervin's view of how the committee's probes should be run. He matched Ervin in this regard as, in less happy circumstances, the dour Roy Cohn was suitably teamed with Senator McCarthy.

The Fourth Amendment

The Fourth Amendment to the Constitution declares in part that "The right of the people to be secure in their persons, houses, papers, and effects, against unreasonable searches and seizures, shall not be violated . . ." The Supreme Court has said that the amendment restricts the investigatory activities of Congress. But what is the scope of the regimen imposed on Congress by its terms?

Plainly, if Senator Ervin and Sam Dash without subpoena had, by pick and crowbar, entered the residence of Bebe Rebozo to obtain papers relating to the $100,000 Hughes contribution to Mr. Nixon, this conduct would have contravened the Fourth Amendment as well as other provisions of law. The Supreme Court intimated as much in the 1967 case of *Dombrowski* v. [James] *Eastland.** There the Court remanded a damage action for trial on the factual issue of whether the counsel to the Senate Internal Security Subcommittee had collaborated in illegal "raids" by Louisiana officials in violation of Fourth Amendment rights.

A more conclusive decision applying the Fourth Amendment had issued earlier from the District of Columbia Circuit Court of Appeals.† In that case, the Senate Special Committee to Investigate Crime in Interstate Commerce obtained numerous papers from a witness regarding his gambling activities. But no subpoena or other lawful order had been issued for these papers, and the question for resolution was whether the witness had voluntarily supplied them to the committee or whether they had been taken under compulsion in violation of Fourth Amendment proscriptions. The court found the witness had not "freely" turned over these materials, but that the committee, by threats of criminal prosecution, had forced him to produce them. Judge (now Chief Judge) David Bazelon declared with literary flourish that "[The witness's] freedom of choice had been dissolved in a brooding omnipresence of compulsion." Congressional committees, he continued, may not "extort assent to invasions of homes and to seizures of private papers. Assent so extorted is no substitute for lawful process." The witness's conviction on gambling charges was reversed because the trial court had refused to suppress this evidence, allowing instead its introduction by the prosecution.‡

---

* 387 U.S. 82 (1967); see also, *Doe* v. *McMillan*, 412 U.S. 306, 327 (1973) (Douglas, J., concurring) and *Gravel* v. *United States*, 408 U.S. 606, 621 (1972).

† *Nelson* v. *United States*, 208 F. 2d 505 (D.C. Cir. 1953), *cert. denied*, 346 U.S. 827 (1953).

‡ A recent Court of Appeals case held that it is unlawful for a committee to base a subpoena on information gained from an illegal search and seizure by state officials, and that, at the contempt trial

But these cases do not deal with a more common and more important issue: What restrictions does the Fourth Amendment place *on the use of subpoena power* by congressional committees to obtain documents and other records? The short answer is that the Fourth Amendment prohibits subpoenas that are "unreasonable." The term "unreasonable," however, is amorphous. Essentially it refers to subpoenas which are not limited in scope, which seek material irrelevant to the investigation, or which would be unduly burdensome to honor, but a better idea of the protection provided is obtained by examining the cases where the reasonableness standard has been applied.

The most prominent decision is *McPhaul* v. *United States,* decided by the Supreme Court in 1960.* Like so many Supreme Court cases involving the rights of individuals vis-à-vis Congress, this case emanated from a HUAC investigation. Arthur McPhaul was convicted of contempt of Congress for not complying with a HUAC subcommittee subpoena. The subcommittee was investigating the Civil Rights Congress, an organization declared subversive by the Attorney General. The subpoena directed to McPhaul, the Civil Rights Congress's executive secretary, was sweeping, calling for "all records, correspondence and memoranda pertaining to the organization of, the affiliation with other organizations and all monies received or expended by the Civil Rights Congress. . . ."

McPhaul's argument that the subpoena was unreasonable under the Fourth Amendment was rejected by the Court.

> [McPhaul] contends that the subpoena was so broad as to constitute an unreasonable search and seizure in violation of the Fourth Amendment of the Con-

---

for failure to comply with the subpoena, the court erred in allowing the subpoena's introduction into evidence. *United States* v. *McSurely,* 473 F. 2d 1178 (D.C. Cir. 1972).

* 364 U.S. 372 (1960).

stitution. "[A]dequacy or excess in the breadth of the subpoena are matters variable in relation to the nature, purposes and scope of the inquiry" . . . The Subcommittee's inquiry here was a relatively broad one—whether "there has been Communist activity in this vital defense area [Detroit], and if so, the nature, extent, character and objects thereof"—and the permissible scope of materials that could reasonably be sought was necessarily equally broad.

It is not reasonable to suppose that the Subcommittee knew precisely what books and records were kept by the Civil Rights Congress, and therefore the subpoena could only "specif[y] . . . with reasonable particularity, the subjects to which the documents . . . relate" . . . The call of the subpoena for "all records, correspondence and memoranda" of the Civil Rights Congress relating to the three specified subjects describes them "with all of the particularity the nature of the inquiry and the [Subcommittee's] situation would permit" . . . "[T]he description contained in the subpoena was sufficient to enable [McPhaul] to know what particular documents were required and to select them accordingly" . . . If [McPhaul] was in doubt as to what records were required by the subpoena, or found it unduly burdensome, or found it to call for records unrelated to the inquiry, he could and should have so advised the Subcommittee, where the defect, if any, "could easily have been remedied."*

Congressional committees are clearly given considerable leeway by this case. If the scope of the investigation is broad—and the law relating to legislative purpose

---

* There were four dissents in this case but they were based on other grounds. Note further, *See* v. *City of Seattle*, 387 U.S. 541 (1967); *Oklahoma Press Publishing Co.* v. *Walling*, 327 U.S. 186 (1946); *In re Horowitz*, 482 F. 2d 72 (2d Cir. 1973) (Friendly, J.), *cert. denied* 414 U.S. 867 (1973). See also *Shelton* v. *United States*, 404 F. 2d 1292, 1299–1301 (D.C. Cir. 1968) *cert. denied* 393 U.S. 1024 (1968).

allows wide-spectrum probes—subpoenas issued pursuant to the investigation can be likewise broad. In addition, this case appears to put a burden on a subpoena recipient to approach a committee with objections to its demands and thus aid the committee in structuring a production request that is unchallengeable.

McPhaul, however, should be read in conjunction with a later Supreme Court case dealing mainly with the *First* Amendment where the Court said: "The fact that the general scope of the inquiry is authorized and permissible does not compel the conclusion that the investigatory body is free to inquire into or demand all forms of information. Validation of the broad subject matter under investigation does not necessarily carry with it automatic and wholesale validation of all individual questions, subpoenas, and documentary demands."*

Despite the license given congressional committees under the Fourth Amendment, cases do arise where subpoenas exceed the bounds of reasonableness. Such a situation occurred in 1935, when the Senate Special Committee to Investigate Lobbying Activities issued blanket subpoenas to District of Columbia telegraph companies to obtain all telegraph messages transmitted through their offices for a seven-month period. With the aid of the Federal Communications Commission, the committee was actually able to examine these records. Interestingly, the chairman of the special committee was Senator Hugo Black, who, later—as a Supreme Court Justice—was the staunchest of foes to overreaching congressional committees. Before the District of Columbia Court of Appeals, certain parties who had used telegraph services claimed the searches violated their constitutional rights, including those enshrined in the Fourth Amendment. The Court agreed that, in the language of Justice Holmes, "It is contrary to the first principles of justice to allow a search

* *Gibson* v. *Florida Legislative Investigation Committee*, 372 U.S. 539, 545 (1963).

through all the [companies'] records, relevant or irrelevant, in the hope that something will turn up."* In other words, there must be a reasonable belief that a subpoena calls for information related to the investigation at hand. However, it must be recognized, to use the Supreme Court's recent words, that legitimate investigations may lead "up some 'blind alleys' and into nonproductive enterprises. To be a valid legislative inquiry there need be no predictable end result."†

It appears that an individual faced with a subpoena valid in part but also partially invalid need not comply with any of its demands. "One should not be held in contempt under a subpoena that is part good and part bad. The burden is on the court to see that the subpoena is good in its entirety and it is not upon the person who faces punishment to cull the good from the bad."‡ But the *McPhaul* case mutes this proposition somewhat, indicating that a person served with a faulty subpoena must tell the committee why it is bad and thus provide the chance for rectification.

Fourth Amendment problems appeared in several forms

* *Hearst* v. *Black*, 87 F. 2d 68, 71 (D.C. Cir. 1936) quoting from *Federal Trade Commission* v. *American Tobacco Co.*, 264 U.S. 298, 306 (1924). However, the Court of Appeals declined to enjoin the committee from making further use of the materials under subpoena, declaring that the courts, under separation of powers principles, should not impede prospective legislative conduct even if it would be unconstitutional. This ruling should be compared with the same court's more recent opinion in *Sanders* v. *McClellan*, 463 F. 2d 894 (D.C. Cir. 1972).

† *Eastland* v. *United States Servicemen's Fund*, 421 U.S. 491, 509 (1975).

‡ See *United States* v. *Patterson*, 206 F. 2d 433, 434 (D.C. Cir. 1953) and *United States* v. *McSurely*, 473 F. 2d 1178, 1204 (D.C. Cir. 1972) (Wilkey, J., concurring), quoting from *Bowman Dairy Co.* v. *United States*, 341 U.S. 214, 221 (1951). This rule would apply whether the subpoena exceeded the bounds of reasonableness mandated by the Fourth Amendment, went beyond the authority vested by a committee's enabling resolution, or sought records not pertinent to the question under inquiry. See below this chapter for a discussion of the restraints imposed by an enabling resolution and the requirements of pertinency.

during the Ervin committee's investigation. Bebe Rebozo complained that the committee was engaging in an "exploratory witch hunt" with the intention of examining "every business and financial record concerning [his affairs] since 1969"—conduct, he claimed, that violated the Fourth Amendment. District Judge John Lewis Smith, in the lawsuit brought by Rebozo, declined to find that the committee's subpoenas to Rebozo were unlawful, stating that this issue should be resolved in a contempt proceeding for failure to comply, should one materialize.

In the tapes suit, the President, using language frequently employed with Fourth Amendment claims, contended that the subpoena calling for all records concerning the criminal involvement of twenty-five individuals in connection with the 1972 presidential campaign was "unreasonably broad and oppressive" and "would require a complete review of virtually all records in the White House." The committee—with humor that escaped the President's lawyers—responded that this contention was "either very overblown or very disturbing." Judge Gesell eventually ruled that the subpoena "overlooks the restraints of specificity and reasonableness which derive from the Fourth Amendment." In declining to enforce the subpoena, Gesell also concluded that it was "too vague and conclusory to permit a meaningful response" and was "wholly inappropriate given the stringent requirements applicable where a claim of executive privilege has been raised." As authority for his Fourth Amendment ruling, the judge cited the *McPhaul* case.

While Gesell's refusal to enforce the subpoena may have been justified—the committee did not appeal it—his view of the Fourth Amendment deserves some comment. First, it is arguable that the Ervin committee's subpoena was no less specific and reasonable than that approved in *McPhaul*. But there is a more interesting issue. The subpoena was directed to "President Richard M. Nixon" and called for production of records held in his official capacity. And, in the suit that followed, the President claimed that White

House tapes and documents were official records. Although the Fourth Amendment, unlike the Fifth, guards against unreasonable searches of corporate materials, its protection does not shelter official governmental records. The Supreme Court, regarding Fourth and Fifth Amendment assertions, has said that "in the case of public records and official documents, made or kept in the administration of public office, the fact of actual possession or of lawful custody would not justify the officer in resisting inspection, even though the record was made by himself and would supply evidence of his criminal dereliction."* While Nixon as a private citizen had a Fourth Amendment right to protect his privacy, he could not properly invoke that amendment to resist investigation of official records by governmental entities, including congressional committees.†

The First Amendment

No significant First Amendment issues presented themselves during the Ervin committee investigation. Chester Davis urged that requiring Hughes employees to testify in private session violated their rights of free speech, but this argument was not supported by a shred of logic or authority.

During the loyalty investigations, however, serious First Amendment contentions were advanced. The basic claims there were that the investigations were unlawfully forcing witnesses to reveal their beliefs and associations. Reliance on the First Amendment was in part prompted by the vilification that followed a Fifth Amendment claim. Better to resist testifying on another ground and avoid being labeled a Fifth Amendment Communist.

* See *Davis v. United States*, 328 U.S. 582, 587–91 (1946).
† Note that Gesell did not flatly rule that the subpoena contravened the Fourth Amendment, instead stating that the subpoena ignored specificity and reasonableness restraints "which derive from" that amendment.

As with the Fifth, a reading of the First Amendment leaves the impression that it does not pertain to congressional investigations. It says in part, "Congress shall make no law . . . abridging the freedom of speech, or of the press . . . or the right of the people peaceably to assemble and to petition the Government for a redress of grievances." To conduct an investigation is not to "make [a] law." Nonetheless, the amendment has been held applicable to congressional investigations. The Supreme Court has declared:

> Clearly, an investigation is subject to the command that the Congress shall make no law abridging freedom of speech or press or assembly. While it is true that there is no statute to be reviewed, and that an investigation is not a law, nevertheless an investigation is part of lawmaking. It is justified solely as an adjunct to the legislative process. The First Amendment may be invoked against infringement of the protected freedoms by law or by lawmaking.*

Having established that the amendment applies to investigations, the question becomes: In what circumstances will it be applied? This issue is hotly disputed and has been the focus of numerous court cases. A review of the majority and dissenting opinions in several of these litigations will best highlight the difficulties encountered in using the First Amendment to regulate investigations.

Lloyd Barenblatt, a teacher of psychology at Vassar College, was summoned in June 1954 to appear before a HUAC subcommittee. (After he was summoned, his contract with Vassar expired and was not renewed.) When asked by the subcommittee about his Communist Party affiliation, Barenblatt declined to testify. He disclaimed reliance on the Fifth Amendment, but asserted he need not answer because the questions infringed rights protected by

---

* *Watkins v. United States*, 354 U.S. 178, 197 (1957).

the First. Barenblatt was convicted of contempt of Congress, and the Supreme Court, by a 5–4 vote, affirmed, Justice Harlan writing the majority opinion.*

Justice Harlan began his decision by reaffirming the applicability of the First Amendment to legislative investigations.

Undeniably, the First Amendment in some circumstances protects an individual from being compelled to disclose his associational relationships. However, the protections of the First Amendment, unlike a proper claim of privilege against self-incrimination under the Fifth Amendment, do not afford a witness the right to resist inquiry in all circumstances. Where First Amendment rights are asserted to bar governmental interrogation resolution of the issue always involves a balancing by the courts of the competing private and public interests at stake in the particular circumstances shown.

"The first question," Justice Harlan continued, "is whether this investigation was related to a valid legislative purpose, for Congress may not constitutionally require an individual to disclose his political relationships or other private affairs except in relation to such a purpose." The Justice then proceeded to find that Congress had a legitimate interest in investigating Communist Party activities which rested "[i]n the last analysis . . . on the right of self-preservation, 'the ultimate value of any society,' " since the Party sought "the ultimate overthrow of the Government of the United States by force and violence."

Barenblatt's interests, Harlan said, did not outweigh those of the government. He rejected Barenblatt's claim that the investigation aimed at what was taught in the classroom rather than at the revolutionary aspects of Communism. He refused to find that the purpose of the investigation was purely Barenblatt's "exposure." He

* *Barenblatt* v. *United States*, 360 U.S. 109 (1959).

observed that the committee had not attempted to pillory Barenblatt, and that his appearance did not result from indiscriminate dragnet procedures. Instead, there was "probable cause"* to believe that Barenblatt had information helpful to the subcommittee. Harlan concluded that "the balance between the individual and the governmental interests here at stake must be struck in favor of the latter, and that therefore the provisions of the First Amendment have not been offended."

Justice Black dissented in an opinion adopted by Justices Warren and Douglas. "The First Amendment," he asserted, "says in no equivocal language that Congress shall pass no law abridging freedom of speech, press, assembly or petition. The activities of this Committee, authorized by Congress, do precisely that through exposure, obloquy and public scorn. . . . I do not agree that laws directly abridging First Amendment freedoms can be justified by a congressional or judicial balancing process."

Even if a balancing process were proper, Black said, it was misapplied. The Court's balancing, he asserted, "completely leaves out the real interest in Barenblatt's silence, the interest of the people as a whole in being able to join organizations, advocate causes and make political 'mistakes' without later being subjected to governmental penalties for having dared to think for themselves. It is this right, the right to err politically, which keeps us strong as a Nation."

And, Black stated, "I cannot agree with the Court's notion that First Amendment freedoms must be abridged in order to 'preserve' our country. . . . The First Amendment means to me . . . that the only constitutional way our

* For a highly skeptical view of the usefulness of the "probable cause" requirement as applied in another First Amendment case, see Justice Black's dissent in *Wilkinson* v. *United States*, 365 U.S. 399, 418–20 (1961). Criticizing the majority's finding that probable cause to investigate defendant was present because one informant had identified him as a Communist, Justice Black dryly observed, "Every member of this Court has, on one occasion or another, been so designated."

Government can preserve itself is to leave the people the fullest possible freedom to praise, criticize or discuss, as they see fit, all governmental policies and to suggest, if they desire, that even its most fundamental postulates are bad and should be changed."

Justice Brennan dissented separately. He declared that "no purpose for the investigation of Barenblatt is revealed by the record except exposure purely for the sake of exposure." "This is not a purpose," Brennan concluded, "to which Barenblatt's rights under the First Amendment can validly be subordinated."

The Supreme Court in 1961, by the same 5–4 vote, reached similar results in two other cases growing out of HUAC investigations.* But in 1963, after Justice Goldberg replaced Justice Frankfurter on the Court, a case involving a probe by a Florida Legislative Investigation Committee produced a different result, again by a 5–4 vote.† This decision left matters even more clouded.

In November 1959, Theodore Gibson, the president of the Miami branch of the NAACP, was called before the Florida committee and asked to bring NAACP membership and contributions records for use in answering questions. Gibson declined to bring these records, but did testify that fourteen persons with Communist affiliations —who were identified to him by name and photograph— were not associated with the NAACP. For refusing to produce the records, Gibson was convicted of contempt of the legislature under Florida law, sentenced to six months in prison and fined $1,200.

The Supreme Court upset the conviction, with Justice Goldberg delivering the opinion for the majority. He

---

* *Wilkinson* v. *United States*, 365 U.S. 399 (1961); *Braden* v. *United States*, 365 U.S. 431 (1961). See also *Uphaus* v. *Wyman*, 360 U.S. 72 (1959); *United States* v. *Josephson*, 165 F. 2d 82 (2d Cir. 1947) *cert. denied* 333 U.S. 838 (1948); *Barsky* v. *United States*, 167 F. 2d 241 (D.C. Cir. 1948) *cert. denied* 334 U.S. 843 (1948).

† *Gibson* v. *Florida Legislative Investigation Committee*, 372 U.S. 539 (1963).

began by stating that "an essential prerequisite to the validity of an investigation which intrudes into the area of constitutionally protected rights of speech, press, association and petition [is] that the State convincingly show a substantial relation [or nexus] between the information sought and a subject of overriding and compelling state interest." In the *Barenblatt* case, where information about a defendant's own membership in the Communist Party was requested, that interest was present because the Communist Party was not a legitimate political party and membership in it was subject to regulation and legislative overview. But here the NAACP was the object of the investigation and no indication existed that its policies were Communist dominated or influenced. Consequently, Justice Goldberg stated, "Compelling such an organization, engaged in the exercise of First and Fourteenth Amendment rights, to disclose its membership presents . . . a question wholly different from compelling the Communist Party to disclose its own membership."*

Justice Goldberg concluded that "the record in this case is insufficient to show a substantial connection between the Miami branch of the NAACP and Communist *activities* which . . . is an essential prerequisite to demonstrating the immediate, substantial, and subordinating state interest necessary to sustain its rights of inquiry into the membership lists of the association. . . . The strong associational interest in maintaining the privacy of membership lists of groups engaged in the constitutionally protected free trade in ideas and beliefs may not be substantially infringed upon such a slender showing as made here by the [Committee]. * * * Of course, a legislative investigation— as any investigation—must proceed 'step by step,'. . . . but step by step or in totality, an adequate foundation for inquiry must be laid before proceeding in such a manner as will substantially intrude upon and severely curtail or

* The principles of the First Amendment, the Court has held, are made applicable to the conduct of state officials by the Fourteenth Amendment.

inhibit constitutionally protected activities or seriously interfere with similarly protected associational rights. . . ."

Justice Harlan's dissent was joined by Clark, Stewart and White. He said: "[U]ntil today, I had never supposed that any of our decisions relating to state or federal power to investigate in the field of Communist subversion could possibly be taken as suggesting any difference in the degree of governmental investigatory interest as between Communist infiltration *of* organizations and Communist activity *by* organizations . . . Considering the number of congressional inquiries that have been conducted in the field of 'Communist infiltration' since the close of World War II, affecting such diverse interests as 'labor, farmer, veteran, professional, youth, and motion picture groups' . . . , it is indeed strange to find the strength of state interest in the same type of investigation now impugned . . . Given the unsoundness of the basic premise underlying the Court's holding as to the absence of 'nexus,' this decision surely falls of its own weight. For unless 'nexus' requires an investigating agency to prove in advance the very things it is trying to find out, I do not understand how it can be said that the information preliminarily developed by the Committe[e] . . . was not sufficient to satisfy, under any reasonable test, the requirement of 'nexus.' "

Justice Harlan also did not perceive a strong interest in freedom of association in this case because Gibson was not asked to turn over the lists to the committee, but only to use them to refresh his recollection. Additionally, he noted, Gibson was willing to testify from his own memory about the associations of the fourteen subversives with the NAACP.

Justice White filed a biting separate opinion in dissent:

Although one of the classic and recurring activities of the Communist Party is the infiltration and subversion of other organizations, . . . the Court holds that even where a legislature has evidence that a legitimate organization is under assault and even though that organization is itself sounding open and public alarm, an investigating committee is nevertheless forbidden to compel the organization or its members to reveal the fact, or not, of membership in that organization of named Communists assigned to the infiltrating task. . . . As I read the Court's opinion the exposed Communist might well, in the name of associational freedom of the legitimate organization and of its members including himself, successfully shield his activities from legislative inquiry. . . . The net effect of the Court's decision is . . . to insulate from effective legislative inquiry and preventive legislation the time-proven skills of the Communist Party in subverting and eventually controlling legitimate organizations.

Justice White also offered an interesting perspective on associational rights. "I would have thought that the freedom of association . . . would be promoted, not hindered, by disclosure which permits members of an organization to know with whom they are associating and affords them the opportunity to make an intelligent choice as to whether certain of their associates who are Communists should be allowed to continue their membership."*

* For other cases of the *Gibson* type, see *De Gregory* v. *Attorney General of New Hampshire*, 383 U.S. 825 (1966) and *Hentoff* v. *Ichord*, 318 F. Supp. 1175 (D.D.C. 1970). In *De Gregory*, the court, over three dissents, ruled that New Hampshire's "remote and conjectural" interests in "stale" information respecting a defendant's relations with the Communist Party in the distant past did not outweigh his First Amendment rights to protect his associational and political activities from public exposure. In *United States Servicemen's Fund* v. *Eastland*, 488 F. 2d 1252 (D.C. Cir. 1973), the court, by a 2–1 vote, held that a subpoena to a bank seeking records on contributors to the plaintiff Fund—which was vehement in its opposition to the Indochina war—violated First Amendment protections. The Supreme Court reversed on the ground that suit was barred by the speech or debate clause. (See Chapter X.) The Supreme Court has never directly held that a specific investigatory interest of the *federal* legislature was outweighed by First Amendment concerns.

To say that the discordant concatenation of opinions produced in the *Barenblatt* and *Gibson* cases leaves only a shaky notion as to how the balancing test between governmental interests and First Amendment rights should be applied is to understate the matter. One suspects that the result the Court reaches on such questions depends more on the philosophical beliefs of its majority when a matter is decided than on the dispassionate application of relevant principles of law. Thus reliance on the First Amendment in resisting congressional inquiries is, at best, a treacherous business.

Other Limitations

As has become apparent, much of the law relating to the limitations on congressional investigations has developed in the context of contempt prosecutions. The federal courts have not been especially hospitable to these prosecutions. A survey conducted in 1959 showed that, of the 226 contempt citations voted by Congress during 1944–57 (the bulk originating in HUAC), only 44 had resulted in criminal convictions; 122 cases had been terminated by dismissals or verdicts of not guilty; 35 were never brought to court; and 25 were still pending.* None of the seven prosecutions stemming from Senator McCarthy's Permanent Subcommittee on Investigations had been successful. This basic trend continued after the 1959 survey. In 1962 alone the Supreme Court reversed nine contempt convictions. But there have been exceptions, e.g., the 1960 affirmance of conviction in the *McPhaul* case discussed in connection with the Fourth Amendment.

While the tendency of courts in contempt situations where liberty is at stake is to restrict the powers of Congress, judges often couch their opinions in other than constitutional terms. This accords with the Supreme Court's oft-repeated prescription that constitutional rul-

---

* Carl Beck, *Contempt of Congress* (Hauser Press, 1959), p. 243.

ings should be avoided when possible. And this practice displays a recognition that Congress, under the Constitution, has broad powers which—if extended to logical ends —may clash with individual constitutional rights, thus making constitutional adjudication extremely difficult. Consequently, in many cases the courts have been more than content to rest their decisions on nonconstitutional grounds, that is, on the language of statutes or congressional resolutions, or on court-made rules.

A salient example of this judicial predilection is *United States* v. *Rumely*, decided by the Supreme Court in 1953.* *Rumely* stands for the proposition that a congressional committee cannot probe beyond the scope of its authorizing resolution, but it is also a commentary on the pitfalls of constitutional adjudication.

Edward Rumely was the executive secretary of the Committee for Constitutional Government (CCG), a right-wing organization engaged in selling books displaying, in Justice Frankfurter's phrase, "a particular political tendentiousness." Rumely was subpoenaed by the House Select Committee on Lobbying Activities (the Buchanan committee) to produce the names of certain purchasers who bought these books in bulk for further distribution. Rumely would not, and after heated debate, the House cited him for contempt by a 183–175 vote. He was convicted, sentenced to six months in prison, and fined $1,000.

The Buchanan committee's rationale for its subpoena was based on a belief that Rumely had devised a scheme to evade the 1946 Regulation of Lobbying Act, which required disclosure to Congress of all contributions over $500 received or spent to influence legislation "directly or indirectly."† CCG would not accept contributions over $490 unless the donors specified that the money was for the distribution of written materials, and all sums exceed-

---

* 345 U.S. 41 (1953).
† U.S.C. 261 et seq. (1970).

ing $490 were treated by CCG as payments for the sale of literature and not reported. The Buchanan committee suspected that these "payments" were concealed contributions to influence legislation which should have been reported. Thus, it argued, the committee could properly inqure into their sources to determine if its supicions were well-founded.

Justice Frankfurter, who wrote the Court's opinion, was quick to note the difficult constitutional question potentially involved. On the one hand, there was Congress's broad investigatory power which allows searching inquiry into matters of federal interest; on the other, the rights to free speech and press sanctified by the First Amendment. A clash of basic precepts was in the offing.

This confrontation of contending constitutional principles, Justice Frankfurter said, should be sidestepped. As Chief Justice Hughes once said, "if a serious doubt of constitutionality is raised, it is a cardinal principle that this Court will first ascertain whether a construction of the statute is fairly possible by which the question may be avoided."* "Patently," said Justice Frankfurter, "the Court's duty to avoid a constitutional issue, if possible, applies not merely to legislation technically speaking but also to congressional action by way of resolution."

In the *Rumely* case a way out of the constitutional dilemma was available. The Buchanan committee's enabling resolution authorized the study of "all lobbying activities intended to influence, encourage, promote, or retard legislation." Frankfurter chose to define "lobbying" as "representations made directly to the Congress," rejecting Chairman Buchanan's definition, which included attempts "to saturate the thinking of the community." Referring to his own definition, Frankfurter said, "So to interpret [lobbying] is in the candid service of avoiding a serious constitutional doubt." Under this interpretation

* *Crowell v. Benson*, 285 U.S. 22, 62 (1932).

the committee had exceeded the scope of its authority, Rumely's refusal was justified and his conviction could not stand.*

Justices Douglas and Black concurred in the result, but were of the opinion that the enabling resolution did permit the committee's subpoena and therefore the constitutional issue should be reached. Justice Douglas's declaration that free speech and press were offended by the subpoena bears an eloquence that warrants repeating.

[Rumely] represents a segment of the American press. Some may like what his group publishes; others may disapprove. These tracts may be the essence of wisdom to some; to others their point of view and philosophy may be anathema. To some ears their words may be harsh and repulsive; to others they may carry the hope of the future. We have here a publisher who through books and pamphlets seeks to reach the minds and hearts of the American people. He is different in some respects from other publishers. But the differences are minor. Like the publishers of newspapers, magazines, or books, this publisher bids for the minds of men in the market place of ideas. . . .

If the present inquiry were sanctioned, the press would be subjected to harassment that in practical effect might be as serious as censorship. . . . A requirement that a publisher disclose the identity of those who buy his books, pamphlets, or papers is indeed the beginning of surveillance of the press. . . . The finger of government leveled against the press is ominous. Once the government can demand of a publisher the names of the purchasers of his publications, the free press as we know it disappears. Then the spectre of a government agent will look over the shoulder of everyone who reads. The

* See further, *Shelton v. United States,* 327 F. 2d 601 (D.C. Cir. 1963) *cert. denied* 393 U.S. 1024 (1968).

purchase of a book or pamphlet today may result in a subpoena tomorrow. Fear of criticism goes with every person into the bookstall. The subtle, imponderable pressures of the orthodox lay hold. Some will fear to read what is unpopular, what the powers-that-be dislike. When the light of publicity may reach any student, any teacher, inquiry will be discouraged. The books and pamphlets that are critical of the administration, that preach an unpopular policy in domestic or foreign affairs, that are in disrepute in the orthodox school of thought will be suspect and subject to investigation. The press and its readers will pay a heavy price in harassment. But that will be minor in comparison with the menace of the shadow which government will cast over literature that does not follow the dominant party line. If [a purchaser] can be required to disclose what she read yesterday and what she will read tomorrow, fear will take the place of freedom in the libraries, bookstores, and homes of the land. Through the harrassment of hearings, investigations, reports, and subpoenas government will hold a club over speech and over the press. Congress could not do this by law. The power of investigation is also limited.

But our paramount concern here is not with Douglas's views on free speech and press but with the principle that a committee cannot exceed the scope of its authorizing resolution. This is a principle that courts on other occasions have affirmed.* A variation of this requirement is that a resolution must spell out the scope of a committee's jurisdiction with "sufficient particularity" so that both investigators and those under investigation will know the

* *Watkins* v. *United States,* 354 U.S. 178 (1957); *Barenblatt* v. *United States,* 360 U.S. 109 (1959); *Tobin* v. *United States,* 306 F. 2d 270 (D.C. Cir. 1962) *cert. denied* 371 U.S. 902 (1962); *United States* v. *Kamin,* 135 F. Supp. 382 (D. Mass. 1955), 136 F. Supp. 791 (D. Mass 1956).

latitude allowed, and unless the resolution is sufficiently limited, it is impossible to determine whether a committee acts with valid legislative purpose.*

There is, moreover, a subsidiary rule declaring that demands for evidence made by a *subcommittee* must be within the scope of the inquiry authorized by the full committee. The subcommittee's authorization must also designate the scope of its powers with enough specificity to convey the boundaries of the inquiry.†

The proposition that a committee's inquiries are limited by its resolution served as a significant bridle to the Ervin committee's probes. The committee could only examine "illegal, improper or unethical activities . . . in the presidential election of 1972." Consequently Nixon's campaign activities in 1960 and 1968 were out of bounds unless some theory could be devised to demonstrate a relation to the 1972 campaign. In addition, Nixon's malefactions while President which were unrelated to the 1972 campaign were beyond the committee's jurisidction. Thus the committee engaged in no thorough analysis of Nixon's tax returns, which essentially did not concern the campaign, leaving that task to the Joint Committee on Taxation. But there was stretching to pull certain subjects within the committee's jurisdiction; the Ellsberg break-in, for example, was investigated partially on the theory that it showed a prior propensity of White House personnel to authorize and engage in burglaries of the Watergate type. It was, in other words, part of the atmosphere that produced Watergate. Additionally, the cover-up that hid the full Watergate story was also designed to prevent revelation of the Ellsberg episode.

Another important and related restriction on legislative probes requires that questions asked or records sought

---

* E.g., *Watkins* v. *United States*, 354 U.S. 178, 201–07 (1957).
† E.g., *Gojack* v. *United States*, 324 U.S. 702, 713–17 (1966).

be pertinent to the matter under investigation. This requirement derives from the federal contempt statute which punishes a refusal "to answer any question pertinent to the question under inquiry." The government, to convict, must prove pertinency at trial.* While the contempt statute might be read to require only that questions be pertinent, it has been interpreted to demand that records sought be pertinent if a conviction under the statute for failure to produce such records is to prevail.†

A witness is entitled to know why a query asked or material sought is "pertinent to the question under inquiry." He is entitled, in other words, to understand the specific aspect of the committee's jurisdiction under its authorizing resolution to which the question asked relates. This is a matter of fundamental fairness. A witness must decide at the time a question is propounded whether to answer. He acts at his peril. If he erroneously determines—even in good faith—that a question is not pertinent and refuses to answer it, he can later be convicted of contempt. As the Supreme Court has said: "It is obvious that a person compelled to make this choice is entitled to have knowledge of the subject to which the interrogation is deemed pertinent. That knowledge must be available with the same degree of explicitness and clarity that the Due Process Clause requires in the expression of any element of a criminal offense. The 'vice of vagueness' must be avoided here as in all other crimes."‡

The "question under inquiry" may be determined in several ways. It may appear in the authorizing resolution, but authorizing resolutions, especially those of standing committee, are often written in general terms and "gen-

* 2 U.S.C. 192 (1970). *Deutch* v. *United States,* 367 U.S. 456 (1961).

† *United States* v. *McSurely,* 473 F. 2d 1178, 1203 (D.C. Cir. 1972) (Wilkey, J., concurring); *United States* v. *Orman,* 207 F. 2d 148, 153 (3rd Cir. 1953); *Marshall* v. *United States,* 176 F. 2d 473, 474 (D.C. Cir. 1949) *cert. denied* 339 U.S. 933 (1950).

‡ *Watkins* v. *United States,* 354 U.S. 178, 208–9 (1957).

erality must be refined" in some manner to identify the question under inquiry to allow conviction under the contempt statute.* The subject under inquiry may also be found in the remarks of the chairman or other members of the committee, or in the committee's response to objections on the grounds of pertinency. Or the nature of the proceedings, including the questions put to other witnesses, may make the topic under consideration apparent.

The burden is on the committee to illuminate the pertinency of an inquiry. "Unless the subject matter has been made to appear with undisputable clarity, it is the duty of the investigative body, upon objection of the witness on grounds of pertinency, to state for the record the subject under inquiry at that time and the manner in which the propounded questions are pertinent thereto. To be meaningful, the explanation must describe what the topic under inquiry is and the connective reasoning whereby the precise questions asked relate to it."†

These principles formed the basis for the decision in *Watkins* v. *United States*, a compendium of learning on congressional investigations frequently cited in this book. A HUAC subcommittee had asked Watkins whether certain past acquaintances had previously been members of the Communist Party. He declined to respond and was convicted of contempt. The Supreme Court reversed, holding that the pertinency of the query was not made clear. The government claimed that the subject under examination was Communist infiltration of labor, but the Court, looking to the various indicia that give guidance in this regard, found this proposition dubious. It noted, for example, that Watkins had been quizzed about certain individuals who had no relationship with the labor movement and that six of nine witnesses who preceded him were not labor-connected. The Court concluded that Watkins had

---

* *Gojack* v. *United States*, 384 U.S. 702, 712 (1966).
279 U.S. 263 (1929); *Deutch* v. *United States*, 367 U.S. 456 (1961);
† *Watkins* v. *United States*, 354 U.S. 178, 214–15 (1957).

not been accorded a fair opportunity to determine whether he could rightfully refuse to answer, and ruled his conviction invalid under the due process clause.*

The federal courts have relied on other technical grounds in refusing to hold witnesses guilty of contempt. Numerous convictions, for example, have been reversed because the indictments failed to set forth the subject under inquiry during the witness's interrogation. And contempt convictions have been rejected where committees did not unequivocally require that defendants answer the questions involved. A witness is entitled to a clear ruling on his objections to testifying or producing evidence.†

On the other hand, a witness at his hearing should present all known objections to a committee if he is later to rely on them at criminal trial. For example, an objection to the pertinency of a question should initially be made to the interrogating committee.‡ The reason for this requirement is plain. A witness is not permitted to toy with a committee. He must present the committee with challenges to its authority so the committee itself will have opportunity to

* For other cases on the pertinency requirement, see, e.g., *Barenblatt* v. *United States*, 360 U.S. 109 (1959); *Sinclair* v. *United States*, 279 U.S. 263 (1929); *Deutch* v. *United States*, 367 U.S. 456 (1961); *Slagle* v. *Ohio*, 366 U.S. 259 (1961); *Russell* v. *United States*, 369 U.S. 749 (1962); *Bowers* v. *United States*, 202 F. 2d 447 (D.C. Cir. 1953); *Watson* v. *United States*, 280 F. 2d 689 (D.C. Cir 1960); *Knowles* v. *United States*, 280 F. 2d 696 (D.C. Cir 1960).

† See generally, Emerson, Haber, and Dorsen, *Political and Civil Rights in the United States* (Little, Brown & Co., 1967), pp. 411–15.

‡ See generally *Barenblatt* v. *United States*, 360 U.S. 109, 123–24 (1959); *United States* v. *Bryan*, 339 U.S. 323, 332–35 (1950); *Deutch* v. *United States*, 367 U.S. 456, 468–69 (1961). The last-cited case teaches that the government must prove pertinency at trial even if that issue was not raised by the defendant at the congressional hearing. But if the witness does not object on the grounds of pertinency at the hearing, he may not later claim that his due process rights were violated because the committee failed to explain the relationship of the question at issue to the subject under inquiry.

remedy defects.* Relying on this principle, the Ervin committee argued that Nixon had forfeited his right to object
in court to the committee's authority under its enabling
resolution to subpoena him because he did not broach this
issue to the committee when declining to comply with its
subpoenas. The correctness of this proposition was never
tested because the issue was eliminated by the subsequent
passage in November 1973 of another Senate resolution
affirming the committee's right to subpoena the President.

A witness may also find some solace in the traditional
common-law privileges—attorney-client, husband-wife,
doctor-patient, priest-penitent. While no direct holding applying these privileges to congressional proceedings exists,
at least one decision has assumed they are applicable.†
The various social policies that protect communications
between such parties from judicial prying should also safeguard them from legislative scrutiny. Congressional committees in practice have at times recognized the validity of
such privileges. The Ervin committee, however, rejected
several attorney-client privilege claims. Robert Mardian
was required to testify about a conversation with Gordon
Liddy concerning the latter's nefarious escapades after the
committee determined he had no valid lawyer-client relationship with Liddy. After the committee ruled that Bebe
Rebozo never engaged Herbert Kalmbach as his attorney,
Kalmbach was forced to give testimony concerning a conversation with Rebozo relating to the uses made of campaign contributions to Nixon. Furthermore, John Dean,
the former counsel to Nixon, testified before the
committee after Nixon waived any attorney-client privilege
he might have had because of their relationship. It is worth

---

* A defendant in a contempt case may be able to rely on a serious
defect in committee procedure not objected to at the committee
hearing if he was not aware of the defect at that time. See *Yellin* v.
United States, 374 U.S. 109, 122–23 (1963), discussed in the next
chapter.

† *United States* v. *Keeney,* 111 F. Supp. 233 (D.D.C. 1953) (Holt-
zoff, J.) *reversed on other grounds,* 218 F. 2d 843 (D.C. Cir. 1954).
But see *Stewart* v. *Blaine,* 1 MacArthur 453 (D.D.C. 1874).

noting that as a general rule the various common-law privileges are of no avail where the communications involved were made in furtherance of criminal conduct.

A final prescription affords considerable protection to those called before a congressional committee: the requirement that a committee follow its published rules of procedure established to protect the rights of those under scrutiny. This requirement has special relevance to the regulation of committee hearing procedures. It and other standards that govern the conduct of committee hearings are next considered.

·VIII·
Hearing Procedures and Individual Rights

In 1948 J. Parnell Thomas, chairman of the House Un-American Activities Committee, told a hapless witness: "The rights you have are the rights given you by this Committee. We will determine what rights you have and what rights you have not got before the committee."

This view—at least in regard to hearing procedures—gained wide acceptance. In 1955 Telford Taylor in *Grand Inquest* summed up the state of the law: "As a matter of general principle, the chilly and comfortless observation of Congressman Thomas . . . is quite correct as applied to questions of procedure. * * * The witness has no procedural rights that the committee is bound to respect."*

Whatever the accuracy of those observations when Taylor made them, they are no longer correct. Today's witnesses

---

* See at pp. 242, 244.

before congressional committees have substantial procedural rights because of the confluence of several related
legal principles.

The first is the requirement that committees adopt and
publish rules governing their procedures. This mandate as
it pertains to the Senate was established by the 1946
Legislative Reorganization Act.* The requirement for
House committees is found in the Rules of the House of
Representatives.† The Reorganization Act and the House
Rules serve as a partial delegation of the power given each
house by the constitutional provision declaring that "Each
House may determine the rules of its proceedings."‡

The second precept is that committee rules must be
consistent with statutory law and the rules of the parent
house, a requirement also embodied in the Legislative
Reorganization Act and the House Rules.§ While the
House in 1955 adopted basic rules (which have subsequently been amended) for the conduct of committee
hearings, the Senate has not. Various statutory provisions,
however, regulate both Senate and House committee
procedures.

The third principle is that—once a committee establishes
rules—it must follow those rules which significantly affect
the rights of persons under investigation. This doctrine is
court-made. Its creation probably reflects two strains of
thought: the belief that basic fairness requires committees
to live up to the standards they publish and the recognition
that requiring adherence to committee rules may allow a
court to pretermit tricky constitutional issues. The development of this concept by the Supreme Court merits a
moment's attention.

In January 1958 Edward Yellin was subpoenaed by
HUAC to appear in public session. Yellin had been iden-

---

* 2 U.S.C. §190a–2 (1970).
† Rule XI 2.(a). This rule, however, applies only to *standing*
House committees.
‡ Art. I, Sec. 5, Cl. 2.
§ See 2 U.S.C. 190a–2 (1970) and House Rule XI 2(a) (2).

tified to the committee as a Communist who had infil-trated a Gary, Indiana, steel mill to proselytize for the Party. By telegram, he asked the committee to allow him to appear in executive session to avoid adverse publicity. There was at the time a HUAC rule which stated, "If a majority of the Committee . . . believes that the interroga-tion of a witness in a public hearing might . . . unjustly injure his reputation . . . the Committee shall interrogate such witness in an Executive Session for the purpose of determining the necessity or advisability of conducting such interrogation thereafter in a public hearing." After Yellin's request for private hearing was denied, he refused for various reasons to respond to questions and subsequently was convicted of contempt.

Evidence at Yellin's trial showed two things: that the committee did not consider injury to Yellin's reputation before determining to call him in public session, and that it failed to act upon Yellin's express request to appear in executive session. Regarding the second finding, the evi-dence revealed that Yellin's entreaty had been denied by the committee's staff director, who lacked authority to take such action.

The Court—Chief Justice Warren writing the majority opinion—found that the committee, by holding a public hearing without considering Yellin's reputation and his efforts to protect it, had violated its own rules.* Reversing his conviction, the Court said: "Yellin might not prevail [on his request for private session], even if the Commit-tee takes note of the risk of injury to his reputation or his request for an executive session. But he is at least entitled to have the Committee follow its rules and give him con-sideration according to the standards it has adopted . . ."

The Court rejected the government's argument that Yel-lin's rights were forfeited because he failed to make clear at the hearing that his refusal to testify was based on the committee's departure from its rule. Yellin, the Court

* See *Yellin v. United States*, 374 U.S. 109 (1963).

observed, did not know until he heard the testimony at his trial that the committee's rule had been violated. At the hearing the committee had conveyed the impression that his reputation had been taken into account when a public hearing was first ordered and that his subsequent request for executive session had been properly considered and denied. The Court stated: "When reading a copy of the Committee's rules . . . the witness' reasonable expectation is that the Committee actually does what it purports to do, adhere to its own rules. To foreclose a defense based upon those rules, simply because the witness was deceived by the Committee's appearance of regularity, is not fair."

Four Justices—White, Clark, Harlan, and Stewart—dissented on the grounds that at the hearing Yellin had not specifically refused to testify because the session was public. The dissenters were also of the view that the committee had properly determined that a public hearing would not "unjustly injure" Yellin's reputation and thus had obeyed its rules in deciding on public session.

However, the next Supreme Court decision concerning compliance with committee rules was handed down without dissent. In 1955 John Gojack refused to answer certain questions before a HUAC subcommittee, including inquiries relating to his affiliation with the Communist Party and a so-called Peace Crusade. He was convicted of contempt, but in 1962 the Supreme Court reversed because the indictment did not allege the subject under inquiry at the time he was questioned.* Gojack was reindicted and convicted, but in 1966 the Supreme Court again reversed, this time partially on the grounds that the subcommittee had not followed HUAC's rules of procedure.†

HUAC rules provided that "No major investigation shall be initiated without approval of a majority of the

---

* See *Russell* v. *United States,* 369 U.S. 749 (1961) and Chapter VII.

† *Gojack* v. *United States,* 384 U.S. 702 (1966).

Committee." The investigation involving Gojack was indisputedly a major one. But, the Court found, a majority of the committee had not authorized it. Citing the *Yellin* case, the Court (Justice Fortas) wrote: "The House Committee on Un-American Activities has itself recognized the fundamental importance of specific authorization by providing in its [rules] that a major inquiry must be initiated by vote of a majority of the Committee. When a committee rule relates to a matter of such importance, it must be strictly observed. . . . Since the present inquiry is concededly part of a 'major investigation' and the Committee did not authorize it as required by its own (rules), this prosecution must fail."*

These cases are of immense importance, especially when read in conjunction with the requirements that committees adopt their own rules and that these rules conform to standards laid down by their parent body and statutes. This convergence of principles is especially significant where House committees are concerned because the full House has adopted a detailed set of procedures for committee activity. To some degree, the House Rules reflect attempts to rectify the abuses of the loyalty investigation period. The current rules show considerable sensitivity for the rights of individuals that is miles apart from the callousness portrayed by the "chilly and comfortless" remark of HUAC's Congressman Parnell with which this chapter began.

---

* See also *Christoffel* v. *United States*, 338 U.S. 84 (1949); *Shelton* v. *United States*, 327 F. 2d 601 (D.C. Cir. 1963), *cert. denied* 393 U.S. 1024 (1968); *Liveright* v. *United States*, 347 F. 2d 473 (D.C. Cir. 1965); *United States* v. *Grumman*, 227 F. Supp. 227 (D.D.C. 1964). However, court decisions also indicate that a committee's construction of its own rule is entitled to considerable weight and that there is a presumption that a committee has proceeded with regularity in conducting its affairs. See, e.g., *Barry* v. *United States ex rel. Cunningham*, 279 U.S. 597, 619 (1929) ; *United States* v. *Smith*, 286 U.S. 6, 33, 48 (1932); *Yellin* v. *United States*, 374 U.S. 109, 146–47 (1963) (White, J., dissenting).

A few selected examples indicate the scope and tenor of the House Rules.* At the beginning of an investigative hearing, the chairman must announce the subject of the investigation in an opening statement. Subpoenas can be issued only when authorized by a majority of the committee, except that minority party members have certain rights to call witnesses even if members of the dominant party object. A copy of the committee's rules must be made available to witnesses. The committee may allow witnesses to submit brief, pertinent, sworn statements. A quorum for taking testimony can be no less than two committee members.† Witnesses have the right to transcripts of their testimony at public session. If a committee determines that evidence at a hearing may tend to defame, degrade, or incriminate a person, the committee must give that person the opportunity to appear voluntarily and must consider his request to subpoena other witnesses. Other rules dealing with public and executive sessions, broadcasting of hearings, right to counsel, and protection of confidential information are dealt with below.

Because the Senate has no comprehensive rules spelling out committee procedures, Senate committees have more leeway concerning their rules of conduct, although certain statutory restrictions do control their hearings. Nonetheless, some Senate committees have adopted regulations that are fairly detailed in nature.

The provisions of the Ervin committee's *Rules of Procedure* and its *Guidelines* (a supplemental set of standards) serve as suitable illustrations. Subpoenas could be authorized by the chairman, vice chairman, or a majority of the committee. (Additionally, a federal statute gives a majority of the minority members of a Senate committee

* See generally Rule XI.
† The rules of the House Select Committee on Intelligence specify that at least one minority member must be present when testimony is received.

the right to call witnesses.)* A witness subpoenaed to appear was entitled to a reasonable time to prepare—not less than twenty-four hours. All persons subpoenaed were furnished a copy of the committee's enabling resolution and *Rules of Procedure*. A quorum for taking testimony was one committee member. Witnesses were allowed to file written statements and make uninterrupted opening and closing oral statements. While the committee *Guidelines* restricted opening statements to twenty minutes, this time limitation was not enforced; John Dean's opening statement, droned on for six hours, and Boston attorney Gerald Alch, whose major aim was to defend himself against charges of professional misconduct by his former client James McCord, was allowed to remonstrate for one and a half hours.† Persons mentioned in testimony could file sworn statements relevant to that testimony and could request the opportunity to appear. A witness was allowed to make technical (not substantive) corrections in the transcript of his sworn testimony and had the right to a copy of his public testimony. Additionally, the committee's *Rules* and *Guidelines* contained extensive provisions relating to public and executive sessions, regulation of the media, the right to and role of counsel, and the safeguarding of confidential information.

To review in detail all the various rules that govern committee procedures would be tedious. Instead, the remainder of this chapter concentrates on two critical problem areas: (1) what considerations determine whether committee hearings are held publicly or privately, and if public, what regulation of the media is in order; (2) what rights have witnesses to counsel and to

---

* 2 U.S.C. 190a–1(c) (1970). The Senate Committee on Appropriations is not covered by this provision.

† The Ervin committee's practice should be contrasted with the conduct in the case of Owen Lattimore, who, before the Senate Internal Security Subcommittee in 1952, was repeatedly and rudely interrupted by senators and counsel as he attempted to read his opening statement. See Alan Barth, *Government by Investigation* (Viking Press, 1955), pp. 99–102.

what lengths can counsel go to protect his client. The next chapter deals with that bane of congressional hearings: the problem of protecting information received in confidence.

Public versus Private Hearings: Control of Media Coverage

Senator Daniel Inouye is an impressive interrogator. His questions are brief and incisive, his voice resonant, his gaze penetrating. After a round of Inouye's productive and professional questioning of John Ehrlichman, I slipped into Senator Herman Talmadge's vacant chair and said, "Good job, Senator." Inouye, palpably annoyed by Ehrlichman's answers, turned toward me abruptly by rotating his swivel chair, and forgetting to cover his microphone with his left hand—his only hand—exclaimed, "What a liar!" Unfortunately his remark was heard not only by me but also by those in the hearing room and millions more tuned in to television and radio.

John Wilson, Ehrlichman's aging but feisty lawyer, was furious. He retaliated by calling Inouye a "little Jap," a reference to the war hero's Japanese ancestry, and for several days the little Jap flap was the big news from the hearings.

The day after the incident I apologized to Inouye for provoking his remark. Unperturbed, he responded, "Don't worry about it. It was the only truthful thing said all day." Inouye also observed that from then on he would make his private comments only in Hawaiian.

A funny story perhaps—although undoubtedly not to John Ehrlichman, now convicted of lying to a grand jury. But this occurrence also demonstrates anew the dangers intrinsic in public hearings covered by the broadcast media, even when those hearings are conducted by well-intentioned persons. While there may be no design to stage a legislative trial or affect future criminal proceedings, the potential for public disgrace and rebuke is ever-present. Nonetheless, the prevailing penchant—embodied in both House and Senate rules—is for open hearings.

No constitutional provision, however, demands that congressional investigatory hearings be open. Chester Davis argued strenuously that the due process clause forced this result, but his contentions were based on a misconception of the nature of the investigatory process. The normal legislative hearing is not a trial where rights are adjudicated. There are no plaintiffs or prosecutors or defendants. Its purpose is not to assess guilt or liability. Rather, its functions are investigatory—to acquire information to aid the lawmaking process, to oversee the executive branch, to inform the public of the condition of government. When Congress assumes a quasi-judicial or adjudicating role—as in impeachment, contempt, or censure proceedings, or in hearings to determine the results of contested elections—it may be argued that due process, at least at some stage, requires open hearings. But the standards are different in purely investigatory endeavors.*

The Supreme Court has commented on the flexibility inherent in the due process requirement. " 'Due process' is an elusive concept. Its exact boundaries are undefinable, and its content varies according to specific factual contexts. Thus, when governmental agencies adjudicate or make binding determinations which directly affect the legal rights of individuals, it is imperative that those agencies use the procedures that have traditionally been associated with the judicial process. On the other hand, when governmental action does not partake of an adjudication, as for example, when a general fact-finding investigation is being conducted, it is not necessary that the full panoply of judicial procedures be used. Therefore, as a

* As discussed in Chapter IV, it would unconstitutionally exceed legislative powers if an investigating committee conducted a "legislative trial" where guilt was assessed and an attempt made to punish witnesses or others by public disgrace.

generalization, it can be said that due process embodies the differing rules of fair play, which through the years have become associated with differing types of proceedings. . . ."* The case quoted from—which, among other things, held that witnesses in an investigative administrative proceeding conducted to develop facts for legislative judgments had no right to confront or learn the identity of their accusers—strongly suggests that due process does not require the opening of congressional investigatory hearings.†

As we have noted, however, congressional rules do express a preference for open hearings. At one time provisions of the federal code provided that Senate committee hearings must be public unless a committee determined that its hearings would relate to national security matters, reflect adversely on individual reputations, or reveal material made confidential by law or regulation. It was this requirement that Chester Davis relied on to argue that Hughes employees should be examined in public—an argument defeated when the Ervin committee passed a resolution closing its sessions because public interrogations might injure reputations or reveal national security matters. However, the statutory provisions have recently been replaced by a similar Standing Rule of the Senate which allows a committee to close hearings to avoid (1) disclosing national defense and foreign relations secrets, (2) charging individuals with crimes, subjecting them to disgrace, or unduly invading their privacy, (3) hindering law enforcement efforts, (4) revealing trade and financial secrets, and (5) divulging matters made confidential by law or regulation.‡

---

* *Hannah* v. *Larche*, 363 U.S. 420, 442 (1960); compare *Jenkins* v. *McKeithen*, 395 U.S. 411, 425–27 (1969).

† Others cases dealing with administrative proceedings compel the same conclusion. See, e.g., *Fitzgerald* v. *Hampton*, 467 F. 2d 755 (D.C. Cir. 1972) and cases cited.

‡ See Rule xxv, par. 7 (b).

It is significant that the Rule gives a committee discretion to close hearings. A witness is not relieved of the obligation to testify publicly because he fears his testimony will harm him. In fact, a related statutory provision says, "No witness is privileged to refuse to testify to any fact, or to produce any paper, respecting which he shall be examined . . . by any committee of either House, upon the ground that his testimony to such fact or his production of such paper may tend to disgrace him or otherwise render him infamous."*

This latter provision applies to the House as well as the Senate. But the House also has rules allowing resort to private hearings. One rule declares, "Each hearing conducted by [a] committee . . . shall be open to the public except when the committee . . . determines by roll call vote that [the hearing] shall be closed to the public because disclosure of testimony, evidence, or other matters . . . would endanger the national security or would violate any law or rule of the House . . ." This provision must be read in conjunction with another House rule stating that "If the committee determines that evidence or testimony at an investigative hearing may tend to defame, degrade, or incriminate any person, it shall . . . receive such evidence or testimony in executive session."†

Actually, the various provisions discussed may not give Senate or House committees enough authority to close hearings. Instances may arise, for example, where reputations, trade secrets, law enforcement, or national security are not factors, yet efficient investigating techniques mandate nonpublic hearings. In some situations the wise course is to receive evidence in executive session to prevent leads from drying up or witnesses from disappearing. Similarly, it may be advantageous to hold back the testi-

---

* 2 U.S.C. 193 (1970). But under the Fifth Amendment, a witness whose testimony would incriminate him may refuse (unless given immunity) to testify in any setting. See Chapters III and VII.

† See Rule XI 2.(g) (2) and Rule XI 2.(k) (5) (A).

mony of a witness to prevent future witnesses from tailoring their statements. And executive sessions are useful to determine the credibility of witnesses and weed out evidence not worth presenting at public hearing.

Recognition of these considerations led the Ervin committee to recommend that the law be amended to allow a Senate committee to shut its hearings when efficient investigatory techniques so require. But because the committee recognized the salutary policy behind open hearings—letting the people in on the business of government—the recommendation also specified that the results of hearings closed for reasons of efficiency should be made public as soon as proper investigatory techniques no longer dictated secrecy.

The presence of the broadcast media adds another dimension to the question whether to hold public hearings. Television and radio are mixed blessings. They allow Congress to fulfill its salient responsibility of informing the public about the business of government. But they also provide unparalleled opportunities for injuring reputations, damaging fair trials, and grandstanding by congressmen and staff. To appear before cameras and microphones can be a distracting, indeed terrifying, experience for witnesses. Not surprisingly, various congressional rules have evolved that regulate broadcast coverage of committee hearings, and litigation over such coverage has occurred.

Discretion to allow broadcast coverage of hearings is left to Senate committees by the Senate's Standing Rules. Senate committees also have full authority under the Rules to adopt their own standards regulating broadcast coverage.* The Ervin committee's *Rules of Procedure* gave the chairman power to ensure that media coverage was "orderly and unobtrusive." Its *Guidelines* specified that all still photography must be completed before a witness

---

* See Rule xxv 7(b), which replaced 2 U.S.C. 190a–1(b) (1970).

actually testified. And the rules provided that a witness "on grounds of distraction, harassment, or physical discomfort" could request that cameras and lights not be directed toward him during his testimony. Requests of this nature were to be ruled on by the committee.

Not content with these protections, Senator Robert Dole of Kansas, a former chairman of the Republican National Committee, introduced a Senate resolution in September 1973 to "turn off the TV lights in the Ervin committee hearing room." "It is time, Dole said, "to move the Watergate investigation from the living rooms of America." Dole's resolution found little support in the Senate and was not passed.

The House Rules, formulated in the Legislative Reorganization Act of 1970, are quite solicitous of witnesses confronted with cameras and microphones.* The House Rules permit a committee by majority vote to allow media coverage of hearings. But a committee must promulgate regulations governing media coverage which conform to the House Rules. These rules set out strict standards to ensure that dignity of proceedings, decorum, and courtesy to witnesses are observed, and that the media does not interfere with the orderly conduct of the hearings. Additionally, they provide that no radio or television tapes of a hearing may be utilized in political campaigns and that live radio and television coverage must be "conducted and presented without commercial sponsorship."

Perhaps most important, the rules declare that "No witness served with a subpena by the committee shall be required against his or her will to be photographed at any hearing or to give evidence or testimony while the broadcasting of that hearing, by radio or television, is being conducted. At the request of any such witness who does not wish to be subjected to radio, television, or still photography coverage, all lenses shall be covered and all microphones used for coverage turned off." The rules of

---

* See generally Rule XI 3, and 84 Stat. 1153 (1970).

the Senate Select Committee to study Government Operations with Respect To Intelligence Activities contain similar protections.

These prescriptions are reminiscent of the treatment given underworld kingpin Frank Costello when he appeared before the Kefauver committee in New York in March 1951. Costello's lawyer vigorously objected to televising his client's testimony on the grounds that it would force Costello to submit to a "spectacle" and would prevent proper conferences with his attorney. Senator Herbert R. O'Conor, who was presiding, prohibited televising Costello's face while he testified. But the nation was treated to the memorable "spectacle" of Costello's hands nervously twisting as he gave evidence.

There are other instances where television cameras have been forbidden even though a hearing was open to the public. One notable situation involved the proceedings of the select committee chaired by Senator Arthur V. Watkins of Michigan which considered the censure of Senator McCarthy. Cameras were excluded from these hearings because of their quasi-judicial nature. Despite the careful manner in which the committee proceeded, McCarthy referred to its members—who had been appointed by Vice President Richard Nixon and included Sam Ervin—as "unwitting handmaidens" of the Communist Party.

The presence of cameras and microphones at congressional hearings has precipitated a variety of litigation. We have discussed the unsuccessful efforts by Special Prosecutor Cox to ban broadcast coverage of the testimony of John Dean and Jeb Magruder and the equally unavailing attempts by Rabbi Korff to stop the Ervin committee's public televised proceedings in toto. And we have considered Judge Gesell's opinion in the tapes case where, with media coverage in mind, he refused tapes to the committee in order to avoid "the blazing atmosphere of ex parte publicity directed to issues that are immediately and intimately related to pending criminal proceedings." The media issue has also arisen in the context of contempt of Congress prosecutions.

Of special interest is a case spawned by the Special Senate Committee investigating crime in interstate commerce* Morris Kleinman and Louis Rothkopf, allegedly big-time gamblers, were convicted of contempt for refusing to testify before the committee. Neither had taken the Fifth, but each had claimed that his constitutional rights would be violated if required to testify before cameras and microphones.

Judge Henry A. Schweinhaut, who tried the case without jury, acquitted the defendants, but not on constitutional grounds. Holding that the defendants' refusals to respond to questions were justified, he said:

> When the power of the court to punish is invoked, it necessarily follows in order properly to determine the guilt or innocence of the accused, that the court must examine the entire situation confronting the witness at the time he was called upon to testify. Only thus can it be determined whether his refusal was capricious and arbitrary and therefore a wilful, unjustified obstruction of a legitimate function of the legislature or was a justifiable disobedience of the legislative command. . . .
>
> *   *   *
>
> In the cases now to be decided, the stipulation of facts discloses that there were, in close proximity to the witness, television cameras, newsreel cameras, news photographers with their concomitant flashbulbs, radio microphones, a large and crowded hearing room with spectators standing along the walls, etc. The obdurate stand taken by these two defendants must be viewed in the context of all of these conditions. The concentration of all of these elements seems to me necessarily so to disturb and distract any witness to the point that

---

* *United States* v. *Kleinman*, 107 F. Supp. 407 (D.D.C. 1952).

he might say today something that next week he will realize was erroneous. And the mistake could get him in trouble all over again.

Judge Schweinhaut's decision, which seems to assume that extensive media coverage makes thoughtful answers impossible, was aberrational and has not been followed. With the increasing prevalence of televised hearings, there is understandable reticence to reject contempt convictions for all those who refuse to testify under the cameras' gaze. A more representative statement of judicial sentiment is undoubtedly contained in a 1961 opinion by District Judge Julius H. Miner resulting from a televised proceeding of the Senate Committee on Banking and Currency.*

In this case the defendant moved to dismiss the contempt indictment against him on the grounds that the mere presence of mass communication media in the hearing room justified his silence. Judge Miner rejected this claim. "[T]here is," he said, "a valid legislative purpose in informing and educating the public to the end that they may exercise an informed judgment and render all possible aid to Congress in the investigations and deliberations which are the essence of the legislative function. There is, undeniably, a valid legislative purpose in admitting to the conference room the eyes and ears of the nation."

Furthermore, he wrote:

Ruling on how congressional hearings shall be conducted is the task of the Congress. The courts have no right to dictate either the procedures for Congress to follow in performing its functions, or the composition and conduct of the persons and paraphernalia admitted by Congress to its hearings. This court has no power to impose upon Congress, a coordinate branch

* *United States* v. *Hintz*, 193 F. Supp. 325 (N.D. Ill. 1961).

of our government, either a proscription against or a prescription for radio, television, movies or photographs. This court is of the opinion that the mere presence of such mechanisms at an investigative hearing does not infect the proceeding with impropriety.

Judge Miner concluded that contempt charges against a defendant should fail only upon a showing by competent evidence that unwarranted media conditions caused or permitted by Congress "actually deprived [a defendant] of his normal facilities to respond intelligently with clarity and accuracy."*

The Supreme Court, in the variety of contempt cases it has heard, has never indicated that the mere presence of the media justifies refusal to answer congressional inquiries. The most it has said is that legislative trials aimed at the punishment of witnesses and hearings conducted solely to expose private affairs—activities aided by broadcast coverage—are unlawful. In any event, the problem of media distraction should no longer exist regarding *House* hearings, since a witness, under its standing rules has an absolute right to have cameras and microphones covered. As to those Senate hearings where like protections are not available, a witness unsuccessfully objecting at hearing time to the diverting and disturbing presence of the media may still be able to mount a valid defense against prosecution for silence.

Counsel and His Role

To a large degree the question whether the Constitution gives a congressional witness the right to counsel is academic, for counsel is allowed in almost all situations†

---

* See also *United States* v. *Orman*, 207 F. 2d 148 (3d Cir. 1953); *United States* v. *Moran*, 194 F. 2d 623, 627 (2d Cir. 1952), *cert. denied* 343 U.S. 965 (1952).

† Some early state decisions, following British practice, held there was no right to counsel in state legislative investigations. *People ex*

The live question is what functions can counsel perform. How far beyond merely advising his client may he go? May he insist that his client be allowed to confront those who accuse him and that cross-examination be permitted? May he question his own client and call other witnesses to present his client's point of view? May he object to questions put his client and others on the grounds that they seek irrelevant or hearsay testimony, or exceed the scope of the committee's resolution?

The lawsuit brought by Rabbi Korff raised (but did not decide) some of these issues. He argued that the committee's public hearings were improper and should be enjoined because witnesses were allowed to give hearsay testimony about criminal conduct and because persons accused of unlawful activities were not allowed to confront and cross-examine their detractors.

That great champion of civil liberties—former Vice President Spiro Agnew—went beyond Korff's position in a June 1973 speech to the National Association of Attorneys General. Along with calling for the right of cross-examination and a ban on hearsay testimony, Agnew advocated allowing rebuttal testimony and the introduction of evidence to impeach an accuser's credibility. He also urged the prohibition of testimony that contained inferences, impressions, and speculations. "Lacking such safeguards," Agnew expostulated, "the committee, I am sad to say, can hardly hope to find the truth and can hardly fail to muddy the waters of justice beyond redemption."*

---

rel. Keeler v. *McDonald*, 99 N.Y. 463, 2 N.E. 615 (1885); *In re Falvey*, 7 Wis. 630 (1858). It seems likely, however, that federal courts would rule that the rudiments of due process at least allow a witness to have the advice of counsel during testimony so that his basic rights may be protected. The rules of the Senate select committee on intelligence activities require that panel to attempt to obtain voluntary counsel for witnesses unable to do so on their own. But the failure to secure counsel does not excuse a witness from testifying.

* In fairness, it must be observed that a number of prominent lawyers and legal scholars have recommended the imposition of certain trial procedures on legislative hearings.

That the Agnew-Korff stance does not represent prevailing law is demonstrated by a 1971 case decided by the District of Columbia Circuit Court of Appeals involving one Jeff Fort, a vice president of a Chicago "youth gang" called the Blackstone Rangers.* The investigation concerned was a Senate Permanent Investigations Subcommittee inquiry into a job-training program for youth gangs funded by the Office of Economic Opportunity. The committee had received allegations that federal monies funneled into the program—which totaled almost a million dollars—had been grossly misused. Fort was a "Center Chief" for the Woodlawn program and drew a yearly salary of $6,000.

Called before the subcommittee, Fort made a formal request to allow his counsel to cross-examine any person who had given evidence defaming him. When this was denied, Fort refused to testify upon counsel's advice. He was convicted of contempt and the Court of Appeals affirmed.

A witness in an investigatory proceeding, the court said, has no constitutional right to confront and cross-examine his accuser.

> The right to present evidence in one's own behalf and to confront and cross examine one's accusers are rights designed to protect the individual's interests when the Government seeks to impose criminal sanctions upon him. But the plain fact is that the congressional investigation with which we are here concerned is an investigative proceeding and not a criminal proceeding, and in such proceeding Congress is not empowered to adjudicate criminal sanctions on the witness. These are the distinguishing features of a congressional investigation that cause such proceedings to be outside the guarantees of the due process clause of the Fifth Amendment and the confrontation right guar-

---

* *United States* v. *Fort*, 443 F. 2d 670 (D.C. Cir. 1971).

anteed in criminal proceedings by the Sixth Amendment.*

Quoting from a 1960 Supreme Court decision, the Court of Appeals observed:

The investigative function of [legislative] committees is as old as the Republic . . . The procedures adopted by legislative investigating committees have varied over the course of years. Yet, the history of these committees clearly demonstrates that only infrequently have witnesses appearing before congressional committees been afforded the procedural rights normally associated with an adjudicative proceeding. In the vast majority of instances, congressional committees have not given witnesses detailed notice or an opportunity to confront, cross-examine and call other witnesses.†

In this same case the Supreme Court advanced some very practical reasons why the functions of counsel in investigatory proceedings should be limited:

[T]he investigative process could be completely disrupted if investigative hearings were transformed into trial-like proceedings, and if persons who might be indirectly affected by an investigation were given an absolute right to cross-examine every witness called to testify. Fact-finding agencies without any power to adjudicate would be diverted from their legitimate duties and would be plagued by the injection of collateral issues that would make the investigation inter-

---

* The statement that the due process clause has no application to congressional hearings appears to go too far. As suggested above, a federal court might well rule that due process principles at least allow a congressional witness to have counsel to advise him of his rights. Compare *Hannah* v. *Larche*, 363 U.S. 420, 442 (1960).

† *Hannah* v. *Larche*, 363 U.S. 420, 444–45 (1960).

minable. Even a person not called as a witness could demand the right to appear at the hearing, cross-examine any witness whose testimony or sworn affidavit allegedly defamed or incriminated him and call an unlimited number of witnesses of his own selection. This type of proceeding would make a shambles of the investigation and stifle the agency in its gathering of facts.*

The view of practicalities and law put forth by these decisions is reflected in the various rules of procedure regulating committee proceedings. The standing rules of the House provide that "Witnesses at investigative hearings may be accompanied by their own counsel for the purpose of advising them concerning their constitutional rights."† This rather costive affirmation of the right to counsel, first adopted in 1955, leaves undefined the precise functions counsel can fulfill. Seizing on this omission, HUAC, in its *Rules of Procedure*, placed explicit restrictions on the role of counsel: "The participation of counsel during the course of any hearing and while the witness is testifying shall be limited to advising said witness as to his legal rights. Counsel shall not be permitted to engage in oral argument with the Committee, but shall confine his activity to the area of legal advice to his client."‡

Rules of procedure established by Senate committees have also contained limitations on the right of counsel. The rules of the Senate select committee on intelligence activities and the Permanent Investigations Subcommittee, for instance, expressly prohibit examination or cross-examination of witnesses by private attorneys.

The *Rules of Procedure* and *Guidelines* of the Ervin committee contained detailed provisions concerning counsel's latitude to participate in its proceedings. The rules gave a witness the right to counsel whose "sole and exclusive prerogative shall be to advise such witness while he

* 363 U.S. at 443–44.
† See Rule XI 2.(k) (2).
‡ See Rule No. VIII, HUAC's 1965 *Rules of Procedure*.

is testifying of his legal and constitutional rights." "Counsel for the witness," the rules stated, shall not "coach the witness, answer for the witness, or put words in the witness' mouth." After a witness testified, his counsel could request that the committee hear the testimony of additional witnesses or receive other evidence. Resolution of such requests was left to the committee's discretion.

The rules provided that "there shall be no direct or cross-examination by counsel appearing for a witness. However, the counsel may submit in writing any questions he wishes propounded to his client or to any other witness." Similarly a person who was the subject of an investigation could submit written questions for a witness. The propriety of such requests was ruled on by the committee. Utilizing these provisions, the White House proffered questions for John Dean which were dutifully—albeit not enthusiastically—asked by Senator Inouye.

Notwithstanding the provision that counsel's "sole and exclusive prerogative" was to advise his client of his rights, the committee's rules also declared that counsel could raise objections "to procedures or to the admissibility of testimony and evidence" which would be passed on by the chair or, in the case of disagreement, by a majority of the committee present. Counsel frequently availed themselves of this opportunity, sometimes with success. On occasion, testimony was barred because it was irrelevant under the committee's resolution. But the committee frequently allowed hearsay evidence and testimony containing opinions and speculations.

Legislative committees are, of course, not bound by the strict rules of evidence that control courtroom proceedings. Hearsay and opinion testimony—normally taboo in courts of law—are frequently accepted in legislative proceedings, and such evidence can be extremely useful to committees in making legislative judgments. Actually much hearsay testimony offered during the Ervin committee's hearings would have been admissible in court under the well-accepted theory that conspirator statements during the course and in furtherance of a conspiracy are admissible against all conspirators as long as other evidence shows the fact of, and membership in, the conspiracy. Thus, James McCord's testimony about G. Gordon Liddy's statements concerning participation in planning the Gemstone operations by John Mitchell, Jeb Magruder, and John Dean would have been admissible against those men in a criminal conspiracy trial.*

Another provision in the committee's *Guidelines,* inserted largely to deal with executive privilege contentions, gave the committee discretion to allow counsel to argue claims of privilege asserted by witnesses. Additionally, the White House could have its own counsel accompany testifying White House aides for the purpose of invoking executive privilege for the President. The White House frequently took advantage of this prerogative: James St. Clair, Fred Buzhardt, Douglas Parker, and others were familiar guests of the committee. But the committee's regulations preserved for the committee the right to rule on the validity of all claims of privilege.

Other committees have given counsel more license than the Ervin committee. In some instances, committees have granted the right to call witnesses and cross-examine. General Arthur St. Clair and others were allowed to call witnesses in the House's investigation of his Ohio frontier defeat. During the Senate investigation of the Justice Department's involvement in the Teapot Dome scandal, counsel for Attorney General Harry Daugherty was permitted to examine adverse witnesses. Senator McCarthy, at the Army-McCarthy hearings where charges between him and the Army were vituperatively traded, had a limited right of cross-examination. (McCarthy had temporarily resigned from the Permanent Investigations Sub-

---

* *E.g., United States* v. *Annunziato,* 293 F. 2d 373 (2d Cir. 1961); *United States* v. *Pugliese,* 153 F. 2d 497 (2d Cir. 1945), (Learned Hand, J.). The newly adopted *Federal Rules of Evidence* recognize that such statements by a co-conspirator are admissible in conspiracy trials. See Rule 801(d) (2) (E).

committee, which conducted the hearing.) Later at the Watkins committee's hearings on his censure, McCarthy's counsel (Edward Bennett Williams) was given the right to call witnesses as well as cross-examine. Similar practices have been followed during various stages of impeachment proceedings. Nixon's attorney, James St. Clair, was permitted to cross-examine during the House Judiciary Committee's investigation of his client. Where congressional proceedings are directed toward the adjudication of rights as in impeachment, contempt, or censure proceedings or in hearings considering contested elections, the propriety and desirability of courtroom techniques and prerogatives become more manifest.*

While rights to present testimony and cross-examination were not allowed by the Ervin committee, its hearings on the whole did represent a determined effort to be fair to all concerned. As noted, those affected by the hearings could request that other witnesses be called and submit questions for witnesses on the stand. And, in practice, counsel for witnesses had expansive rights to object to committee questions. The atmosphere was totally different, for instance, from that prevailing during Senator McCarran's Internal Security Committee investigation of Owen Lattimore where Lattimore's counsel, Abe Fortas—later a Supreme Court Justice—was pointedly instructed that he could not object to committee inquiries. In fact, counsel at that proceeding were informed that they would be removed from the hearing room if they ventured to do more than merely advise their clients.†

Admittedly, certain witnesses before the Ervin committee were made to feel uncomfortable. Some questions were

---

* Compare *Jenkins* v. *McKeithen*, 395 U.S. 411 (1969) and *Groppi* v. *Leslie*, 404 U.S. 496 (1972).

† As various committee rules of procedure recognize, a committee may discipline lawyers before it who are obstreperous, fail to abide by its rules, or are otherwise contemptuous. See, e.g., House Rule XI 2.(k) (4). But in doing so, a committee must follow its own rules of procedure. See *Kinoy* v. *District of Columbia*, 400 F. 2d 761 (D.C. Cir. 1968).

tough, although a more frequent criticism from lawyers was that they were not biting enough. Some grandstanding occurred and witnesses were not immune from sermonettes from several sources. And there was the problem of leaks (dealt with in the next chapter). But, shortcomings notwithstanding, viewed overall the hearings were fairly run, especially in comparison with some of their well-publicized predecessors from loyalty investigation days.

Perhaps the spirit in which the Ervin committee's investigations were conducted is summed up by the following exchange during the public testimony of H.R. Haldeman.

Senator INOUYE . . . Mr. Haldeman, have you ever been cited by any court in the United States for illegal or unethical campaign activities?

Mr. HALDEMAN. I am not sure what "cited" means, Senator. My name was included, although I was not a defendant, in a suit relating to the . . . 1962 campaigns for Governor of California.

Senator INOUYE. In a judgment rendered on November 2, 1964, the court did cite you and others for carrying out illegal and unethical campaign activities and did enjoin you from ever using such tactics again, and the case was never appealed. Isn't that so?

Mr. HALDEMAN. I have not seen that judgment. I have seen press references to that that said I was, I guess "cited" is the correct term, as having had knowledge of the matter that was under . . . judgment there.

Senator Inouye then proceeded to compare depositions given by Haldeman and another individual in that case.

Mr. WILSON (lawyer for Haldeman). Mr. Chairman— excuse me, Senator . . . I have not interfered up to this point with respect to the question of relevancy. I think it stands out in bold relief. I would like to say that I think this is outside the scope of your resolution.

Senator INOUYE. Mr. Chairman, may I respond to that, sir?

Senator ERVIN. Well, it may be relevant but I believe it would be advisable, I hate to say this, but to refrain from interrogating that far back.

Senator INOUYE. May I respond, sir, Mr. Chairman?

Senator ERVIN. Yes, sir.

Senator INOUYE. I believe it is relevant to the investigation to have some understanding of Mr. Haldeman's approach to political campaigning, and, second, Mr. Chairman, these hearings began on May 17, 1973, and since then I believe we have had 32 days of intensive questioning of witnesses and we have had before us men and women of high standing in our community, men and women supposedly with unimpeachable characters, and to the confusion of all of us here, Mr. Chairman, many of these witnesses have time and again contradicted other witnesses, in other words, suggesting that one witness was faulty in his recollection or committed outright perjury, and I think it is relevant to this investigation to determine a witness' credibility.

For example, when Mr. Dean was before us, no one objected to a question posed about reasons for his dismissal from his first job and I believe this touched his credibility.

Senator ERVIN. Well, Senator, I would approximate this to the rule in criminal cases, though we are not trying a criminal case, but it is a good guide to follow. I do think you can ask the witness about his attitude but I do not believe we ought to go back that far to ask him about specific acts just like trying a man for one thing and then proving he did some other things. If we do this with Mr. Haldeman, then anybody in the committee would be entitled to recall every witness here and do the same thing, go back into their past actions and things, and I just think it is unwise to open the door and—

Senator INOUYE. I shall abide by the Chair's rulings. . . .

Considering the relaxed standards of relevancy pertaining to congressional probes, Senator Ervin clearly bent over backwards—to a position of extreme contortion, some might argue—to be fair to Haldeman.

There remains for examination a critical aspect of committee business: the procedures for handling information given Congress in confidence. This and the troublesome, aggravating, and at times thoroughly disgusting subject of leaks are the topics of the next chapter.

·IX·
Leaks

"The Ervin Committee," mused its vice chairman, Senator Howard Baker, "did not invent the leak, but we elevated it to its highest art form."

As Senator Baker's quip suggests, Congress has long been plagued by improper or injudicious release of information received in confidence. One of Congress's earliest contempt citations was directed to Nathaniel Rounsavell, editor of the Alexandria, Virginia, *Herald*, who in 1812 refused to answer questions about leaks from a secret House session. The Radical Republicans on the Joint Committee on the Conduct of the [Civil] War publicized information gathered in closed sessions when it suited their purposes. This conduct prompted General Robert E. Lee to observe that the committee was worth about two divisions of Confederate troops. During World War II Senator Burton K. Wheeler, an extreme isolationist, revealed the Navy's occupation of Iceland while the operation was still in progress and Navy forces were vulnerable to enemy attack. After closed sessions of his investigation of the Signal Corps Engineering Laboratories at Fort Monmouth, New Jersey, Senator McCarthy regularly gave the press his version of what had occurred, thus provoking sensational media accounts proclaiming that the military establishment was brimming with spies. It later appeared, however, that his descriptions bore little resemblance to actual testimony.

Even the House Judiciary Committee's impeachment investigation of Mr. Nixon, generally conducted in exemplary fashion, had its lapses. For example, the entire transcript of that committee's version of the September 15, 1972, meeting between Nixon, Haldeman, and Dean was leaked to the press.

But never, it is safe to say, has Congress experienced such a frenetic outpouring of supposedly confidential information as emated from the Ervin committee. Recognizing that Senator Baker's remark was whimsical, it nonetheless greatly understated the gravity of the matter. The leaks were the major stain on the committee's performance. They severely jeopardized its credibility and the integrity of its proceedings. At times they made committee members and staff—including those *not* leaking—appear as publicity-grabbing buffoons incapable of keeping their own counsel and conducting conscientious investigations into serious matters. Moreover, the leaks were illegal in that they violated the committee's own rules, and arguably some of them had criminal implications. And, sadly, the leaks blemished the final major senatorial efforts of Sam Ervin, who did not deserve to have the committee he chaired brought into disrepute by irresponsible conduct.

This chapter discusses some of the committee's major leaks and the legal ramifications of this activity. No attempt is made to be inclusive; fully to document all the committee's leaks would take a separate volume.

This discussion, however, must begin with a caveat. The Watergate game was played for high stakes. The Machiavellianism abounding during the investigations should not be underestimated. Leaks seeming to come from the committee may well have emerged from those under scrutiny or other sources. A well-placed leak could discredit the committee's endeavors by making it appear negligent or reckless in protecting its confidences. Or a leak could injure upcoming witnesses, publicize an aspect of a witness's testimony favorable to him, or divert attention from major issues. Because leakers do not as a rule tout their improper activities, and newsmen—the usual recipients of leaks—do not broadcast their confidential contacts, it was often impossible to pinpoint whether a particular leak came from committee or outside sources. Nevertheless, it can be said with assurance that senators and staff were the funnels for much of the confidential information that mysteriously appeared in the public domain during the committee's probes.

The leaks from the committee began in earnest shortly after its first major witness, James McCord, appeared in executive session on March 28, 1973. *Washington Post* newsmen Bob Woodward and Carl Bernstein candidly reported these early leaks in their book, *All The President's Men;**

> The committee session with McCord lasted four and a half hours. Afterward, Senator Howard Baker of Tennessee, the Republican vice chairman of the committee, announced that McCord had provided "significant information . . . covering a lot of territory."
> Bernstein and Woodward began the ritual phone calls, starting with Senators. "Okay, I'm going to help you on this one," one told Woodward. "McCord testified that

* Simon and Schuster, 1974, pp. 280–81.

Liddy told him the plans and budget for the Watergate operation were approved by Mitchell in February, when he was still Attorney General. And he said that Colson knew about Watergate in advance."

But, in answer to Woodward's questions, he added that McCord had only secondhand information for his allegations, as well as for his earlier accusations that Dean and Magruder had had prior knowledge.

"However," the Senator said, "he was very convincing."

[*Post* Executive Editor Benjamin] Bradlee was able to get a second Senator to corroborate the story, and Bernstein received the same version from a staff member.

*   *   *

The flood of "McCord says" stories continued. McCord appeared again on Thursday, and the reporters went through the same exercise. McCord stated that Liddy had told him that charts outlining the Watergate operation had been shown to Mitchell in February. Three sources gave identical versions of the testimony.

Leaking reached fever pitch during the week before John Dean testified at public hearing. Dean first appeared in executive session on Saturday, June 16, 1973. At that time his public session was scheduled for Tuesday, June 19. The hope was that the short time lag between private and public session would permit control of leaks.

Alas, a futile hope! Matters of foreign affairs intervened. The week of June 18 was the period of Party Secretary Leonid Brezhnev's visit to the United States. On June 18 Senators Mike Mansfield and Hugh Scott, the Democratic and Republican leaders of the Senate, wrote Senator Ervin asking that the hearings be postponed during the state visit. They argued that a delay would "give Mr. Nixon and Mr. Brezhnev the opportunity to reconcile differences, arrive at mutual agreements, and in the field of foreign policy, be able to achieve results which would be beneficial not only to our two countries but, hopefully, to all mankind."

The committee acceded to this request with, according to Senator Ervin, "some degree of reluctance." Senator Weicker voted against postponement, contending that while "the Brezhnev visit is important, this particular exercise in democracy [the hearings] is important also. I don't know why the two can't move along together. They might give an idea to Brezhnev of the strength of our kind of government."

Dean's public testimony was postponed until June 25. Between June 16 and June 25, information about Dean's private testimony flowed from the committee like rainwater. A staff summary of Dean's entire secret testimony—which contained many of his charges against Nixon, Haldeman, Ehrlichman, and Mitchell—leaked. A log prepared for the committee by the White House concerning Dean's conversations with the President was also given to the press.

Special media attention focused on Dean's admission that he had taken, and later replaced, $4,850 from campaign funds to pay for his 1972 wedding and honeymoon. This revelation provided ammunition for those inclined to disparage Dean's testimony and assail his character. Railed Senator Hugh Scott: "Nothing is so incredible that this turncoat will not be willing to testify to it in exchange for a reward . . . [A] man who can embezzle can easily tell lies."

Dean's attorney, Charles Shaffer, professed outrage over the leaks. On June 19 he announced that his client would make no more statements to the committee in closed session. Schaffer rightly calculated that with public hearings on the horizon, no contempt citation would result from this stiff-necked stand.

Measures were taken to see that further unauthorized disclosures about Dean's testimony were blocked. On June 24 I transported Dean's lengthy opening statement under armed guard from his lawyer's office to the committee's facilities, where it was reproduced. Armed protection may now seem an extreme, perhaps melodramatic, precaution, but those were days when passions ran high and rumors persisted that a steep price had been offered by a news organization for an advance look at Dean's statement.

But by June 24 the damage was done. The pot shots at Dean had increased, his credibility was injured, and the committee once again had been portrayed as unable or unwilling to safeguard sensitive evidence. An unidentified committee member, referring to the release of the summary of Dean's testimony, remarked disdainfully: "This is not just a bit of a leak. This is a hemorrhage." And Senator Mansfield was moved publicly to call upon the committee to adopt "stricter procedures" to quell the flow of leaks.

The most galling leak never resulted in a news story. On Friday, July 13, Alexander Butterfield told committee staff in private session that President Nixon had taped certain conversations—a revelation Butterfield repeated in public session on Monday, July 16. Although only a weekend was involved, the committee more than once pointed to the "fact" that this startling information was kept secret until Butterfield testified publicly as indication that the committee was capable of protecting sensitive material. The basis for this paltry boast, however, was shattered by a few lines from Woodward and Bernstein's *All The President's Men*:*

By May 17, 1973, when the Senate hearings opened, Bernstein and Woodward had gotten lazy. Their night-time visits were scarcer, and, increasingly, they had begun to rely on a relatively easy access to the Senate committee's staff investigators and attorneys. . . .

* See pp. 330–31.

On Saturday the 14th, Woodward received a phone call at home from a senior member of the committee's investigative staff. . . . [H]e said. . . . "We interviewed Butterfield. He told the whole story."
"What whole story?"
"Nixon bugged himself."

Incredibly, this sensational piece of news did not appear in the *Post* until Butterfield repeated it at public session. According to Woodward and Bernstein, the executive editor of the *Post*, Benjamin Bradlee, did not initially think the story merited much attention. That the story was not prematurely bannered in the press was thus not the fault of the loquacious staff member who blurted this information to a newsman even before many committee members and senior staff knew about it.

The leaks spewing from the Hughes-Rebozo investigation, which in part prompted lawsuits by Rebozo and the Hughes forces, have already been mentioned. There is no need to recount all the specifics of these leaks, which began shortly after the committee's investigation was instigated in August 1973 and appeared with disturbing frequency until the committee's report on the subject was published in July 1974. It is enough to observe that during this period there were numerous accounts in the media concerning the circumstances under which the $100,000 Hughes gift to Nixon was consummated, the possible use made of that money while in Rebozo's possession, the government favors Hughes may have received for his contribution, the facts surrounding the return of $100,000 (actually $100,*100*) to Hughes representatives, and numerous other aspects of the investigation. These reports often divulged confidential information in minute details that could have come only from persons intimately familiar with the investigation. A number of these accounts appeared in *The New*

York Times under the by-line of Seymour Hersh, who has since gained more fame by his revelations of misdeeds within the CIA.

———————

As the committee's tenure waned and its staff began to prepare the final report, the leaks increased to ludicrous proportions. Larry Meyer of *The Washington Post* reported that on two occasions senators seeking to release material they described as "previously undisclosed documents" were told by a reporter that the documents had been made public by the committee months before. And, Meyer wrote, "On another occasion, one senator's aide leaked committee material to several newspaper and television reporters with an embargo to insure that the leak was reported simultaneously by the news media."* The running joke on Capitol Hill was that, if a certain senator's Xerox machine malfunctioned, the congressional press corps would go out of business.

Every draft section of the committee's final report was released to the press within moments after being sent to committee members for review.† Syndicated columnist James Kilpatrick reported on the CBS program *Agronsky and Company* that the draft on the milk fund affair was in reporters' hands less than two minutes after it arrived in the senators' offices. Before the initial draft of the chapter dealing with the Watergate break-in and cover-up was dispensed, Daniel Schorr of CBS told Sam Dash he had been promised a copy. When Dash delivered the draft to the senators, he enclosed a note repeating Schorr's remark with the observation that he hoped Schorr was only boasting or joking because it would be unfortunate if the draft was released before approval by the committee. CBS not

———

* *The Washington Post*, September 30, 1974, p. A8.

† The draft report on the Hughes-Rebozo affair was actually given to the press on the committee's authorization. The press was salivating for this document and the committee realized there was no way to prevent its leaking.

only obtained the draft but also Dash's note, which Schorr's colleague, Lesley Stahl, read in part on the air.

The leakage of report drafts was shamefully unfair to certain persons under investigation. The draft of the Watergate break-in and cover-up chapter—the first chapter prepared—was written under instructions to draw conclusions about the involvement in criminal acts of persons yet to be tried for that conduct. This instruction was later wisely reversed partially because the committee recognized it should not risk prejudicing upcoming trials by firm conclusions on criminal guilt. Generally speaking, the final report presented the facts the committee had uncovered without ultimate resolutions as to criminal culpability. There are two ways to portray a horse, Senator Ervin said. You can draw a picture of a horse and under it write, "This is a horse." Or you can draw the picture and delete the inscription. In its final report, the senator remarked, his committee just drew the picture. But the initial draft of the Watergate chapter included the inscription. For example, it proclaimed in essence that John Mitchell had approved the Watergate break-in and that John Ehrlichman had authorized the Ellsberg burglary. These "conclusions" were reported in the media throughout the country, a result surely disquieting to Mitchell and Ehrlichman, who had yet to stand trial for offenses connected with those episodes.*

The affront to Senator Hubert Humphrey was equally unfortunate. The draft report on his presidential campaign unjustifiably suggested that Humphrey had committed a felony by giving more than $5,000 of his personal money to a single committee supporting his own campaign. At the time of this "gift," federal law made it unlawful for anyone to make a contribution over $5,000 to any presidential

---

* A draft section on Nixon's involvement in the Watergate cover-up was also prepared. But this document—which was obviously highly sensitive in light of the impending impeachment proceedings —was, at Dash's instruction, never sent to committee members and was never leaked.

candidate or committee acting on his behalf. But there was absolutely no authority suggesting that a candidate's gift to a committee established to promote his candidacy came under the statute, and common sense counseled otherwise. The committee's final report made clear that Humphrey had not committed a felony, but the leaked misconceived draft prompted numerous news stories causing him much discomfort.

———————

Witnesses claiming victimization by leaks reacted in different ways. Almost invariably they expressed resentment and concern for the damage done their reputations. The following excerpt is from the second executive session of General Alexander Haig, then President Nixon's chief of staff:

General HAIG. . . . I think I personally have been very chagrined about [his first executive session]. I have been chagrined about it because I have read in the press that I refused to answer a number of questions which suggested to the reader that I had knowledge that I don't believe I had, which is bothersome to me personally.

I also must say, Senator, that before I was called to this committee I was notified by the New York Times that I would be, and it was the day after that I received notification that I should come. That bothered me a great deal.

The day I left here last, by the time I got back to my office, on the wires were first a report that I had refused to answer over 100 questions involving the Rebozo matter. Well, to any layman in this country that reads that they can only assume General Haig is involved in illegal activity on the Rebozo matter.

Then the next lead that came out was a little more precise but equally damaging because the questions that were asked for the record here were given lock, stock, and barrel to the press. I personally resented that very much. I still do.

*   *   *

What bothers me, if I enter into an executive session, by the very rules of this committee I expect it to be processed that way.

Mr. DASH. You have every right to believe that.

Senator WEICKER. You have every right to believe it and unfortunately, General Haig, from what direction the news comes is something we cannot fathom any better than you can, and I would dare say if we knew the record, both of us, we would find it comes in equal proportions from both sides.

Whatever opinion may be held of General Haig, it is possible to sympathize with the concerns he expressed.

Leaks pushed some witnesses into silence. The statement below is by J.D. Williams, an attorney representing Joseph Johnson, former chairman of the Mills for President Committee, and other Mills associates. Williams spoke in conjunction with Johnson's assertion of his Fifth Amendment privilege.

. . . I don't mean to be disrespectful to the committee, Senator . . . but we first started coming up here and our people appeared voluntarily and it was only shortly thereafter that we began to read in the national newspapers about all this and we, that is, people connected with the campaign, began to get calls from reporters, where they either had read to them or received verbatim transcripts of investigators' reports about certain activities. That is when we just said that our voluntary cooperation was going to cease because there is just no point in coming up here and talking about things and then reading about them in the newspapers, particularly where there are inaccuracies in the newspapers.

*   *   *

[The committee's investigators want] to get back into the milk thing and our position on that is he is not going to testify. This is the subject of grand jury investigation. We have no assurance and indeed no assurance can be made by even this committee that this won't appear in the newspapers in a distorted form. The grand jury is not sequestered and they could read this and they could form the wrong interpretation and Mr. Johnson could be summoned before the grand jury and there is just no telling what could happen.

Other witnesses used the occasion of leaks to attack the committee. Most observers felt that former Nixon speechwriter Patrick Buchanan skillfully put the committee on the defensive when he appeared before it. Leaks gave him his best weapon. This is how he began his testimony:

Of [great] concern to me . . . has been an apparent campaign orchestrated from within the committee staff to malign my reputation in the public press prior to my appearance. In the hours immediately following my well-publicized invitation there appeared in the Washington Post, the New York Times, the Baltimore Sun, the Chicago Tribune, and on the national networks, separate stories all attributed to committee sources alleging that I was the architect of a campaign of political espionage or dirty tricks. According to the Post, committee sources were in possession of my memorandums recommending infiltrating the opposition.

In the Times the charge was that the committee had a series of Buchanan memorandums suggesting "political espionage and sabotage against Edmund S. Muskie of Maine and other candidates for the Presidential nomination."

One wire service stated that Mr. Buchanan would be questioned about "blueprints and plans concerning the scandal."

In the Chicago Tribune, the headline read: "Nixon Speech Writer Blamed for Muskie Plot." The story read, and I quote: "Senate investigators have evidence that Patrick J. Buchanan, one of the President Nixon's favorite speechwriters, was the secret author of a political sabotage scheme."

In the Baltimore Sun under a major front page headline reading: "Buchanan Linked to 1972 Dirty Tricks," the story ran thus: "Patrick J. Buchanan, a Presidential consultant, may emerge as yet another architect of the 1972 White House dirty tricks strategy, according to congressional sources."

Mr. Chairman, this covert campaign of vilification carried on by staff members of your committee is in direct violation of rule 40 of the Rules of Procedure for the Select Committee. That rule strictly prohibits staff members from leaking substantive materials. Repeatedly, I have asked of Mr. Dash and Mr. Lenzner information that they might have to justify such allegations. Repeatedly, they have denied to me that they have such documents. When I asked Mr. Lenzner who on the committee staff was responsible, he responded, "Mr. Buchanan, you ought to know that you cannot believe everything you read in the newspapers." It was his joke and my reputation.

So it seems fair to me to ask how can this Select Committee set itself up as the ultimate arbiter of American political ethics if it cannot even control the character assassination in its own ranks.

One does not have to agree with Buchanan's characterizations of committee staff to appreciate that leaks allowed him to enter the hearing in a position of strength—to appear more a victim of "dirty tricks" than a perpetrator.

Some speculation on the motives that prompted the leaks is in order. The reasons appear diverse. There was a point of view—woefully naïve in my judgment*—that the investigations should be totally open. Perhaps the desire to bring the public in provoked putting secret evidence out. Politicians and their staffs may have felt that giving choice tidbits to newsmen (thus assuring them air time or a prominent place in their publications) would cultivate favorable attitudes in the press quite useful in some later political campaign. Staff members may have wished to publicize their particular investigations for their own self-aggrandizement. There may have been conscious designs to injure a witness or individual under investigation; from surface appearances, this seemed the case concerning many of the Dean leaks. Some may have believed that a leak would prime the press and public for upcoming testimony, thereby increasing comprehension of its import. Or, when the committee was deciding whether to have further public hearings and what areas to cover, staff members may have believed that a well-publicized leak would ensure that their work was included in the hearings.

In regard to this last consideration, I was told by a reporter that a senator's aide had remarked that I had the wrong "strategy." I didn't recognize, the aide purportedly said, that senators do not think something is important unless they see it in the headlines. By not leaking, he suggested, I was destroying the chance for public hearings of my investigations.

A more cynical, perverted view of a staff lawyer's role would be difficult to construct. Staff attorneys are paid to investigate, gather facts, come to conclusions about their propriety and present their findings and recommendations to their committee, which must determine whether public hearings or other actions are justified. They are not employed to engage in "strategies"—especially those contrary

* See Chapter VIII.

to the rules of their committee—to promote their own prestige or ensure that their findings are ventilated.

While the leakers must bear chief responsibility for the unseemly mire the leaks produced, the actions and attitudes of the press also warrant examination. Siphoning leaks from an investigating committee is not investigative reporting in any true sense. A gaping difference exists between (1) enticing White House officials to divulge information regarding executive malefactions that the administration dearly hopes to keep secret and (2) revealing facts uncovered by an investigative body that in all probability will eventually be publicized in orderly fashion. (The Ervin committee was not seriously criticized for withholding information. In fact, if it erred, it erred on the side of revealing information of dubious pertinency under its enabling resolution.)

Woodward and Bernstein recognized this distinction in *All the President's Men.** Referring to their perceptions as the Ervin committee investigations began, they remarked: "It was no longer a matter of 'investigative' reporting, putting pieces in a puzzle, disclosing what had been obscured. They [reporters] would be merely trying to find out in advance the testimony of witnesses who would eventually take the stand in public." But, they commented, "If some papers or networks searched out leaks, all the reporters would feel bound to compete."

This last insight was prescient. The coverage of the Ervin committee investigations was marked by strenuous competition among newsmen for confidential information. For a reporter to obtain a major leak was viewed in the press as a badge of honor. Woodward and Bernstein in their book recount Bernstein's "frustration" at being beaten on a Watergate story.† Reporters for the *Washington Star-News* were under intense pressure from their editors

* See p. 280.
† See pp. 276–77.

to secure some of the leaks that usually went to the more established *Washington Post* and *New York Times*. But the competition was not only among news organizations. Little could please CBS correspondent Lesley Stahl more than scooping her more experienced colleague Daniel Schorr with a juicy leak from a committee source.

Reporters' tactics varied. Some would beg, badger, wheedle, demand. The press has its sycophants as well as those who appeared to believe they were entitled to leaks by Divine Right.* Some requests approached the absurd. Shortly after the committee filed suit against the President, one reporter asked me "on a confidential basis" to tell him the major weaknesses in our case.

This discussion should not be taken as undifferentiated criticism of the press. The public owes the media a great debt: without the press, Wategate might never have unfolded and Nixon might yet be in the White House. Much of the coverage of the Watergate hearings was thoughtful, fair, and incisive. At times newsmen would provide facts or suggest avenues of interrogation that had escaped the investigators. And many questions put to staff members—about, for example, scheduling of public hearings, past public testimony, the nature of the committee's legal positions—were legitimate.†

But too little serious thought has been given to the role of the press in the leaking process. It is insufficient for a newspaper like *The Washington Post* to criticize Ervin committee leaking—as it has done‡—without mentioning the part played by its reporters. Certainly no paper benefited more from leaks than the *Post*, and it and other media

---

* "It has generally been held that the First Amendment does not guarantee the press a constitutional right of special access to information not available to the public generally."—*Branzburg* v. *Hayes*, 408 U.S. 665, 684 (1972).

† Questions of this sort should have been directed to a press aide, an official the committee unfortunately did not have. The Senate select committee investigating intelligence activities has a flat ban on unauthorized staff personnel talking to the press.

‡ See *The Washington Post*, January 29, 1975, p. A 20.

outlets must bear at least partial blame for whatever disrupted investigations and injured reputations the leaks caused. The claim that a news organization must print or broadcast leaks because its competition does so is not adequate justification for indiscriminate publicizing of confidential information. And while the public's right to know is a powerful consideration influencing media conduct, the need to act responsibly to promote effective, fair governmental functioning is also present.

The seepage of information from the committee caused great heartache to Senator Ervin. He and Sam Dash instituted procedures to stop the leaks. Highly confidential materials were kept in the secure area of the Joint Committee on Atomic Energy; items stored there generally escaped improper release. Less sensitive information was housed in the committee's secure area under lock and key. But access to this material was not difficult. Staff members with a need to know could obtain the material they desired, and in any event, those actually working on an investigation knew what they had uncovered. Additionally, committee members or their aides could normally secure information if a senator requested it. In such circumstances the principal protection against leaking was individual integrity, a commodity often sorely lacking.

Ervin, with resignation born of long experience in Congress, recognized the difficulties in silencing those prone to break confidences. "Being in Washington," he said, "I've learned you can't keep secrets. No sooner has something reached someone's ears here than it comes out his mouth." On another occasion he remarked: "I know of no way to stop men from talking. The only way men who have responsibility for keeping secrets can do so is by exercising will power, and if they refrain from using will power, then no one can force them to do so."

Senator Talmadge was not so philosophical. To mention leaks to him was to see him turn the color of his native Georgia clay. "It's the damnedest thing I've ever seen," he fulminated near the end of the committee's work. "I've been in the Senate seventeen and a half years and never has anything leaked from my staff. The Select Committee was like a sieve. My opinion is that Senators more than staff were guilty."

Guilty of what? Most certainly of violations of the Committee's *Rules of Procedure*. But beyond that, interesting questions arise as to whether leaks may transgress even weightier proscriptions.

That the leaks contravened relevant portions of the committee's rules is demonstrated by their recitation. The rules provided that "No testimony taken or material presented in an executive session, or any summary or excerpt thereof shall be made available to other than the committee members and committee staff and no such material or testimony shall be made public or presented at a public hearing, either in whole or in part, unless authorized by a majority of the committee members or as otherwise provided for in these rules." The rules also stated, "No evidence or testimony, or any summary or excerpt thereof given in executive session which the committee determines may tend to defame, degrade or incriminate any person shall be released, or presented at a public hearing unless such person shall have been afforded the opportunity to testify or file a statement in rebuttal, and any pertinent evidence or testimony given by such person, or on his behalf, is made a part of the transcript, summary, or excerpt prior to the public release of such portion of the testimony."* And the rules declared:

> All information developed by or made known to any member of the committee staff shall be deemed to be confidential. No member of the committee staff shall

---

* Note that this provision required a committee determination to activate its protections.

communicate to any person, other than a member of the committee or another member of the committee staff, any substantive information with respect to any substantive matter related to the activities of the committee. All communications with the press and other persons not on the committee or committee staff in respect to confidential substantive matters shall be by members of the committee only. Official releases of information to the press on behalf of the committee shall be made only with the express consent of the Chairman and Vice Chairman.*

These provisions were not unique. The standing rules of the House, for instance, provide that "No evidence or testimony taken in executive session may be released or used in public session without the consent of the committee."† Similarly, the rules of the Senate Permanent Investigations Subcommittee state, "All testimony taken in executive session shall be kept secret and will not be released for public information without the approval of a majority of the Subcommittee." The Senate select committee studying the intelligence agencies has a rule declaring that any staff member caught leaking will be immediately fired.

On occasion it seemed that the no-leak provisions of the Ervin committee's rules were more honored in the breach than in the observance. But the full legal implications of the rampant violations of these rules appear not to be generally appreciated.

Particularly significant here is a principle discussed in the preceding chapter. Witnesses before a congressional committee have a right to expect that the committee will adhere to its rules established for the protection of indi-

* The rules also provided that, unless authorized, the names of witnesses subpoenaed—and information relating to the witness or the subpoena to him—could not be released prior to the time set for his appearance.

† Rule XI 2.(k) (7).

vidual rights. If a committee ignores its rules, a witness may be justified in refusing to testify or produce evidence.

No case applies this principle to a committee derelict in protecting its confidences, but the possible application is evident. No-leak rules are established in part to protect the reputations of witnesses and others under examination. If a pattern of leaks has developed—if, in other words, a witness can demonstrate that the chances are slim or nil that information taken in confidence will remain confidential—he may be justified in refusing to cooperate. In such circumstances, a court might well conclude that a prosecution for contempt of Congress was inappropriate because the recalcitrant witness was fully within his rights.

But mere speculation that leaks might result should not justify refusal to produce evidence. This much is suggested by the following passage from Judge Sirica's decision turning over the Watergate grand jury's report to the House Judiciary Committee.

> . . . The [House Judiciary] Committee has taken elaborate precautions to insure against unnecessary and inappropriate disclosure of these materials. Nonetheless, counsel for the indicted defendants, some having lived for a considerable time in Washington, D.C., are not persuaded that disclosure to the Committee can have any result but prejudicial publicity for their clients. The Court, however, cannot justify non-disclosure on the basis of *speculation* that leaks will occur, added to the further *speculation* that resultant publicity would prejudice the rights of defendants. . . . We have no basis on which to assume that the Committee's use of the Report will be injudicious or that it will disregard the plea contained therein that defendants' rights to fair trials be respected.*

* This decision is as yet unreported. In *Haldeman* v. *Sirica*, 501 F. 2d 714 (D.C. Cir. 1974) the Court of Appeals declined to disturb Sirica's ruling in this case.

Serious leaking also presents the opportunity for direct action by the Senate and House under their self-help contempt authority and their powers of expulsion and dismissal. Congress has intrinsic power to punish acts that obstruct or impede the performance of its legislative duties.* Clearly, unchecked leaking can have this effect. Leaks can draw a committee into disrepute, prod potential witnesses to obduracy or disappearance, allow subsequent witnesses improperly to conform their testimony or conjure up devious explanations or excuses, and cause confidential sources to evaporate.

The standing rules of the Senate recognize that contempt and other remedies are available to discourage leaking. Rule XXVI 4., which the Senate Committee on Rules and Administration has interpreted as applying to committee activities,† provides that "Any Senator or officer of the Senate who shall disclose the secret or confidential business or proceedings of the Senate shall be liable, if a Senator, to suffer expulsion from the body; and if an officer, to dismissal from the service of the Senate, and to punishment for contempt."

An intriguing question is whether a reporter or news organization that publishes leaks obstructing or impeding the performance of Congress's legislative functions could be punished for contempt under the self-help powers. Undoubtedly, if Congress had the temerity to take such action, claims of First Amendment rights of free press would ring to the heavens. How these claims would be resolved is not certain and might depend largely on the specific facts involved, but a recent admonition of the Supreme Court may be relevant:

It is clear that the First Amendment does not invalidate every incidental burdening of the press that may

---

* See Chapter III.

† See the committee's report, *Rules of Procedure for Senate Investigating Committees*, 84th Cong., 1st Sess., (January 10, 1955) pp. 39–40.

result from the enforcement of civil or criminal statutes of general applicability. Under prior cases, otherwise valid laws serving substantial public interests may be enforced against the press as against others, despite the possible burden that may be imposed. The Court has emphasized that '[t]he publisher of a newspaper has no special immunity from the application of general laws' . . . .

The prevailing view is that the press is not free to publish with impunity everything and anything it desires to publish. . . . A newspaper or a journalist may . . . be punished for contempt of court, in appropriate circumstances. . . .*

On June 3, 1974, Charles Colson pleaded guilty to obstructing justice by leaking materials intended to prejudice the criminal trial of Daniel Ellsberg on charges relating to his obtaining and releasing the Pentagon Papers. The plea prompted the gratuitous remark by White House press spokesman Gerald Warren that Colson's misdeeds were no worse than the conduct of the "felons" on the Ervin committee and its staff. Mr. Warren's attack as reported was highly indiscriminate, making no distinction between those who were leaking and those who were not. But his uncharitable comment does serve to raise the question whether leaking may have consequences in terms of the criminal law.

In this lawsuit against the committee, Bebe Rebozo charged that the barrage of leaks by staff members concerning the Hughes-Rebozo investigation violated two specific criminal statutes. The leaks, he alleged, constitured an obstruction of justice under a statute, similar to that used in the Colson case, making it a felony "corruptly" to influence, obstruct or impede—or attempt to influence, obstruct or impede—the "due and proper"

* *Branzburg* v. *Hayes*, 408 U.S. 665, 682–84 (1972).

administration of the law in a federal proceeding or the "due and proper" exercise of the power of inquiry by Congress.* Moreover, Rebozo claimed, the staff leaks offended a provision condemning unauthorized disclosure by federal employees of various types of business and financial information acquired in the course of official duties.† In the proper factual settings these statutes could be applied to persons leaking certain types of information received in confidence by a congressional committee.‡ Conceivably, for instance, releasing information deemed confidential by committee rules could constitute a corrupt impediment to a congressional inquiry.§ So, too, in appropriate circumstances, could provisions of the espionage laws be invoked to punish the leaking of certain types of classified and other sensitive information.¶

There may be, moreover, another statute that could be applied to deal generally with the problem raised by the gush of leaks from an investigating committee. A provision of the code penalizes conspiracies "to defraud the United States."** Despite the wording of the statute, it has been interpreted to interdict conspiracies to impair, obstruct or defeat lawful government functions. An early statement of the elements of this crime comes from a 1924 opinion by Chief Justice (former President) William Howard Taft:††

---

* 18 U.S.C. 1505 (1970).

† 18 U.S.C. 1905 (1970). This crime is a misdemeanor.

‡ Since leaking is not a valid part of legislative duties, it appears that the speech or debate clause would provide no protection against charges brought to penalize such conduct. See Chapter X.

§ "Corruptly" as used in a related provision of the relevant statute has recently been defined as acting "with improper motive, a bad and evil purpose." See *United States* v. *Abrams*, 427 F. 2d 86 (2d Cir. 1970) *cert. denied* 400 U.S. 832 (1970).

¶ See generally, 18 U.S.C. 792–99 (1970).

** 18 U.S.C. 371 (1970). Under the statute—and under general conspiracy law—one overt act in furtherance of a conspiracy is needed to comprise the crime. No attempt has been made to catalogue all criminal statutes that possibly, in suitable circumstances, might apply to leaking from a congressional committee.

†† *Hammerschmidt* v. *United States*, 265 U.S. 182, 188 (1924).

To conspire to defraud the United States means primarily to cheat the Government out of property or money, but it also means to interfere with or obstruct one of its lawful governmental functions by deceit, craft or trickery, or at least by means that are dishonest. It is not necessary that the Government shall be subjected to property or pecuniary loss by the fraud, but only that its legitimate official action and purpose shall be defeated by misrepresentation, chicane or the over-reaching of those charged with carrying out the governmental intention. . . .

Later cases indicate that "misrepresentation or deceit" are not essential components of the crime.*

The Ervin committee's final report suggested that this statute might pertain to the conduct revolving around White House machinations to use the instruments of federal government as tools to reelect Nixon. Could it also be applied to agreements to leak confidential information obtained during a congressional investigation?

Several cases indicate that it could. Of special importance is a 1910 Supreme Court case where the Court was asked to rule on the legal sufficiency of an indictment charging a conspiracy between a Department of Agriculture statistician and two other defendants.† The indictment alleged in part that, pursuant to the conspiracy and in violation of his official duty under Department "custom practices and regulations," the statistician secretly released information received in his official capacity concerning the probable content of forthcoming cotton crop reports. Armed with advance knowledge, the other defendants were able to speculate with unfair advantage in the open market.

---

* *Dennis v. United States*, 384 U.S. 855, 861 (1966); *United States v. Johnson*, 337 F. 2d 180, 185–86 (4th Cir. 1964) *affirmed as to that issue*, 383 U.S. 169, 172 (1966).
† *Hass v. Henkel*, 216 U.S. 462 (1910).

The indictment, the Court said, adequately alleged a conspiracy to defraud the United States.

These counts do not expressly charge that the conspiracy included any direct pecuniary loss to the United States, but as it is averred that the acquiring of the information and its intelligent computation, with deductions, comparisons and explanations involved great expense, it is clear that practices of this kind would deprive these reports of most of their value to the public and degrade the department in general estimation, and that there would be a real financial loss. But it is not essential that such a conspiracy shall contemplate a financial loss or that one shall result. The statute is broad enough in its terms to include any conspiracy for the purpose of impairing, obstructing or defeating the lawful function of any department of Government. Assuming, as we have, for it has not been challenged, that this statistical side of the Department of Agriculture is the exercise of a function within the purview of the Constitution, it must follow that any conspiracy which is calculated to obstruct or impair its efficiency and destroy the value of its operations and reports as fair, impartial and reasonably accurate, would be to defraud the United States by depriving it of its lawful right and duty of promulgating or diffusing the information so officially acquired in the way and at the time required by law or departmental regulation. . . .

Recently, a federal court of appeals sustained under the statute a conviction of an attorney who conspired with a Securities and Exchange Commission branch chief to obtain confidential SEC information that allowed the attorney to make a "tidy profit."* The court said: "An agreement whereby a federal employee will act to pro-

* *United States* v. *Peltz*, 433 F. 2d 48 (2d Cir. 1970), *cert. denied* 401 U.S. 955 (1971).

mote private benefit in breach of his duty . . . comes within the statute if the proper functioning of government is significantly affected thereby. . . . The very making of a plan whereby a government employee will divulge material information which he knows he should not is 'dishonest' within Chief Justice Taft's language [quoted above] regardless whether such plan is secured by consideration."*

It takes no great imagination to reach the conclusion that, if agreements to leak confidential Agriculture and SEC information can constitute conspiracies to defraud the United States, then an agreement with upcoming witnesses, the press, or other interested parties to leak information deemed confidential under congressional regulations could also, in certain circumstances, comprise a conspiracy of this nature. Certainly leaks can seriously "impair" or "obstruct" the exercise of the investigatory function.

The suggestion that the press might have some criminal liability for leaks will not go well in some circles. If the law developed along this line, several Washington reporters might be looking for work. Some undoubtedly would feel that any prosecution would be infirm under the free-press provision of the First Amendent. This view, however, experiences difficulty when juxtaposed with a recent pronouncement by the Supreme Court.

> It would be frivolous to assert . . . that the First Amendment, in the interest of serving news or otherwise, confers a license on either the reporter or his news sources to violate valid criminal laws. Although stealing documents or private wiretapping could provide newsworthy information, neither reporter nor source is immune from conviction for such conduct, whatever

---

* Daniel Ellsberg and Anthony Russo were indicted under the conspiracy statute for conduct surrounding the leak of the Pentagon Papers. Their case, however, never came to trial, but was dismissed for government improprieties.

the impact on the flow of news . . . . The Amendment does not reach so far as to override the interest of the public in ensuring that neither reporter nor source is invading the rights of other citizens through reprehensible conduct forbidden to all other persons. . . .*

This commentary should not be interpreted to imply that every congressional leak is a crime, nor construed as a recommendation for wholesale prosecutions for leaking under the conspiracy statute or any other law discussed. Arguably only the most reprehensible crimes—those where investigations in fact have been seriously impaired or obstructed—should be tried, because the potential exists for abusive prosecutions. The phrase "interfere with or obstruct . . . lawful governmental functions" used in connection with the conspiracy statute is vague and has been only partially adumbrated by case law. So also is there difficulty in delineating the precise boundaries of the statute that proscribes the corrupt influencing, obstructing, or impeding of congressional inquiries. An overzealous or corrupt prosecutor could use unwarranted prosecutions to harass congressmen and their staff. Or court action could be used to chill the rights of free press.†

What this discussion is intended to do is galvanize thinking about the seriousness of leaks from investigating committees. During Watergate, attitudes on the committee

---

* *Branzburg* v. *Hays*, 408 U.S. 665, 691–92 (1972). See also *New York Times Co.* v. *United States*, 403 U.S. 713, 735–37 (1971) (White, J., concurring).

† Prosecutions could also be employed by an administration, unhappy with leaks about corruption in its own house, against its own employees. However, leaking material revealing governmental corruption which otherwise would be hidden is *not* interfering with a lawful government function—indeed, it may be the only feasible course to ensure that government acts within the law. Leaks taking the lid off wrongdoing such as came from the White House during Watergate are a far cry from disruptive leaks seeping from an investigating body attempting to carry on an orderly inquiry.

and in the press were too cavalier. Leaks were accepted as endemic to the Washington scene—a phenomenon to be expected and not fretted about unduly. This perspective needs changing. What must be understood is that leaks often unfairly injure reputations and impair investigations, and may have severe legal repercussions that well-intentioned, law-abiding citizens should wish to avoid.

·X·
Court Review of Congressional Abuses

The last several chapters demonstrate that persons under legislative investigation have numerous rights deriving from the Constitution, statutes, congressional rules and court decisions which afford considerable protection. Well and good, but how and when can these rights be asserted?

The first forum is the committee. The law normally requires that aggrieved persons initially raise their specific complaints with the offending committee. But congressional committees are often unsympathetic tribunals. They may see objections—even valid ones—as attempts to delay and disrupt their hearings. And a committee's parent body may hold similar views. Consequently, satisfactory review of committee procedures may come only in a court of law.

Historically, court review of congressional actions has

been precipitated most frequently in two ways.* Upon committee recommendation, a house of Congress may send a refusal to comply with committee orders or subpoenas to a grand jury. If indictment and prosecution follow, the witness-turned-defendant may ventilate his contentions before judge and jury.

A house may also remedy contempt of its authority by directing its sergeant at arms to arrest and imprison the offender until he cooperates or the session of Congress ends. The individual detained can test this action in court by seeking a writ of habeas corpus to free himself from custody or bringing a damage action against the sergeant at arms.

If these avenues to gain court review are exclusive, a witness is presented with unpalatable alternatives. He can succumb to committee demands and thus forfeit the rights he claims. Or, to test his contentions, he can resist and subject himself to criminal trial or imprisonment by the sergeant at arms. That he may have opportunity to convince the committee's parent body that criminal proceedings or the exercise of self-help powers are not warranted is little consolation.

No wonder then that persons under scrutiny—such as Rebozo and the Hughes employees—have sought to adjudicate their rights in civil actions against congressmen and their aides before criminal contempt or self-help procedures are employed. No need to risk unpleasant sanctions if another remedy is available.

Litigations against congressmen and their staffs have been instigated on numerous occasions. But often these suits have foundered on the shoals of various legal doctrines, two of which are particularly relevant. The first concerns the Constitution's speech or debate clause; the second, the so-called doctrine of comity, which teaches that a court normally should not exercise its equity powers to interfere with the conduct of legislative investiga-

* See Chapter III.

tions, especially where the issues involved may later be raised in contempt proceedings.

The archaic phrasing of the speech or debate clause reflects its early beginnings. It states, "for any Speech or Debate in either House, they [Senators and Representatives] shall not be questioned in any other Place."* The clause had its roots in English history, deriving from the English Bill of Rights of 1689 which declared "That the Freedom of Speech, and Debate or Proceedings in Parliament, ought not to be impeached or questioned in any Court or Place out of Parliament." Behind this declaration was a long struggle between the Tudor and Stuart kings and the House of Commons over the suppression and intimidation of critical legislators by the monarchy and judges under royal control. In 1688 the Glorious Revolution expelled the last of the Stuarts and established a new dynasty, and in 1689 the Bill of Rights was promulgated by Parliament and assented to by the crown.

The abuses that the English speech or debate clause were intended to correct are aptly illustrated by the case of Richard Strode, a member of Commons from Devonshire. Apparently motivated by personal interests, Strode in 1512 introduced a bill regulating tin miners. He was promptly prosecuted in a Stannary Court—a court with special jurisdiction over tin miners—for violating a local law making it criminal to obstruct tin mining. Strode was convicted and imprisoned until Parliament released him by the passage of a special bill

Also significant is a 1629 case where Sir John Elliot and other members of Commons who had spoken out against the crown in Parliament were prosecuted by Charles I and imprisoned in the Tower of London in part for "a conspiracy between the defendants to slander the state, and to raise sedition and discord between the king, his peers and people." Thirty-eight years later, in 1668, after Parliament had resolved that the conviction "was an ille-

---

* United States Constitution, Art. I, Sec. 6, Cl. 1.

gal judgment, and against the freedom and privilege of Parliament," the House of Lords finally reversed the convictions.

The principle of legislative freedom of speech and debate was thus well established by the time of the American Revolution. Indeed, the Constitution's speech or debate clause was approved at the Constitutional Convention without discussion or opposition. A similar clause had been contained in Article V of the Articles of Confederation.

As this spare look at history indicates, the speech or debate clause was primarily intended to guard congressmen against prosecution by an unfriendly executive and conviction by a hostile judiciary. The following statement of James Wilson, who was responsible for the clause's inclusion in the Constitution, reflects this purpose: "In order to enable and encourage a representative of the publick to discharge his publick trust with firmness and success, it is indispensably necessary, that he should be protected from the resentment of every one, however powerful, to whom the exercise of that liberty may occasion offence."* Moreover, as Wilson's statement also suggests, the clause protects against suits by private parties. Chief Justice Burger has said: "[The clause] has enabled reckless men to slander and even destroy others with impunity, but that was the conscious choice of the Framers. . . . 'The injury to the reputation of a private citizen is of less importance to the [nation], than the free and unreserved exercise of the duties of a representative, unawed by the fear of legal prosecutions.' "†

---

* R. McCloskey, ed., *Works of James Wilson* (Belknap Press, 1967), p. 42.

† *United States* v. *Brewster*, 408 U.S. 501, 516 and n. 11 (1972), quoting *Coffin* v. *Coffin*, 4 Mass 1, 28 (1808). See also, on the history of the clause, *Kilbourn* v. *Thompson*, 103 U.S. 168 (1881); *Tenney* v. *Brandhove*, 341 U.S. 367 (1951); *United States* v. *Johnson*, 383 U.S. 169 (1966); *Powell* v. *McCormack*, 395 U.S. 486 (1969); *Gravel* v. *United States*, 408 U.S. 606 (1972); *Doe* v. *McMillan*, 412 U.S. 306 (1973).

As should now be apparent, the clause exists not for the personal benefit of congressmen but to protect the integrity and independence of the legislative process. The clause, however, has never been thought to insulate legislative acts from review. For example, statutes can be tested for constitutionality, and committee actions challenged in contempt trials or habeas corpus proceedings. As the Supreme Court has said, "The purpose of the protection afforded legislators is not to forestall judicial review of legislative action but to insure that legislators are not distracted from or hindered in the performance of their legislative tasks by being called into court to defend their actions."*

To read the clause gives the impression that its protection is narrow—that it only safeguards utterances in the course of "Speech or Debate in either House." But the Supreme Court disabused this notion in the first matter regarding the clause that came before it—the well-known case of *Kilbourn* v. *Thompson.*† Ruling that members of the House could not be sued for authorizing Kilbourn's arrest by its sergeant at arms, the Court stated: "It would be a narrow view of the constitutional provision to limit it to words spoken in debate. . . . In short, [it applies] to things generally done in a session of the House by one of its members in relation to the business before it." Since *Kilbourn* the Court has broadly held that the clause precludes inquiries into legislative acts or the motives of a legislator in performing them. A legislative act has been defined as an act done in Congress (not necessarily in the physical confines of a house's chamber) in relation to the business before it or as part of "the deliberative and communicative processes by which Members participate in committee and House proceedings."‡

* *Powell* v. *McCormack*, 395 U.S. 486, 505 (1969).

† 103 U.S. 168 (1881). See Chapters III and IV.

‡ See, e.g., *Eastland* v. *United States Servicemen's Fund*, 421 U.S. 491, 501–2 (1975); *United States* v. *Brewster*, 408 U.S. 501, 512–16, 525 (1972); *Gravel* v. *United States*, 408 U.S. 606, 625 (1972); *Con-*

Numerous activities are protected under this formulation. The clause shields voting, authorization of investigations, issuance of subpoenas, conduct of committee hearings, publication of committee reports, and dissemination
of committee reports to congressmen, other committees,
and legislative functionaries. Actions taken in "the legislative sphere," the Supreme Court has said, are protected
even "if performed in other than legislative contexts,
[they] would . . . be unconstitutional or otherwise contrary to criminal or civil statutes."* But this statement
should be compared with the Court's previous declaration that congressmen would receive no protection under
the clause for executing "an invalid resolution by themselves carrying out an illegal arrest, or if, in order to
secure information for a hearing, [they] seized the property or invaded the privacy of a citizen."† The distinction
seems to be between taking an illegal legislative act such
as voting an unlawful resolution—protected—and preparing for or implementing that legislative act by additional
illegal conduct which is not "essential to legislating"—
unprotected.‡

Furthermore, certain activities of congressmen that are
more "political" than "legislative" in nature and only
"casually or incidentally related to legislative affairs" are
not covered by the clause. For instance, though they
may be legitimate endeavors, no protection exists for performing errands for constituents, making appointments
with government agencies, assisting in securing government contracts, preparing "newsletters" for constituents,
reproducing privately materials made public at committee

---

sumers *Union of United States, Inc. v. Periodical Correspondents'
Association,* 515 F. 2d 1341 (D.C. Cir. 1975); *United States v. Ehrlichman,* 389 F. Supp. 95 (1974).

* *Doe v. McMillan,* 412 U.S. 306, 312–13 (1973).

† *Gravel v. United States,* 408 U.S. 606, 621 (1972).

‡ See *Eastland v. United States Servicemen's Fund* 421 U.S. 491,
507–8 (1975).

hearings, or making speeches on the stump.* Also, one would presume, the clause does not shield leaking confidential material to the press.

Accepting a bribe to do a legislative act is not protected by the clause. In the case of former Maryland Senator Daniel Brewster,† the Supreme Court upheld an indictment—based on a criminal statute specifically relating to members of Congress—alleging in part that Brewster solicited, received, and agreed to receive money "in return for being influenced . . . in respect to his action, vote, and decision on postage rate legislation." "Taking a bribe," the Court said, straining to make fine distinctions, "is, obviously, no part of the legislative process or function; it is not a legislative act. . . . Nor is inquiry into a legislative act or the motivation for a legislative act necessary to a prosecution under this statute or this indictment. When a bribe is taken, it does not matter whether the promise for which the bribe was given was for the performance of a legislative act. . . . To make a prima facie case under this indictment, the Government need not show any act of [defendant] subsequent to the corrupt promise for payment, for it is *taking* the bribe, not performance of the illicit compact, that is a criminal act." The Court added that proof in such a bribery case must be truncated; the clause, it said, "precludes any showing of how [Brewster] acted, voted, or decided."‡

A case more closely connected with the investigatory

* See generally, *Doe* v. *McMillan*, 412 U.S. 306 (1973); *United States* v. *Brewster*, 408 U.S. 501, 512–13, 528 (1972); *Gravel* v. *United States*, 408 U.S. 606 (1972).

† *United States* v. *Brewster*, 408 U.S. 501 (1972).

‡ Compare *United States* v. *Johnson*, 383 U.S. 169 (1966). In *Brewster*, the Court, on similar reasoning, upheld another count of the indictment based on a separate code provision alleging that Brewster solicited, received, and agreed to receive money because of his *previous* action on postal rate legislation. Justices Brennan, Douglas, and White dissented in *Brewster* partially on the grounds that the prosecution involved an inquiry into legislative acts and motivations.

process illustrating the difficulty in deciding what conduct qualifies for speech or debate protection is *Doe* v. *McMillan*,* examined above in regard to the informing function. *Doe* presented the question whether distributing a committee report damaging the reputations of schoolchildren to the public at large went beyond the valid requirements of the legislative process and thus constituted a nonlegislative, unprotected act. The informing function notwithstanding, the Supreme Court remanded the case to the District Court for a determination whether "the legitimate legislative needs of Congress" had been exceeded. But three Justices—Douglas, Brennan, and Marshall—were ready to determine on the facts before them that dissemination of the report beyond the halls of Congress exceeded the sphere of legitimate legislative activity and consequently was not shielded by the clause.†

The dissenters—Burger, Blackmun, Rehnquist, and Stewart—concluded the contrary. Their basic view was that distribution of the report was, as an exercise of the informing function, a legislative act and therefore protected. Chief Justice Burger wrote, "I cannot accept the proposition that the judiciary has power to carry on a continuing surveillance of what Congress may and may not publish by way of reports on inquiry into subjects plainly within the legislative powers conferred on Congress by the Constitution." Justice Blackmun, writing also for Burger, denounced "[s]tationing the federal judiciary at the doors of the Houses of Congress for the purpose of sanitizing congressional documents in accord with this

---

* 412 U.S. 306 (1973).

† In *Gravel* v. *United States*, 408 U.S. 606 (1972), the Court held that the private reproduction and publication of materials presented at a Senate subcommittee hearing was not a legislative act (despite claims that such conduct was in furtherance of the informing function) and consequently had no constitutional protection. The dissenting views of Justices Douglas, Brennan, and Marshall in that case should be compared with those expressed by them in *Doe*. See also *Hentoff* v. *Ichord*, 318 F. Supp. 1175 (D.D.C. 1970).

Court's concept of wise legislative decisionmaking policy."
And Justice Rehnquist, for Burger, Blackmun, and Stewart also, trenchantly remarked: "While there is no reason for a rigid, mechanical application of the Speech or Debate Clause, there would seem to be equally little reason for a . . . factual determination in each case of public distribution as to whether that distribution served the 'legitimate legislative needs of Congress.' A supposed privilege against being held judicially accountable for an act is of virtually no use to the claimant of the privilege if it may only be sustained after elaborate judicial inquiry into the circumstances under which the act was performed."

A recent case where more unanimity was reached is *Eastland* v. *United States Servicemen's Fund.** Plaintiffs sued nine senators to enjoin enforcement of a Senate Internal Security Subcommittee subpoena to a bank calling for records relating to the Fund's donors. Eight Justices agreed that the speech or debate clause barred suit, since issuance of a subpoena was clearly a legislative act. The five Justices joining in the Court's opinion—Burger, Stewart, White, Blackmun, and Powell—stated that the clause must be "read . . . broadly to effectuate its purposes" and decried the fact that a legislative inquiry had been frustrated for five years while this suit (which plaintiffs had won in the Court of Appeals) was pending. The three concurring Justices—Marshall, Brennan, Stewart—noted that the decision left open the question whether suit could have been properly maintained against the bank, which was not a party to the action, even though the congressional defendants were protected.†

---

* 421 U.S. 491 (1975). Chief Justice Burger wrote the majority opinion in this case. Justices Marshall, Brennan, and Stewart concurred in the judgment, but filed a separate opinion.

† In August 1975 District Judge William Bryant issued a temporary restraining order against eight administrative agencies forbidding them from complying with subpoenas issued by a subcommittee of the House Commerce Committee which called for *all* copies of answers and working papers relating to wide-ranging ques-

The *Eastland* case notwithstanding, an examination of
the disparate views expressed in the Supreme Court's
cases indicates that the precise scope of the safeguards
afforded congressmen by the speech or debate clause
remains an issue fraught with uncertainty. Furthermore,
additional confusion exists concerning the extent to which
the clause protects the conduct of legislative aides. The
Supreme Court has stated that "for the purpose of construing the privilege a member and his aide are to be
'treated as one' . . ." Although the terms of the clause
refer only to congressmen, this provision, the Court has
said, "applies not only to a Member but also to his aides
insofar as the conduct of the latter would be a protected
legislative act if performed by himself." The rationale for
this holding is based on the recognition "that it is literally
impossible, in view of the complexities of the modern
legislative process, with Congress almost constantly in
session and matters of legislative concern constantly proliferating, for Members of Congress to perform their legislative tasks without the help of aides and assistants; that
the day-to-day work of such aides is so critical to the
Members' performance that they must be treated as the
latter's alter egos; and that if they are not so recognized,
the central role of the Speech or Debate Clause—to prevent intimidation of legislators by the Executive and
accountability before a possibly hostile judiciary . . . will
inevitably be diminished and frustrated."*

---

tionnaires sent the agencies by the subcommittee. *Television Digest
v. Federal Communications Commission*, Civ. No. 75–1281 (D.D.C.,
August 6, 1975). The plaintiffs were news organizations which previously had sought certain of the materials subpoenaed from the
eight agencies under the Freedom of Information Act. The subpoenas
were intended to prevent the news organizations from obtaining any
material relating to the questionnaires. The subcommittee's chairman, Representative John Moss of California, was a principal author
of the Freedom of Information Act. After Judge Bryant's ruling the
subpoenas were rescinded.

* *Gravel v. United States*, 408 U.S. 606, 616–17 (1972). See also
Doe v. McMillan, 412 U.S. 306, 324 (1973); *Eastland v. United States
Servicemen's Fund*, 421 U.S. 491, 507 (1975).

These flat pronouncements by the Court were surprising because just five years earlier it had indicated that the protection of the clause was "less absolute" for legislative aides than for congressmen. "[T]he doctrine," the Court had said, "in respect of a legislator, 'deserves greater respect than where an official acting on behalf of the legislature is sued' . . ."*

On occasion, congressional aides have in fact been afforded some protection under the clause. In the *Eastland* case, the Court held that a staff counsel who had participated in the issuance of the subpoena in question was immune from suit. An aide for Senator Mike Gravel of Alaska was excused by the Supreme Court from testifying before a grand jury concerning various acts of Gravel and his staff relating to the Senate subcommittee hearing where the senator made his now famous reading from the Pentagon Papers. But the Court also held that the aide could be required to testify about Gravel's source for these documents, his arrangements for their republication by a private firm, and other third-party conduct under investigation by the grand jury, so long as the inquiry did not implicate legislative acts.†

At other times congressional aides have not fared so well. In the *Kilbourn* case the Court held that the sergeant at arms who performed the illegal arrest could be held liable, although the members of Congress who authorized that conduct were immune. In the well-publicized suit by Adam Clayton Powell to regain his seat and back pay after his exclusion by the House of Representatives, the Court held that the action could proceed against the House sergeant at arms, doorkeeper, and clerk but could not be maintained against several congressmen, including

---

* *Dombrowski* v. *Eastland*, 387 U.S. 82, 85 (1967). Note also *Tenney* v. *Brandhove*, 341 U.S. 367, 378 (1951), which deals with the judicially created doctrine of official immunity that would protect legislative conduct even if an express constitutional provision did not exist. And see *Wheeldin* v. *Wheeler*, 373 U.S. 647 (1963).

† *Gravel* v. *United States*, 408 U.S. 606, 625–27 (1972).

House Speaker John McCormack. This result was reached even though the three functionaries were only following the illegal instructions they had received.* In its recent decision in *Doe* v. *McMillan* the Court allowed the action to proceed against the Public Printer and the Superintendent of Documents—who, the Court found, as distributors of the controversial report were only acting as arms of Congress—while dismissing the action against congressman defendants who had sought and voted for dissemination of that document.‡

The various rationales the Supreme Court has adopted in allowing agents of Congress to be sued while protecting congressmen are not always satisfying or wholly consistent. Several considerations, however, have been prominent. The cases reveal the view that the legislative authorization of an illegal act is somehow different in kind from the actual execution of the unlawful instruction. Moreover, there is the feeling that persons with legitimate grievances should have recourse against someone. In several cases the Supreme Court has ruled that allowing the suit in question to proceed against aides will permit redress of wrongs but will not subject legislators to intimidation by a hostile executive or judicial branch, nor distract them from legislative tasks.‡ (This view, of course, does not square with the Court's rationale, quoted above, for giving the clause's protection to aides.) The Court on more than one occasion has left undecided the issue whether an action might be maintained against congressmen if no legislative agents had participated in the offending action and no remedy for the wrong committed was otherwise available.§

* *Powell* v. *McCormack*, 395 U.S. 486, 501–06 (1969).

† See also *Hentoff* v. *Ichord*, 318 F. Supp. 1175 (D.D.C. 1970).

‡ *Doe* v. *McMillan*, 412 U.S. 306, 316–17 (1973); *Powell* v. *McCormack*, 395 U.S. 486, 505 (1969).

§ *Gravel* v. *United States*, 408 U.S. 606, 620 (1972); *Powell* v. *McCormack*, 395 U.S. 486, 506 (1969); *Kilbourn* v. *Thompson*, 103 U.S. 168, 204–05 (1881). Compare *Eastland* v. *United States Servicemen's Fund*, 421 U.S. 491, 509–11 (1975).

The Ervin committee urged that the speech or debate clause immunized it from suit in the Korff, Rebozo, and Hughes litigations. However, in only one suit—that brought by Rabbi Korff—did the district court rely on the clause to dismiss the action. The committee argued vigorously that the other two suits also essentially presented challenges to legislative acts—the issuance of subpoenas and the conduct of legislative hearings and investigations—and thus speech or debate protection should attach. (The since decided *Eastland* case supports this argument.) That the judges in those cases failed to rule on this ground may reflect the view that the Supreme Court had so obfuscated the law relating to the clause that reliance on it was precarious and tempted reversal.

The judges in the Rebozo and Hughes litigations relied in part on another concept, the doctrine of comity, in dismissing those suits. The doctrine of comity—a rule of judicial making—takes its signal from a pronouncement in the 1962 Supreme Court case involving labor leader Maurice Hutcheson: "[I]t is appropriate to observe that just as the Constitution forbids the Congress to enter fields reserved to the Executive and Judiciary, it imposes on the Judiciary the reciprocal duty of not lightly interfering with Congress' exercise of its legitimate powers."* In essence the doctrine states that a court—in the absence of a showing of serious, irreparable, and imminent injury—should not leap to intervene in a congressional proceeding, particularly where the issues involved may later be resolved in contempt proceedings.

An illustrative case concerned a subpoena issued to the publisher of a journal called *Black Politics* by the Senate Permanent Investigations Subcommittee while investigating riots, insurrection, and other violent disturbances.† The subpoena called for materials relating to a "George Prosser" (a fictitious name) who, in articles in the journal,

* *Hutcheson* v. *United States*, 369 U.S. 599, 622 (1962). See Chapter V.
† *Sanders* v. *McClellan*, 463 F. 2d 894 (D.C. Cir. 1972).

had "detail[ed] how to accomplish sabotage and terror-
ism, suggest[ed] various targets, and explain[ed] how to
manufacture explosives." The publisher filed suit for
injunctive and declaratory relief against the committee's
members and its general counsel, claiming that free-press
freedoms, particularly the right to keep confidential the
true names of article contributors, would be violated if the
subpoena was enforced.

The Court of Appeals for the District of Columbia
Circuit refused to block enforcement of the subpoena and
dismissed the action. It said:

> We first note the existence, apart from resort to our
> jurisdiction in equity, of an orderly and often approved
> means of vindicating constitutional claims arising from a
> legislative investigation. A witness may address his
> claims to the Subcommittee, which may sustain objec-
> tions. Were the Subcommittee to insist, however, upon
> some response beyond the witness' conception of his
> obligation, and he refused to comply, no punitive action
> could be taken against him unless the full Committee
> obtained from the Senate as a whole a citation of the
> witness for contempt, the citation had been referred to
> the United States Attorney, and an indictment returned
> or information filed. Should prosecution occur, the wit-
> ness' claims could then be raised before the trial
> court. . . .

"The judiciary," the court stated, "has the duty 'of not
lightly interfering with Congress' exercise of its legitimate
powers'. . . . [T]he court must not intervene prematurely
or unnecessarily. . . ." And, it continued, "[W]e think no
case is made for the court in the exercise of its equity
power to excuse [plaintiff] from appearing in response to
the subpoena. . . . [T]here is no irreparable injury of
'great and immediate' character, and the possibility or
even probability that his appearance may indirectly and
incidentally inhibit the flow of information from confiden-

tial sources is not a bar to congressional pursuit by the subpoena of its investigation of rioting, other disorders . . . and their causes."*

Only a year earlier the same court had made similar declarations in another case seeking emergency relief to enjoin a Senate subpoena.† "The courts," it said, in denying the request, "avoid use of extraordinary remedies that involve 'needless friction' with a coordinate branch of government." And the court, remarking that the relief sought would precede the subcommittee's hearing, declared that it "cannot assume .. . that the members of the committee will fail to give consideration to constitutional claims they consider may have merit. On the contrary, we may rightly assume that the legislators are sensitive to, and will endeavor to act conformably to, the principle that the Bill of Rights applies to the legislature's investigations as well as to its enactments." The court also observed that plaintiffs could raise their constitutional claims in connection with any contempt proceeding that might be instituted against them.

However, in *United States Servicemen's Fund v. Eastland*‡ the same court concluded that comity principles did not preclude the entrance of a declaratory judgment against congressional defendants blocking enforcement of a Senate Internal Security Subcommittee subpoena. This conclusion was required, the court said, because the subpoena had been served on a third-party bank and plaintiffs thus had no opportunity to test the subpoena by defying it and provoking a contempt prosecution. Although the Supreme Court reversed on the ground that suit was prohibited by the speech or debate clause, it agreed that

* The court did, however, hold that the matter was "justiciable." See Chapter VI and compare *Powell* v. *McCormack*, 395 U.S. 486 (1969) with *Davis* v. *Ichord*, 442 F. 2d 1207 (D.C. Cir. 1970), *Pauling* v. *Eastland*, 288 F. 2d 126 (D.C. Cir. 1960), *Hearst* v. *Black*, 87 F. 2d 68 (D.C. Cir. 1936) and *Stamler* v. *Willis*, 415 F. 2d 1365 (7th Cir. 1969), *cert. denied sub. nom. Ichord* v. *Stamler* 399 U.S. 929 (1970).

† *Ansara* v. *Eastland*, 442 F. 2d 751 (D.C. Cir. 1971).

‡ 488 F. 2d 1252 (D.C. Cir. 1973).

comity principles did not prevent maintenance of the suit, since plaintiffs were unable to have their contentions resolved in a contempt proceeding.*

The frequent inability to sustain suits against congressional defendants, coupled with the realization that it may be unfair to force a witness to test constitutional claims in the crucible of a contempt action, has precipitated various recommendations for a federal statute allowing challenge to congressional conduct through civil litigation. The Court of Appeals for the District of Columbia Circuit on several occasions† has repeated its call for "sympathetic consideration" of a plea by District Judge Luther Youngdahl, who, in a 1961 case, wrote:

> During the House debate on the contempt citation, the Committee inserted in the *Congressional Record* a memorandum purporting to show that declaratory judgment procedures were not an available means for procuring judicial resolution of the basic issues in dispute in this case. Although this question is not before the Court, it does feel that if contempt is, indeed, the only existing method, Congress should consider creating a method of allowing these issues to be settled by declaratory judgment. Even though it may be constitutional to put a man to guessing how a court will rule on difficult questions like those raised in good faith in this

---

* *Eastland* v. *United States Servicemen's Fund*, 421 U.S. 491, 501 & n. 14 (1975). Compare *Stamler* v. *Willis*, 415 F. 2d 1365 (7th Cir. 1969) *cert. denied sub. nom. Ichord* v. *Stamler*, 399 U.S. 929 (1970), where the court, allowing a civil First Amendment challenge to a HUAC rule to take precedence over criminal proceedings raising similar issues, remarked, "Plaintiffs should not be compelled to go through years of criminal litigation" to achieve resolution of their constitutional claims.

† *United States* v. *Fort*, 443 F. 2d 670, 677–78 (D.C. Cir. 1971); *Tobin* v. *United States*, 306 F. 2d 270, 276 (D.C. Cir. 1962), *cert. denied* 371 U.S. 902 (1962).

suit, what is constitutional is not necessarily most desirable.*

It is easy to surmise why Congress has not responded positively to recommendations giving persons under scrutiny the right to attack its proceedings as plaintiffs in civil suits. Certain applications of such a statute might offend the speech or debate clause. But practical considerations may be weightier than constitutional ones. Congressional investigations are often spur-of-the-moment activities. Frequently information is needed yesterday, if not sooner. Congress is understandably reluctant to confer on private parties a mechanism that could promote dilatory tactics and perhaps destroy the efficacy of hearings.

But a variant solution may have more chance of passage and be more constitutionally desirable. Congressmen and congressional bodies could be given the right to initiate actions to achieve declaratory judgments on the scope of their powers without extending authority to bring such litigations to private parties. The statute would be similar to that advocated regarding suits by congressional plaintiffs against executive branch officials.† It would provide that the federal courts have jurisdiction to hear cases against private parties brought by congressional litigants and that such actions must be expedited. Criminal contempt and self-help powers would remain available to rectify disregard of congressional authority in appropriate situations.

Congress is jealous of its prerogatives and would undoubtedly be hesitant to call on the judiciary for instructions on legislative powers. But on occasion congressmen and staff may want a court determination on the precise extent of congressional rights without resorting to contempt procedures. An example where a civil action

---

* *United States* v. *Tobin*, 195 F. Supp. 588, 616–17 (D.D.C. 1961) reversed, 306 F. 2d 270 (D.C. Cir. 1962), *cert. denied* 371 U.S. 902 (1962).
† See Chapter VI.

would have been far preferable is the case in which Judge Youngdahl wrote. There the executive director of the Port of New York Authority, an agency established by interstate compact, was prosecuted for refusing to produce documents subpoenaed by a House subcommittee, although that official was acting under direct orders of the authority's board of commissioners, which, in turn, proceeded under instructions from the governors of New York and New Jersey. The Court of Appeals, reversing the conviction on highly technical grounds, pointedly observed that the defendant "is no criminal and no one seriously considers him one."*

Numerous factors may make the contempt process distasteful to congressmen themselves. A great many congressmen are attuned to individual concerns and desire to be fair. And there is also the painfully evident fact that judicial reaction has often been hostile to congressional claims in contempt proceedings. The courts might well be more sympathetic to congressional contentions in civil proceedings than in the contempt milieu where liberty is at jeopardy. Also, a civil proceeding providing injunctive and declaratory relief could allow an investigatory panel quickly to obtain evidence that a drawn-out criminal prosecution would never produce. In the long run, therefore, Congress might fare better through the civil route.†

---

* 306 F. 2d at 274. The Court of Appeals held that the subpoena exceeded the subcommittee's authority under its parent's authoriizng resolutions.

† A civil proceeding, with its more flexible rules of evidence and discovery procedures, may also be more suitable than a criminal prosecution for the resolution of many constitutional questions. See *Stamler* v. *Willis*, 415 F. 2d 1365, 1369 (7th Cir. 1969) *cert. denied sub. nom. Ichord* v. *Stamler*, 399 U.S. 929 (1970).

·XI·
Final Thoughts

This book began with the remark that the problems to be
discussed were not theoretical issues lacking practical
import. True to this forecast, we have dealt with the live
issues that have permeated past congressional investigations and daily confronted congressmen, staff, witnesses,
and counsel. In particular, we have examined various
litigations involving the Ervin and other committees because here the issues intrinsic in the investigatory process
have been sharpened in adversary contexts.

These issues are not controversies of the past that can
be safely left to grow moldy with age. That they exist
today is demonstrated by the congressional investigations
currently receiving the most interest—the inquiries of
select Senate and House committees into the nation's
intelligence apparatus.

The paramount issue presented by those investigations is

the right of Congress to probe the inner workings of the
executive branch. Simply put, the question is, Will Congress get the information it needs to perform its lawmaking, oversight, and informing functions? The intelligence
agencies should not be allowed to run loose, free from congressional supervision.

Complicating the situation is the fact that these inquiries concern information which the executive has traditionally sought and often been allowed to protect—for
example, sensitive military and foreign affairs secrets and
various investigatory files. The committees and the Ford
administration have frequently squabbled over the committees' rights to information.*

Another crucial set of problems concerns how the committees use the information they receive. An obvious
tension exists between Congress's responsibility to inform
the public about the intelligence agencies—especially
about their shortcomings—and the need to protect information that could endanger lives, wreck investigations, and
perhaps imperil the safety of the nation. From the brief
glance the Ervin committee took at the CIA respecting
that agency's link with the Watergate and Ellsberg episodes, it became clear that reckless publication of facts
concerning the CIA's operations could have unfortunate
ramifications, such as endangering the physical safety of
overseas operatives. How much to reveal about the agency's
affairs is not an easy question.

That highly sensitive matters are involved in these
investigations raises another central issue: How will leaks
be controlled? In several respects the problem here is
more troublesome than in the Watergate investigation.
In Watergate there were reputations to be lost; here there

---

* Just before this book went to press, the House intelligence committee voted to cite Secretary of State Henry Kissinger for criminal
contempt for failing to supply subpoenaed documents. This action
followed on the heels of a similar contempt vote by a House Commerce subcommittee against Secretary of Commerce Rogers Morton,
who had refused to produce information to the subcommittee.

are lives. Moreover, in Watergate it was likely that all relevant information would eventually be released. Here Congress will be under immense pressures to hold back data where revelation would have calamitous effects. Because all information that comes to Congress will not ultimately be disclosed, the temptations for selective leaking are heightened.

These considerations highlight again the role of the media. The press has manifested extreme fascination with the intelligence agencies. Unfortunately, the danger exists that some members of the media will try to pry into sensitive national security secrets by teasing leaks from disgruntled agency employees or loose-tongued congressmen and their aides. There is a possibility that a newspaper, coming upon highly sensitive facts that by any reasonable standard should remain confidential, will not act responsibly, but—seduced by the lure of the scoop—will rush to headlines.

Other problems—legal and practical—could be suggested, but the above collection is sufficient to demonstrate the range of issues the intelligence investigations present. The CIA inquiries, however, are mentioned only as an example. The discussion need not be limited to the topical, for similar issues will arise so long as Congress continues to probe deeply into the nooks and crannies of executive operations.

———

A fitting ending for this book would be to suggest how future congressional investigations can be both effective and fair, how Congress can fully do its job yet not trample on other rights that demand respect under our form of government. Unfortunately, there is no sweeping panacea. It will help if those involved in the process—Congress, staff, witnesses, counsel, the press—know the ground rules. The participants should understand the scope of Congress's powers and the limitations on its searches. They should comprehend the basic rights of witnesses. They should realize that severe legal and practical consequences may follow the unauthorized release of confidential information. If the legal strictures in which congressional probes function are fully understood, the chances are increased that investigations will be efficient, just, and law-abiding.

But a proper appreciation of governing principles will not alone ensure that investigations are conducted with effectiveness and restraint. In the last analysis, the way in which an investigation proceeds turns largely on the characters and capabilities of the men in charge—on their prudence, integrity, and sense of fairness and proportion. The rules that govern congressional inquiries provide important safeguards, but they do not ensure that investigations will be wise and productive and not be used for demagoguery or the undue pursuit of partisan advantage. There is room within the rules to injure reputations and careers—to harass, abuse, and grandstand. The protections afforded by the courts, which may not lightly interfere with legislative proceedings, are limited.

In a democracy the ultimate responsibility for proper investigations rests with the voters. The Supreme Court has recognized this. Twenty-five years ago, Justice Frankfurter wrote: "In times of political passion, dishonest or vindictive motives are readily attributed to legislative conduct and as readily believed. Courts are not the place for such controversies. Self-discipline and the voters must be the ultimate reliance for discouraging or correcting such abuses."*

More recently, Justice Blackmun has bemoaned the "lack of confidence in our political processes" and stated: "It is inevitable that occasionally . . . there will be unwise and even harmful choices made by Congress in fulfilling its legislative responsibility. That, however, is the price we pay for representative government. I am firmly convinced that the abuses we countenance in our system are

---

* *Tenney* v. *Brandhove*, 341 U.S. 367, 378 (1951).

vastly outweighed by the demonstrated ability of the political process to correct overzealousness on the part of elected representatives."*

If men of ability and probity who will surround themselves with aides of like stature are put in Congress, the quality of investigations will improve. But if the public insists on choosing the Joe McCarthys over the Sam Ervins of this world, the conduct of investigations will suffer. The advent of the television age at least helps the public know who the McCarthys and the Ervins are and who is a competent representative and who is not. It may be no coincidence that several members of the House Judiciary Committee who considered Nixon's impeachment in televised sessions were not successful in their next ventures at the polls.

To those immediately abused by a congressional investigation the chance for vindication or revenge in distant elections may offer little solace. But the vote is the sanction by which transgressions by public officials are often remedied. The process of judgment is slow but effective. No small comfort, then, that in a democracy the people are the final arbiters of Congress's exercise of the power to probe.

---

* *Doe* v. *McMillan*, 412 U.S. 306, 338 (1973) (Blackmun, J., concurring in part and dissenting in part).

Index

About the Author

JAMES HAMILTON is a native of Chester, South Carolina, and holds degrees from Davidson College (A.B., 1960), Yale Law School (LL.B., 1963) and the University of London (LL.M., 1966). From late 1966 to March 1973 he was associated with the Washington law firm of Covington and Burling. In April 1973 he became assistant chief counsel to Senator Sam Ervin's Senate Select Committee on Presidential Campaign Activities. In this capacity he was responsible for the committee's investigation of the Watergate break-in and cover-up, as well as the committee's major litigations, and jointly responsible for its probe of the Nixon administration's overall plan to use federal resources to reelect the President—the so-called Responsiveness Program—and the committee's investigations of certain aspects of the presidential campaigns of Senator Hubert Humphrey and Congressman Wilbur Mills.

Mr. Hamilton is now a partner in the Washington law firm of Ginsburg, Feldman and Bress.